Semantics

Semantics
A Cognitive Account of Linguistic Meaning

Zeki Hamawand

SHEFFIELD UK   BRISTOL CT

Published by Equinox Publishing Ltd.

UK: Office 415, The Workstation, 15 Paternoster Row, Sheffield, South Yorkshire
      S1 2BX

USA: ISD, 70 Enterprise Drive, Bristol, CT 06010

www.equinoxpub.com

First published 2016

British Library Cataloguing-in-Publication Data
A catalogue record for this book is available from the British Library.

ISBN-13 978 1 78179 248 3 (hardback)
        978 1 78179 249 0 (paperback)

Library of Congress Cataloging-in-Publication Data
Hamawand, Zeki, author.
Semantics: a cognitive account of linguistic meaning / Zeki Hamawand.
    pages cm
Includes bibliographical references and index.
ISBN 978-1-78179-248-3 (hb) – ISBN 978-1-78179-249-0 (pb)
1. Semantics–Psychological aspects. 2. Cognitive grammar. 3. Meaning
(Psychology) 4. Psycholinguistics. I. Title.
P325.5.P78H363 2015
401'.43–dc23
                    2015010608

Typeset by S.J.I. Services, New Delhi
Printed and bound in Great Britain by Lightning Source Inc. (La Vergne, TN), Lightning
Source UK Ltd. (Milton Keynes), Lightning Source AU Pty. (Scoresby, Victoria)

Contents

Preface

Approach

Semantics: *A Cognitive Account of Linguistic Meaning* is a textbook which provides an in-depth analysis of English **semantics**, a branch of linguistics which specializes in the study of meaning. The approach adopted is **Cognitive Semantics**, the study of the cognitive aspects of meaning. It provides the basic techniques of determining the meanings of lexical and sentential expressions in a systematic way. It attempts to unify the two spheres of how language conveys meaning and how language relates to context. It tries to demonstrate the ways the mind processes language to organize experience, and vice-versa. It aims to explain the relationship between experience, the conceptual structure and the semantic structure encoded by language. Experience is knowledge gained from seeing, feeling or doing things. Conceptual structure is knowledge representation, including concepts organized in the human conceptual system. Semantic structure is the linguistic form that conceptual structure takes in language. Cognitive semanticists employ language as the lens through which cognitive phenomena can be investigated. Thus, it represents the newest development within the field of Cognitive Linguistics.

Goals

The textbook introduces the topic of semantics, taking a step-by-step approach. To that end, it links theory with practice in the study of meaning. It has, therefore, two goals: theoretical and practical. The **theoretical goal** is to acquaint students with the theories of meaning, introduce the key concepts used in the study of meaning, and elaborate on the two essential units of meaning: word and sentence. In categorization, linguistic expressions are shown to have multiple meanings, which gather around prototypical examples, and so display minimal differences in meaning. In configuration, linguistic expressions denoting the same concept are shown to form domains, in which they represent discrete facets, and so have different roles in the language. In conceptualization, linguistic expressions which look similar are shown to be distinguishable in meaning, and so distinctive in use. The **practical goal** is to develop the skills of the students in analysing linguistic expressions, familiarize them with the mechanisms used in constructing meaning, and inform them of the techniques employed to account for their interpretation.

Contents

The textbook is divided into three parts. Part I is entitled 'Fundamentals', which serves to introduce the major terms involved in the field of semantics. It consists of three chapters. Chapter 1 relates to the nature of meaning. Chapter 2 deals with lexical semantics. Chapter 3 pertains to sentential semantics. Part II sheds light on the cognitive framework in which the study of meaning is carried out. It offers a synthesis of the leading tenets of the cognitive framework. It consists of three chapters. Chapter 4 introduces the cognitive assumptions. Chapter 5 touches upon the conceptual structures. Chapter 6 addresses the cognitive mechanisms. Part III addresses the cognitive processes involved in the construction of meaning. It consists of three chapters. Chapter 7 copes with categorization. Chapter 8 grapples with configuration. Chapter 9 tackles conceptualization. Each chapter begins with an overview, where the subject matter, the objective and the procedures are stated. The overview aims to help the student to understand the content of the chapter before delving into the details. Each chapter is divided into sections. Each section closes with an exercise. The exercises are meant to reinforce the material presented or introduce new material for investigation.

Audiences

To achieve its mission, the textbook uses an approachable style and sums up the information in figures and tables. It uses actual data, offers numerous examples and gives vivid explanations. As a textbook, it targets two classes of audience. Primarily, it targets undergraduate students taking degree courses in linguistics. It provides them with a thorough discussion of the pivotal issues involved in the study of linguistic semantics. It informs them more fully about such areas in semantics as word meaning and sentence meaning. Secondarily, it targets students at English departments. It helps them to understand the meanings of expressions and grasp the conditions under which they are used. As a guidebook, it targets two classes of audience. First, it targets linguists. Of central significance for them are the cognitive tools employed to account for semantic data. Second, it targets scholars from neighbouring disciplines. Of special interest for them is the description of an area in language study from a new perspective.

Notes

To teachers

To make maximum use of the textbook and achieve the goals of the course, teachers should consider two points. Concerning lesson plans, the textbook is organized in such a way that it allows teachers flexibility in designing a semantic course to meet teaching requirements. The textbook is ideal for a one-semester course of 12–14 teaching weeks. In this case, teachers are recommended to cover one chapter per week. However, the recommendations made here can be adjusted to meet different requirements. Therefore, teachers are free to use the textbook in a way that suits the level of the course they teach and/or the time available. Concerning the data, it is taken exclusively from English. The main source for the choice and analysis of the data is the British National Corpus. The corpus provides example sentences and collocation patterns. However, the general principles discussed here can be extended to apply to other languages. Therefore, teachers are free to use cross-linguistic data in their lessons. Just for convenience, the following is a possible format of a one-semester course.

Week	Topic	Reading	Week	Topic	Reading
1	Linguistics		8	Cognitive mechanisms	Ch. 6
2	Nature of meaning	Ch. 1	9	Review/Exam	
3	Lexical Semantics	Ch. 2	10	Categorization	Ch. 7
4	Sentential Semantics	Ch. 3	11	Configuration	Ch. 8
5	Review/Exam		12	Conceptualization	Ch. 9
6	Guiding assumptions	Ch. 4	13	Review/Exam	
7	Conceptual structures	Ch. 5	14	General Review	

To students

The textbook, which is couched within the theory of Cognitive Linguistics, is meant to give students an insight into the nature of linguistic meaning and the principles which govern its mechanism. It does not necessarily presuppose any foreknowledge of the topic. The definitions which it presents and the distinctions which it suggests should not be taken as a hard-and-fast criterion, but rather as a rule of thumb. To get a grasp of any section or subsection, the students are advised to study its content carefully, make a brief summary of it, and then tackle the exercise which it contains. The purpose of this is twofold. First, it attracts attention to the core of the section. Second, it tests comprehension of the material presented. Finally, further reading and bibliographical sources are included at the end of the textbook. The purpose of this is twofold. First, it provides guidance on further reading on the topics covered in the analysis. Second, it acknowledges work which contributed in one way or another to the present discussion.

Conventions

- Bold face is used to introduce technical terms at their first occurrence, and thereafter ordinary type face is used unless particular emphasis justifies its repetition.
- Italics are used to cite a word or a sentence as a linguistic example to illustrate the terms.
- Asterisks are used to indicate that a word or an expression is semantically unacceptable.
- Single quotation marks are used to enclose a phrase to indicate the definition of a morpheme or word.
- The mark = is used to indicate that two words or phrases have the same value as each other.
- The mark [ ] is used to represent schemas and semantic structures of derivational morphemes.
- The mark / / is used to represent phonological structures of derivational morphemes.
- The mark () is used to enclose words.
- The mark { } is used to enclose alternatives.

Acknowledgements

In writing this textbook, I have accumulated many debts to people who contributed in one way or another to its completion, none of whom has responsibility for any flaws. First, I owe Struan Robertson a deep debt of gratitude for reading the manuscript in its entirety, making acute observations and giving useful feedback. Second, I would like to express my deepest appreciation to Ronald Langacker, Dirk Geeraerts and Paul Chilton for devoting their time to reading parts of the work. In fact, their crucial questions, constructive comments and valuable suggestions produced noticeable improvements in the work. I am particularly indebted to Karin Guth whose words have boosted my morale while working on the project in difficult circumstances. I would also like to acknowledge the support of Janet Joyce and Valerie Hall at Equinox for their patience during the long gestation period of the manuscript. Finally, my greatest debt of all is to Suhad. I thank her for her courtesy, patience and support. The book is dedicated to her.

Zeki Hamawand

Part I

Fundamentals

Linguistics is the scientific study of human **language**, a set of vocal sounds or written marks used in communication. Within linguistics, there are two main fields that study meaning. **Semantics** is the study of context-independent meanings of linguistic expressions. It defines the literal meanings which linguistic expressions have and identifies the relations which they hold. **Pragmatics** is the study of the context-dependent meanings of linguistic expressions. It defines the non-literal meanings which linguistic expressions have and identifies the relations which they hold. Semantics and pragmatics are then two sides of the same coin. Semantics deals with meaning which an expression has independently of context. For example, *There is a car coming* signals a statement meaning out of context that a car is coming. Pragmatics deals with the meaning which an expression has in a particular context. For example, *There is a car coming* signals a warning on a specific occasion against stepping onto a road. In a cognitive analysis of language, the two fields form a continuum and study the meanings of linguistic expressions in and out of context.

As a lexical word, **semantics** comes from the Greek adjective *semantikos* meaning 'related to signs', based on the noun *sēmeion* meaning 'sign'. As a linguistic term, **semantics** is the study of the linguistic meaning of words and sentences. The linguist who is interested in the study of meaning is called a **semanticist**. Semantics is an essential branch in linguistics. Its general goal is to study the ways in which meaning can be analysed in language. **Meaning** is the idea that a piece of language represents. It is the thing that the speaker wishes to communicate to the hearer by language. Its specific goal is twofold. The first is to mark the common semantic relations which exist between words. The study of word meanings and the relations among them is the concern of **Lexical Semantics**. The second is to define the common semantic relations which exist between sentences. The study of sentence meanings and the relations among them is the concern of **Sentential Semantics**. In cognitive terms, **semantics** aims to explain how factors inside and outside language contribute to the meanings of linguistic expressions.

Outline

The Nature of Meaning

Chapter 1 introduces the notion of **meaning** in language, identifies its levels, aspects and types, and reviews different approaches to its definition. The aim is to introduce the basic terminology used in the study of meaning. The chapter is organized as follows. Section 1.1 explains what the notion of meaning is. It consists of two subsections. The first deals with levels of meaning. The second revolves around aspects of meaning. Section 1.2 sheds light on the different types of meaning: descriptive, expressive and social. Section 1.3 addresses the different conceptions of meaning: referential, relational, decompositional which includes componential, conceptual and primitive, and representational. In all the sections, I pursue three steps. First, I introduce the meaning conception. Second, I explain its assumption. Third, I give an example to test its application. Section 1.4 draws a comparison between the two mainstream paradigms of meaning: formalist and cognitive. Section 1.5 summarizes the main points of the chapter.

1.1 Meaning

Language is conveyed in terms of expressions. An **expression** is a meaningful unit of language such as an affix, word, phrase or sentence. A **unit** is any simple or complex expression that carries a lexical or grammatical pattern and serves a particular purpose. A linguistic expression has two aspects. One is **substance**, which consists of two facades: form and meaning. **Form** is the orthographic representation associated with a linguistic expression. **Meaning** is the semantic content associated with a linguistic expression. The form serves to indicate meaning. The other is **use**, the purpose for or way in which a linguistic expression is employed. The use of a linguistic expression is determined by the way the **language user** describes a situation, which differs relative to the demands of discourse. The substance of a linguistic expression is activated as a response to language use. Meaning is the characteristic of a linguistic form which is used to pick out some aspect of the non-linguistic world. Meaning is what the speaker communicates or conveys in a message and what the receiver decodes or infers from its use in a context. In essence, meaning is the heart of language. Meaning is what language is for.

1.1.1 Levels

A linguistic expression has two levels of meaning. The first is **expression meaning**, the meaning of a linguistic expression, word or sentence, taken out of context. **Word meaning** is the literal meaning of a word taken out of context, which is derived from the morphemes it consists of. The meaning of the word *unanswerable*, for example, is built up out of the meanings of the morphemes it contains, which are un + answer + able meaning 'cannot be answered'. **Sentence meaning** is the literal meaning of a sentence taken out of context, which is built up from the meanings of the words it contains. The meaning of the sentence *The argument is unanswerable*, for example, is that the argument cannot be answered. The second is **utterance meaning**, the non-literal meaning of an expression, word or sentence, which is derived from the context in which it is used. The meaning of the utterance *The argument is unanswerable*, for example, is that the argument cannot be proved wrong and must therefore be accepted. The distinction drawn above between sentence meaning and utterance meaning is linked to the distinction between semantics and pragmatics. In the approach adopted in this study, the distinction is not recognized. The central aim of semantics is, therefore, to uncover the meanings of linguistic expressions when they are used both in and out of context.

Exercise 1.1

State what the utterance meaning of each of the following sentences is.

1. That is just what I needed!
2. You have been a great help!
3. That will be extremely useful!
4. You are a very tidy cook, I see!
5. You have been working hard!

1.1.2 Aspects

Linguists distinguish different aspects of meaning. These include reference, sense, denotation and connotation. These aspects set important contrasts within the meaning of a linguistic expression. Reference contrasts with sense, whereas denotation contrasts with connotation.

proper noun denotes an individual. A common noun denotes a set of individuals. A verb denotes an action. An adjective denotes a property of the individual. An adverb denotes a property of the action. The meaning of a sentence denotes a situation or event. Second, reference is a momentary relationship. Denotation is a stable relationship. For example, the referent of the word *musician* changes according to context, which could be Mozart, Beethoven, and the like, whereas its denotation remains the same, which is a person who writes music or plays a musical instrument, especially professionally.

Exercise 1.2

The following words denote animals but connote disapproving traits of persons. Give the connotation of each.

1. pig
2. fox
3. mule
4. sheep
5. snake

1.2 Types of meaning

As the study of the meanings of linguistic expressions, semantics discusses not only what words and sentences in the human language explicitly mean but also what they implicitly convey. An accurate semantic analysis of a linguistic expression should then consider all aspects of what it means. The semantic aspects of a linguistic expression can be classified under three main headings: descriptive, expressive and social meaning. The descriptive meaning of a linguistic expression conveys factual information about a particular state of affairs. The expressive meaning of a linguistic expression reflects the subjective reactions of the speaker uttering it. The social meaning of a linguistic expression maintains social relations among participants in talk exchanges.

1.2.1 Descriptive

The descriptive meaning of a word, or its propositional meaning, refers to that part of its meaning which bears on reference and truth. It includes the act of both referring to something and stating its truth. It is the definition that is given in a dictionary. For example, the descriptive meaning of the word *hawk* includes both reference to it as a bird, and truth of it as a living creature. Its meaning might be extended to include some of its characteristics like the ability to hunt and kill other creatures for food. The descriptive meaning of a sentence is a concept for a certain kind of situation. Content words contribute to the descriptive meaning of sentence meaning. The descriptive meaning of a noun is a concept for a certain kind of entity. The descriptive meaning of a verb is a concept for a certain kind of event. The descriptive meaning of an adjective is a concept for a certain kind of quality. For example, the descriptive meaning of the sentence *She writes a letter* includes both its reference and truth. The reference of the sentence is a kind of situation. The references of the components it contains are: objects which are represented by the pronoun *she* and the noun *letter*, and event which is represented by the verb *write*. The truth of the sentence is the conditions under which it is true. The sentence is true because each of its components is linked to a particular referent.

Exercise 1.3

Define the descriptive meaning of each of the following expressions. Then, identify the type of referent of each.

1. relax
2. ring
3. blue
4. linguist
5. I am sick

1.2.2 *Expressive*

The expressive meaning of an expression refers to its semantic quality independently of the context in which it is used. Expressive words or phrases serve to reflect personal attitudes, feelings or opinions. Their use is just a matter of personal emotion, judgement or sensation. The expressive meaning of a word neither contributes to its propositional content nor influences its truth value. For example, the descriptive meaning of the word *idiot* is a person, whereas its expressive meaning is that of contempt. Expressive meaning is exemplified by certain phrases whose functions are the showing of strong feelings: (a) interjections, a short sound, word or phrase spoken suddenly to express an emotion, as in *ow*! which expresses a sudden pain; and (b) exclamations, a clause or sentence structure beginning with *what* or *how*, as in *What bloody awful weather!* and *How lovely she looks*! There are, in addition, other expressions which produce personal reactions to a situation. as in *Thank God you're safe!* conveying happiness, *My goodness, you have spent a lot!* conveying surprise, *Good heavens, what a mess!* conveying annoyance, and *Damn, I've spilt coffee down my blouse*! conveying anger. There exist some words, which have descriptive as well as expressive meanings, as in *Hi, honey, I'm home!* and *Happy birthday, sweetheart!*

The term **expressive** overlaps with other terms like connotative, affective and emotive. The **connotative** meaning of an expression refers to the additional meanings that a word has which goes beyond its denotative meaning. The denotative meaning of the word *child* is what it literally means: a young human being. The connotative meaning of the word *child* includes the other general concepts associated with it: affection or nuisance. The **affective** meaning of an expression refers to the speaker's feelings *vis-à-vis* an expression, which differs from one person to another. For example, the affective meaning of the word *child* differs from one person to another. A person enjoying the company of a *child* would associate positive emotions with it, whereas a person not enjoying the company of a *child* would associate negative emotions with it. The **emotive** meaning of an expression refers to the strong feelings, especially of anger, which a subject, statement or use of language has on the people like *child abuse*.

Exercise 1.4

Below is a list of some interjections in English. Write what each of them expresses.

1. ah!
2. alas!
3. hey!
4. ugh!
5. wow!

1.2.3 *Social*

The social meaning of a word refers to that part of its meaning whose use is governed by the social rules of interaction. It refers to the use of a particular expression in language which indicates the social relationship between the speaker and the addressee. Unlike an expression with descriptive meaning which is governed by rules of factual adequacy, an expression with social meaning is governed by the social rules of conduct. This is found particularly in social rituals such as acknowledging, apologizing, addressing, blessing, greeting or sympathizing. For each ritual, there is a social rule that defines the circumstances under which a certain linguistic expression fits, usually having a positive effect. In English, social differentiation is reflected by the two levels of formality, formal indicating distance, and informal indicating familiarity. To express social relationship, English provides two linguistic devices. The first relates to forms of address. In addressing a person, the speaker can choose between two ways: either a surname with title for a formal relationship as in *Mr. John/Professor John/Sir John,* or just a first name for an informal relationship, as in *John.*

Exercise 1.5

Name the social ritual of each of the following utterances and then indicate the level of formality each represents.

1. a. Hi
   b. Good morning.
2. a. How's it going?
   b. How are you?
3. a. Thanks.
   b. I am grateful to you.
4. a. What?
   b. I beg your pardon?
5. a. What's the time?
   b. Could you tell me the time, please?

The second device pertains to the choice of vocabulary, which is influenced by a phenomenon in language called **euphemism,** the phenomenon in which a word or phrase is used instead of another to avoid being unpleasant, indecent or offensive. The word or phrase that is unpleasant, indecent or offensive is described as being **politically incorrect**. The word or phrase that avoids being unpleasant, indecent or offensive is described as being **politically correct**. As an example of a word, some people prefer to use the politically correct word *firefighter* instead of *fireman* which can be construed as sexist. Linguistically expressed, the word *firefighter* is a euphemism for the word *fireman*. As an example of a phrase, some people prefer to use the politically correct phrase *senior citizen* instead of *old person*. Euphemism is used in many areas within language including sexual activity (*go to bed* instead of *intercourse*), bodily functions (*use the toilet* instead of *defecate*), military (*campaign* instead of *war*), death (*pass away* instead of *die*), politics (*user fees* instead of *taxes*), religion (*heck* instead of *hell*), and so on.

Exercise 1.6

The following are politically incorrect words. Avoid using them by choosing a euphemism for each.

1. sick
2. skinny
3. miserly
4. crippled
5. inquisitive

1.3 Conceptions of meaning

The meaning of a linguistic expression, word or sentence, is so important that it has received attention in many theories of language, but with differences in stance. The stances of the theories follow from differences in their underlying assumptions. These theories seek to provide different answers to the question: what is meaning? The first conception deems meaning referential. This is a characteristic of Traditional Semantics. The second conception considers meaning relational. This is a feature of Structural Semantics. The third conception considers meaning decompositional. Within this, three conceptions have been proposed: componential which is a mark of Structural Semantics, conceptual and primitive which are signs of Generative Semantics. The fourth conception regards meaning representational. This is a hallmark of Cognitive Semantics.

1.3.1 Referential

In view of this conception, the meaning of an expression derives from its reference to an actual object in the external world. This stance stems from the **objectivist** theory of meaning, which views meaning in terms of correlation between what is said and what is seen. For example, the meaning of the word *Susan* is just the person it refers to in the outside world. The act of picking out an entity in the outside world with a word is called **referring**. Thus, one can use the word *library* to **refer to** a building. The entity referred to, in this example *the building*, is called the **referent**. The meaning of a sentence is reduced to the observable features of a situation. There are, however, a number of problems with this view. First, it ignores abstract items like *bravery*. It is impossible to find a referent in the physical world to which it corresponds. Second, it fails to show that the meaning of a word is influenced by extra-linguistic information. This is the case when it fails to account for a word that is ambiguous. For example, it is unable to distinguish between the two interpretations of a word like *pointer*: a device used for pointing or a helpful piece of information. Third, it neglects the difference in meaning between words which share the same referent. For example, in British English the words *pupil* and *student* do not have the same meaning. A pupil is a child who learns in a school, whereas a student is a person who studies at a university. Yet, this conception claims they have the same referent, a person who attends school.

Exercise 1.7

According to the referential conception of meaning, the following nouns share the same referent: a watcher. Despite that, there exist meaning differences which are neglected. Can you identify them?

1. viewer
2. sightseer
3. observer
4. onlooker
5. spectator

1.3.2 Relational

In virtue of this conception, the meaning of an expression is determined by its position in a network in which it is related to other expressions. That is, the semantic value of an expression is the sum total of its sense relations with other expressions in the same **lexical field**, a coherent subset of the vocabulary whose members are interlinked by paradigmatic and syntagmatic relations of sense. The field is partitioned among its members, each of which represents a different semantic value. Knowing any member of a field requires knowing the other members. For example, the verbs *rob, steal, pilfer, filch* and *purloin* are placed in a field denoting *theft*. Yet, each has a different value. *Rob* means 'stealing money or property from a person or place', as in *rob a bank*. *Steal* means 'taking objects from a person or shop', as in *steal jewels*. *Pilfer* means 'stealing things of little value or in small quantities, especially from the place where you work', as in *pilfer stamps from work*. *Filch* means 'stealing something small or not very valuable quickly and secretly', as in *filch an apple from the tray*. *Purloin* means 'stealing something or using it without permission', as in *purloin a pen from office*. This is indeed a valid technique of semantic enquiry, but it is not the whole story. It is true that one aspect of knowing a word is to know how that word is used in relation to other words. In this way, however, the semantic structure of a language becomes a vast calculus of internal relations, with no contact at all with the way speakers conceptualize the world.

Exercise 1.8

Following the relational conception of meaning, the following adjectives express the concept of *weakness*, and so are placed in a set. Nevertheless, there exist meaning differences which are overlooked. Can you pinpoint them?

1. frail
2. weak
3. feeble
4. fragile
5. decrepit

1.3.3 Decompositional

Decomposition refers to the analysis of an expression in terms of semantic components. An expression is built up of smaller components of meaning.

Accordingly, the meaning of a linguistic expression can be defined in terms of **truth conditions**, the conditions of objective external reality against which an expression can be judged true or false. This theory of meaning considers language as corresponding to the world in a literal sense. For example, the sentence *Snow is white* is true if and only if snow is white. This theory can only account for propositions. For example, the sentences *He built a sand castle* and *The sand castle was built by him* mean the same. They stand in a meaning relation of paraphrase. In this regard, the conception of the meaning proposed is **atomistic**, a conception which is founded on the assumption that the meaning of a word can be determined in isolation by its semantic components, and not by its relations with the other words in the language as assumed by **holistic** theories. Words are translated into mathematical-type formulae and then subjected to rigorous truth tests. Within the technique of decomposition, there are three models of analysis: componential, conceptual and primitive.

1.3.3.1   Componential

In terms of this conception, known as **Componential Analysis**, the meaning of an expression can be decomposed into a finite set of **semantic components**, defined as features of meaning which combine to form a complex meaning. It analyses meaning in terms of binary features, with only two possible values of + and −. It is on the basis of these that speakers can describe their experiences in the world. An example is the word *spinster*. This word has a complex meaning which is built up out of the components [female] + [adult] + [human] + [unmarried]. This technique describes only the denotative meaning of the word, and not its connotative meaning which is negative here. This method of analysis is appropriate when dealing with limited areas of phonology or syntax. However, it has two limitations. The first concerns the identification of the semantic components. The question posed is: Do the components cover all the examples of a *chair*, for example, or just some of them? In addition, it seems very difficult to validate the proposed set of components and decide which ones apply and which ones do not. The second concerns its ability to cover all kinds of relations. The question posed is: Can it capture meaning relations such as synonymy or antonymy, for example? As the data show, it is applicable to a limited range of expressions. It cannot account for the meaning of verbs, for example.

> **Exercise 1.9**
>
> Depending on the componential conception of meaning, the following nouns share the semantic components: [human] + [adult] + [+/− male]. Nonetheless, there exist meaning differences which are ignored. Can you diagnose them?
>
> 1. juror
> 2. referee
> 3. reviewer
> 4. surveyor
> 5. arbitrator

1.3.3.2 Conceptual

In the light of this conception, known as **Conceptual Semantics,** the meaning of an expression is a concept in the speaker's mind. The expression is defined by embedding conceptual elements into its arguments. An expression has a conceptual structure with argument slots, which are filled by the syntactic complements of the expression. For example, the sentence *Sara went to school* would be analysed as [Event GO([Thing SARA], [Path TO([Place SCHOOL])])]. Each pair of square brackets represents a concept. The concept of event is represented by *go*, denoting the movement of an object along a path. *Go* has two arguments to be filled: an object argument and a path argument. *Sara* fills the argument position of object, whereas *to school* fills the argument position of path. The concept of thing is represented by *Sara*, denoting a person. The concept of path is represented by *to*, denoting a path to a goal. *To* has an argument which is represented by *school*. The concept of place is represented by *school*, denoting location. Although this theory of meaning is non-objectivist and non-truth-conditional, it suffers from two insufficiencies. First, it carries out linguistic analyses in logical terms or mathematical rules. In doing so, it neglects minute distinctions between seemingly similar expressions. Second, it is unable to account for the meaning of other word classes than verbs.

Exercise 1.10

In conformity with the conceptual conception of meaning, the following verbs share the conceptual element of event, meaning 'to keep away from something'. In spite of that, there exist meaning differences which are unnoticed. Can you establish them?

1. shun
2. avoid
3. evade
4. escape
5. eschew

1.3.3.3   Primitive

As regards this conception, known as **Natural Semantic Metalanguage**, the meaning of an expression can be defined in terms of a small set of **semantic primes** or **primitives**, indivisible atoms of meaning which combine to form a more complex meaning. These primes are expressed linguistically and combined into sentences following syntactic rules. For example, the semantic definition of the word *sky* contains the semantic primes *above* and *far*. The definition goes like this: something is very big, people can see it, it is a place, it is above all other objects, it is far from people. Although this approach is not restricted to the analysis of certain word classes, it has its drawbacks, too. First, the approach is unable to offer precise descriptions of words because the primes are very general and the definitions are therefore rather vague. For example, the definition given for *sky* is not precise because it can also apply to *sun*. Second, the approach is unable to explain meaning relations that hold between primitives denoting synonymy such as *ill* and *sick*, or antonymy such as *big* and *small*, and so on. On the basis of this, the explanations offered in this approach regarding the relations between lexical items cannot be fully accurate.

Exercise 1.11

As reported by the Natural Semantic Metalanguage conception of meaning, the following nouns which describe a 'container' have the same semantic primes. However, there exist meaning differences which are missed. Can you determine them?

1. bag
2. box
3. sack
4. packet
5. wallet

1.3.4   Representational

In connection with this conception, known as **Cognitive Semantics**, the meaning of an expression is linked to a particular mental representation, termed a **concept**. Concepts, in turn, derive from percepts. The link between an expression and its referent is therefore indirect in the mind of the speaker. The meaning of an expression reflects not only the content of a conceived situation, but also how that content is construed by the speaker. In this view, a speaker can view the same situation in different ways. This stance originates as a result of the **subjectivist** theory of meaning, which emphasizes the importance of world experience to the representation of linguistic expressions and recognizes the speaker's capacity to construe a situation in alternative ways. For example, the speaker can view the situation of a sleeping baby either as an activity as in *The baby is sleeping*, or as a state as in *The baby is asleep*. This conception attaches importance to the conceptual processes and embodied experience in the study of meaning. From its perspective, linguistic expressions such as words do not carry meaning(s), but they contribute to the process of meaning construction which takes place at the conceptual level.

When the speaker experiences a thing, the thing experienced activates the conceptual system. In the conceptual system, the thing takes a conceptual structure, which is encoded in language by means of a semantic structure. The **conceptual system** represents our knowledge of the world. It is the repository of the concepts available to a human being. Each concept in the conceptual system can, in principle, be encoded via language. The **conceptual structure** is the concept in the conceptual system which stands for the thing experienced. The **semantic structure** is the meaning which stands for the conceptual structure. The semantic structure is expressed by a linguistic form in language. So, the semantic structure reflects the conceptual structure. The semantic structure subsumes both the open-class system which includes nouns, verbs, adjectives, etc., and the closed-class system which includes idioms and grammatical elements. Accordingly, meaning is derived from conceptual structures which reflect the world human beings experience, not within the linguistic system. Language serves as the lens through which the nature of the conceptual structure is investigated.

To make this clear, let us take an example. In expressing admiration for an entity for having good qualities, the speaker looks for the appropriate concept in the conceptual system. The concept, which is the consequence of the embodied experience, takes the conceptual structure *respect*. This conceptual structure is linguistically expressed by means of semantic structure, which is encoded in language by the two adjectives *respectable* and *respectful*. The semantic structure of each adjective has its distinct value. In *She is a respectable woman from a good family*, the semantic structure of the adjective *respectable* means 'socially acceptable because of her good appearance, character, or manner'. A respectable woman deserves respect by reason of good qualities. In *He taught his children to be respectful of other people*, the semantic structure of the adjective *respectful* means 'showing respect for or marked by deference to others'. A respectful child is deferential towards or shows respect for other people.

Exercise 1.12

According to pre-cognitive conceptions of meaning, the following pairs of words are freely interchangeable. According to the cognitive conception, they are semantically distinctive. Can you show how?

1.	forcible	forceful
2.	displace	misplace
3.	triumphal	triumphant
4.	observance	observation
5.	international	intranational

1.4 Comparison

The different conceptions of meaning can be subsumed under two main-stream paradigms. The first paradigm is labelled **formalist** because it focuses on the formal aspects of language. This paradigm includes the decompositional conceptions of meaning: componential, conceptual and primitive. It considers language a system which should be studied in isolation, both from its users and its cognitive processes. Language is described separately from cognitive faculties and abstracted away from actual use, and so its principles of combination make no reference to system-external factors. For adherents of this paradigm, language faculty is divorced from cognitive influence. Consequently, they exclude the role of the speaker in shaping language. This is due to the theoretical position that divides language into distinct modules, and so its explanation is entirely internal. From the exercises tackled so far, one concludes that the formalist theories are not able to meet the complexities of semantic phenomena in natural language.

The second paradigm is labelled **cognitive** because it underlines the functional aspects of language. This paradigm includes the representational conception of meaning. It considers language as a tool of communication, where language structure reflects what people use language for. The function of conveying meaning has so affected linguistic form that it is senseless to divide it. The way one speaks (semantic structure) is influenced by the way one thinks (conceptual structure). This is to say semantic structure is a reflection of conceptual structure. For proponents of this paradigm, language faculty is influenced by cognitive processes. Consequently, it focuses on the role of the speaker in shaping language. A speaker can choose to view the same situation in different ways. This is due to the theoretical assumption that draws no boundaries between language components, and so its explanation is considerably external.

In addition to the major difference identified above, there are some minor differences between the two paradigms.

1. The formalist conceptions of meaning consider meaning as being derived from correspondence to a given state of affairs in the world. They rely on the technique of decomposition in the definition of a linguistic expression. By contrast, the cognitive conception of meaning considers meaning as being derived from conceptual representations in the mind of the speaker. The meaning of an expression is connected to a concept rather than directly to a physical object in the external

world. It rejects the technique of decomposition in the definition of a linguistic expression.

2. The formalist conception adopts an objectivist approach of meaning, and so sees human thought as disembodied. This is so because linguistic meaning is conceived in terms of states of affairs in the world. By contrast, the cognitive conception of meaning adopts an experientialist or empiricist approach of meaning, and so sees human thought as embodied. This is so because linguistic meaning is conceived in terms of human construal of reality.

3. The formalist conception of meaning assumes a dictionary view of meaning, which aims to provide precise definitions of linguistic expressions. Accordingly, linguistic knowledge is separate from world knowledge. By contrast, the cognitive conception of meaning assumes an encyclopaedic view of meaning, which aims to provide both semantic and pragmatic aspects of the meanings of linguistic expressions.

4. The formalist conception of meaning separates semantics from pragmatics, which is a consequence of the strict separation of linguistic knowledge from world knowledge. This is so because it holds that only semantic meaning, which is purely linguistic, belongs to the lexicon. By contrast, the cognitive conception of meaning rejects this sharp separation between semantics and pragmatics. Both semantic and pragmatic knowledge interact to give an utterance its meaning.

5. The formalist conception of meaning assumes compositionality of meaning. The meaning of a linguistic expression is determined by the lexical meanings of its components. This view implies that non-compositional expressions are the exception rather than the norm. By contrast, the cognitive conception of meaning assumes both compositionality and non-compositionality of meaning. The latter is demonstrated by the use of idioms, for example.

1.5 Summary

In this chapter, I have done three things. First, I addressed the issue of meaning and its aspects and levels. Second, I identified types of meaning. Third, I surveyed the status meaning has within different conceptions. Each conception defines the notion of meaning differently and uses different tools to represent it. In Traditional Semantics, the meaning of a linguistic expression resides in the linkage between its meaning and the object in the real world, a theory referred to as **referential**. In Structural Semantics, the meaning of a linguistic expression is shown in two ways: the relations it has with the other expressions in the language, a theory referred to as **relational**, or the analysis of its components, a theory referred to as **Componential Analysis**. In Generative Semantics, the meaning of a linguistic expression resides in its truth conditions, namely its objective meaning, neglecting the subjective, connotative or emotional ones. Two theories have been introduced: **Conceptual Semantics** and **Semantic Primes**. In **Cognitive Semantics**, the meaning of a linguistic expression refers to a mental representation of the world, a theory referred to as **representational** or **cognitive**. The conceptual structure, which the linguistic expression conjures up, is equated in language with the semantic structure, the conventional meaning which it has.

Table 1.1 Types of meaning

Type	Function	Governing rules
Descriptive	Saying what an entity, event or situation is like	Factuality: based on facts
Expressive	Showing personal attitudes, feelings or sensations	Subjectivity: based on opinions
Social	Indicating social relations between people	Appropriateness: based on circumstances

Table 1.2 Conceptions of meaning

Conception	Premise
Referential	The meaning of a linguistic expression derives from its reference to an actual object in the external world.
Relational	The meaning of a linguistic expression derives from its relation to other linguistic expressions in the same lexical field.
Componential	The meaning of a linguistic expression derives from the semantic components which it comprises.
Conceptual	The meaning of a linguistic expression derives from the conceptual components which fill its arguments.
Primitive	The meaning of a linguistic expression derives from the semantic primes which it evokes.
Representational (Cognitive)	The meaning of a linguistic expression derives from its mental representation of the external world which is subjectively experienced.

2

Lexical Semantics

Chapter 2 explores **lexical semantics**, the branch of semantics which deals with the meanings of words. The aim is to show how the lexicon is organized, how the words of a language are interrelated and how their meanings are consequently interpreted. The chapter addresses two concerns. One relates to terminology. It introduces the terms used in the study of lexical semantics and defines them in a way that is both concise and precise. The other pertains to relation. It introduces the meaning relations which exist between words. The chapter is organized as follows. Section 2.1 focuses on the issue of what the term **word** is and what **word meaning** is. Section 2.2 centres on the types of paradigmatic relations which exist between words. Section 2.3 concentrates on the types of syntagmatic relations which exist between words. Section 2.4 combines both paradigmatic and syntagmatic relations in the description of words. In all the sections, I pursue three steps. First, I introduce the term. Second, I explain its meaning. Third, I devise an exercise to test its application. Section 2.5 summarizes the main points of the chapter.

2.1 Word meaning

The meaning-bearing unit in language with which lexical semantics is concerned is the word. A **word** is a lexical item which is a combination of meaning and form. A word like *car*, for example, has two aspects which cannot be separated: the acoustic image /ka:/ and the concept [CAR]. It refers to a type of vehicle. Words may be simple, composite or compound. A **simple word**, also known as **monomorphemic**, is composed of only one lexical component, which is morphologically indivisible. The word *use*, for example, consists of just one lexical constituent. It is the minimum free form which can stand by itself and act as a meaningful word. A **complex word**, also known as **composite** or **polymorphemic**, is composed of two or more components which is morphologically divisible, one of which is a word. The word *useful*, for example, is a derivation from the lexical components *use* and *-ful*. A **compound word** is composed of two components, namely words, which is morphologically divisible. The word *birthday*, for example, is a combination of the lexical components *birth* and *day*.

A word may then consist of a morpheme or string of morphemes put together by the morphological rules of a language **Word meaning** is the meaning which a word has by virtue of the morphemes it contains and their successive integration, which is calculated independent of context. The meaning of a composite word is the compositional. It is constructed out of the meanings of its component morphemes. For example, the meaning of the word *useful* is the outcome of the meanings of the morphemes *use* and *-ful*, meaning 'full of use'. When a word is used in a context, it functions as a one-word utterance. **Utterance** is a particular piece of language, be it a word, phrase or sentence, which is spoken by a specific speaker on a specific occasion. **Utterance meaning**, alternatively called **speaker meaning**, is the meaning which a word conveys when it is used in a specific context on a specific occasion. For example, the word meaning of *loud* in *loud music* is 'noisy', but its utterance meaning in *loud colour* is 'too bright'.

In order to establish the meanings of words, we need to look at the different types of lexical relation which exist between them. A **lexical relation**, commonly known as a **sense relation**, is a pattern of association that exists between words in a language. Words exhibit two types of lexical relation. The first is paradigmatic, which occurs along a vertical axis. Representatives of such relations are antonymy, polysemy, synonymy and taxonomy. The second is syntagmatic, which occurs along a horizontal axis. Representatives of such relations are anomaly, collocation, colligation and idiomaticity. The two types of relation are important in shedding light on the dynamic nature of vocabulary. At the simple word level, they facilitate our understanding of the links that words have with each other within a language on the basis of their meanings. At the complex word level, they uncover how the morphemes integrate with each other, and how they interact to give a word its identity.

2.2 Paradigmatic relations

One way of establishing word meaning is through a **paradigmatic relation**, a pattern of relation between words which occupy the same position in a linguistic structure. It is based on the criterion of **substitution**, the ability of words to replace each other vertically within a particular context. Paradigmatic relations operate at all levels of language. In the sound system, for example, the phonemes /p/, /l/ and /s/ can all be substituted for /n/ in the context of /-et/. The occurrence of the words of a linguistic structure on a vertical level has some consequences. On the lexical level, a paradigmatic relation uncovers the speech part or the word class which the selected words belong to. For example, in *It is a small/medium/large size*, the words *small*, *medium* and *large* are all adjectives. On the semantic level, a paradigmatic relation allows words denoting a common concept to be grouped together. For example, the words *fit*, *match* and *suit* can be used with clothes. Yet, each word has a use of its own. *Fit* is used with size. *Match* is used with thing. *Suit* is used with colour.

Exercise 2.1

The verbs *banish, discharge, dismiss, expel* and *evict* mean 'send a way' or 'get rid of', but they are used in different ways. Use each verb in the correct form to complete the appropriate sentence.

1. She was – – – – - from school for setting fire to the library.
2. He was – – – – from hospital after recovering from illness.
3. They were – – – – – from the flat for not paying their rent.
4. He was – – – – – from New Zealand for political reasons.
5. She was – – – – – from the firm for calling her boss a liar.

The most important paradigmatic relations are antonymy, polysemy, synonymy, and taxonomy. These sense relations are the different ways in which the meanings of words can be defined. They can be identified in almost all areas of the lexicon.

2.2.1 Antonymy

Antonymy is a lexical relation between two words in which one is the opposite of the other. The word antonymy is derived from the Greek root *anti* which means 'opposite' and denotes opposition in meaning. Representative examples are *short × long, asleep × awake* and *husband × wife*. Antonyms are often divided into primary and marginal types. Primary antonyms are subdivided into in three types: gradable, non-gradable and relational.

The first type is **gradable antonyms**. It is a lexical relation between two words in which the degree of opposition is not absolute. Gradable antonyms normally have a **contrary** relation. Semantically, the quality denoted is present in varying degrees. Linguistically, it can be modified by adverbs like *very*, and used in comparative constructions. Examples of gradable antonyms are *big × little, clever × stupid, brave × cowardly, hot × cold, beautiful × ugly, wide × narrow*, and so on. The denial of one word does not imply the assertion of the other, i.e., its antonym. For example, to say *the house is not big* does not mean *it is little*.

The second type is **non-gradable antonyms**, also called **complementaries** or **binary antonyms**. It is a lexical relation between two words in which the degree of opposition is absolute. Non-gradable antonyms normally have a **contradictory** relation. Semantically, the quality denoted admits of no middle ground. Linguistically, it cannot be modified by adverbs like *very*, or used in comparative constructions. Examples of non-gradable antonyms are *open × closed, dead × alive, married × single, pass × fail, hit × miss*, and so on. The denial of one implies the assertion of the other. For example, to say something is *dead* means it is *not alive*.

The third type is **relational antonyms**. It is a lexical relation between two words which, unlike the gradable ones, are not susceptible to degrees of opposition, and, unlike the non-gradable ones, they are not an either-or matter in character. Examples of relational antonyms are *mother × daughter, parent × offspring, plaintiff × defendant, murderer × victim, father × son*, and so on. Relational antonyms exhibit conversibility and reversibility. **Converse antonyms** exhibit a relation in which the existence of one implies the existence of the other. Examples of converse antonyms are *follow × precede, give × take, buy × sell, borrow × lend, push × pull*, and so on. **Reversive antonyms** exhibit a relation which involves opposition in direction. Examples of reversive antonyms are *up × down, left × right, in × out, forwards × backwards, in front of × behind, above × below*, and so on.

Exercise 2.2

For each pair of the antonyms below, specify the type of relation which it exhibits: gradable, non-gradable or relational.

1. odd × even
2. polite × rude
3. parent × child
4. hit × miss
5. arrive × depart

Marginal antonyms are subdivided into two types: auto-antonyms and anti-antonyms. **Auto-antonyms** are homographs which mean the opposite of each other. For example, the word *shell* has two meanings. As a noun, it refers to the hard outer part that covers something like eggs, nuts or peas, as in *I found a small piece of egg shell in my cake*. As a verb, it refers to the act of removing the shell from something like eggs, nuts or peas, as in *She was shelling peas in the kitchen*. **Anti-antonyms** are pairs of words which mean the same thing although they look the opposite of each other. For example, both *bone* and *debone* refer to the act of taking the bones out of fish or meat, as in *Ask the fishmonger to bone/debone the fish for you*. In such examples, the prefix reiterates the idea of removal, and so serves as an intensifier. A list of other examples includes *deflesh, dehair, dehull, delouse, denude, descale, deworm*, etc.

2.2.2 Polysemy

Polysemy, also called **polysemia**, is a language feature in which a word has several meanings. The name comes from Greek *poly* 'many' and *semy* 'meaning'. A word, also called a **polyseme**, which has more than one distinct but related meaning, is said to be **polysemous** or **polysemic**. For example, the word *head* displays a number of meanings. In *She nodded her head*, it refers to an object: part of the body above the neck. In *She sat at the head of the table*, it refers to location: the beginning or end of something. In *She is a good head taller than her sister*, it refers to a measure: using a person's head as a unit to measure size. In *The thought never entered my head*, it refers to an abstract entity: the mind. In *She resigned as head of department*, it refers to rank: a person who is in charge of a group of people or an organization. In *Their head office is in New York*, it refers to importance: the main office of a company. As can be seen, the multiple senses which the word *head* has are related in some way: the first three are concrete while the last three are abstract.

Polysemy should be distinguished from the other term **homonymy**, the relation between two words which sound alike but differ in meaning, or the relation between two words which have the same spelling but different meaning. Homonyms then are of two types.

Homophony is the relation between two or more words which are pronounced alike but have different spellings and meanings, as in *some/sum* /sʌm/, meat/meet /miːt/, pale/pail /peil/, right/write /rait/, sew/so /səu/, flour/flower /flauə/, bare/bear /beə/, and so on. In a dictionary, homophones are listed as separate entries.

Homography is the relation between two or more words which are spelt alike but have different meanings and different pronunciations, as in *bow* (to move your head forwards and downwards) /bau/ vs. *bow* (a weapon used for shooting arrows) /bɔu/. Other examples include *wind* (air blowing) /wind/ vs. *wind* (make a clock work) /waind/, *bass* (tone) /beis/ vs. *bass* (fish) /bas/, *tear* (rip) /teə/ vs. *tear* (liquid from the eye) /tiə/, *refuse* (reject) /ri'fju:z/ vs. *refuse* (waste material) /'refju:s/, and so on. In a dictionary, homographs are listed as separate entries.

Both polysemy and homonymy deal with multiple meanings of the same phonological form, but with polysemy one form bears two or more related meanings, whereas with homonymy one form bears two or more unrelated meanings. An example of homonymy is the word *coach*. It refers either to a person who trains an athlete or a team in sport or to a vehicle for transporting passengers. In a dictionary, polysemes are listed under one entry, whereas homonyms are listed under different entries.

Exercise 2.3

The following are polysemous words. For each one, give at least three meanings which each displays.

1. plain
2. over
3. foot
4. run
5. mouth

2.2.3 Synonymy

Synonymy is a lexical relation between two words in which the meaning of one is similar, but not identical, to the meaning of the other. A word is said to be a **synonym** of another word when one of its senses is the same or nearly the same as the other. The word *collect* is a synonym of the word *pick up* when talking about going somewhere by car in order to take somebody or something away, as in *I'll collect you/pick you up from the station*. However, they differ in other senses. When talking about collecting things, the word *collect* is used as in *She is collecting coins*. When talking about lifting someone or something from the ground, the word *pick up* is used as in *She picked up the coin lying on the floor*. This amounts to saying that total synonymy is hard to find. Total synonymy means that words can be substituted one for the other in all contexts without signalling a difference in meaning. Pairs of similar-looking words may share the same conceptual sense but they tend to differ along one or more of the following parameters.

- **dialect**. For example, *autumn* is used in Britain, whereas *fall* is used in the United States.
- **style**. For example, *begin* is used in informal language, whereas *commence* is used in formal language.
- **connotation**. For example, both *hide* and *conceal* mean 'to keep something secret', but they are connotatively different. *Hide* may or may not suggest intent as in *He hid the presents in the cupboard*, whereas *conceal* usually implies intent and a refusal to divulge something as in *He concealed the painting in the suitcase*.
- **collocation**. For example, the words *high* and *tall* mean 'above the average in height', but they take different collocations. *High* collocates mostly with things which rise from a base, as in *fence, mountain, wall,* and so on. *Tall* collocates mostly with things which grow high as in *grass, people, trees*, and so on. At other times, two collocates co-occur with the same word, but the meaning is different. For example, *little house*, for instance, has a different meaning from *small house*. *Little* carries connotations of affection that are absent in the more neutral word *small*.
- **grammatical property**. For example, *feed* is used intransitively and transitively, as in *Our kids feed three times a day*, and *Let's feed the kids*, while *nourish* is used only transitively as in *Fresh food nourishes children*.

Exercise 2.4

No two words have exactly the same meaning. Apply this tenet to the following pairs and show how different they are in meaning.

1. thankful   grateful
2. accurate   exact
3. repair   fix
4. quick   prompt
5. steal   rob

2.2.4 Taxonomy

Taxonomy, or **lexical hierarchy**, is a systematic way of classifying words by arranging them into categories. A category of a thing is structured in such a way that the general term at the **superordinate** (higher) level includes the specific terms at the **subordinate** (lower) level. The superordinate term displays a high degree of generality, whereas the subordinate terms display a high degree of specificity. Members of the subordinate level provide detailed information and distinctive properties of the category. Two main sorts of lexical hierarchy exist: hyponymy and meronymy. They differ with respect to the nature of the sense relations which exist between the words.

2.2.4.1 Hyponymy

Hyponymy is a lexical relation between two words in which the meaning of one is included in the meaning of the other. The superordinate word which has a general meaning is called a **hyperonym**. The subordinate word which has a specific meaning is called a **hyponym**. The subordinate word is included in the superordinate word. For example, *fruit* is a hyperonym of *apple*. *Fruit* is general. Therefore, it is superordinate. *Apple* is a hyponym of or a kind of *fruit*. *Apple* is specific. Therefore, it is subordinate. *Fruit* is general because it denotes a particular set in which *apple* is a kind. The set of words which share the same superordinate term are referred to as **co-hyponyms**. For example, *apple, banana* and *orange* are co-hyponyms of *fruit*.

Exercise 2.5

Write three hyponyms for each of the following hyperonyms to indicate the relation of inclusion.

1. cutlery
2. crockery
3. vehicle
4. fish
5. bird

2.2.4.2 Meronymy

Meronymy, also called **partonymy,** is a lexical relation between two words in which the meaning of one names a part of the meaning of the other. This is a part-whole relation between the senses of words. The word naming the part is referred to as **meronym,** and the word naming the whole is referred to as **holonym.** For example, *nose* is a meronym or a part of *face*. Conversely, *face* is a holonym of *nose*. Words naming the parts of the same whole are referred to as **co-meronyms.** For example, *eye, mouth* and *nose* are co-meronyms of *face*. Each meronym serves a different function in the language.

Exercise 2.6

Write three meronyms for each of the following holonyms to indicate the part-whole relation.

1.   camera
2.   computer
3.   car
4.   room
5.   house

2.3   Syntagmatic relations

Another way of establishing word meaning is through a **syntagmatic rela-tion,** a pattern of relation between the words of a linguistic structure in a linear order. It is based on the criterion of **juxtaposition,** the ability of words to combine horizontally. Syntagmatic relations operate at all levels of lan-guage. In the sound system, the phonemes in the word *net*, for example, are so arranged as to make sense. The occurrence of the words of a linguistic structure in sequence has some consequences. On the lexical level, a syn-tagmatic relation between words helps one to understand their combinatorial compatibility. For example, one can say *heavy rain*, but not *strong rain*. On the semantic level, a syntagmatic relation between words helps one to sepa-rate words that are otherwise considered synonymous. For example, both of the words *gain* and *win* can occur with the word *approval*. However, only *gain* is used with *advantage* and only *win* is used with *game*.

Exercise 2.7

Not every word matches a neighbouring word. Choose the correct word that occurs with the word next to it.

1. *burning* occurs with   *blazing* occurs with
2. *broad* occurs with   *wide* occurs with
3. *make* occurs with   *do* occurs with
4. *profound* occurs with   *deep* occurs with
5. *powerful* occurs with   *strong* occurs with

The most important syntagmatic relations are anomaly, collocation, colligation, and idiomaticity. These sense relations are the different ways in which the meanings of sentences can be defined.

2.3.1 Anomaly

Anomaly is a lexical relation in which a word does not match the context in which it is used. The word is not in agreement with the surrounding words which it accompanies. For example, in *a sane chair* the expression is grammatically acceptable because it follows the rules of grammar: determiner + adjective + noun. Yet, it is semantically anomalous because it violates the rules of usage. It is anomalous because the meanings of the words *sane* and *chair* do not go together normally. The expression simply violates the rules of conventional meaning, and so is intuitively rejected by competent speakers of English. As such, anomaly involves the violation of the concept of **selection restrictions**, syntactic-semantic restrictions which govern the co-occurrence of words. It is the tendency of a word to select another word with which it can co-occur. For example, the restriction of the word *sane* to humans as in *a sane person*, and not to non-humans as in *a sane chair* is a selection restriction.

A word can be anomalous, i.e., different from what is normal or expected, in two ways: pleonasm and zeugma. **Pleonasm** is the use of a word to emphasize what is clear without it. For example, in *see with eyes* the words *with eyes* are redundant because they contribute no extra meaning to the word *see*. Other examples of pleonasm include *a new innovation, female actress, dental toothache, return back, end result, invited guest*, and so on. **Zeugma** is the use of a word which has to be interpreted in two different ways at the same time in order to make sense. In *The bread was baking, and so was I*, the word *baking* could refer either to bread being cooked in the oven, or to the person getting fed up with waiting. Other examples of zeugma include *She always pays him the money and compliments, He carried the injured and the responsibility for their lives, He was wearing a puzzled look on his face and a new coat, She could well expire before her club membership does, She held her breath and her father's hand tightly,* and so on.

Exercise 2.8

The examples below are grammatically acceptable but semantically anomalous. Show how they violate selection restrictions.

1. Mutton is meat from cow.
2. I heard a lion barking.
3. The plant passed away.
4. A stallion is a female horse.
5. The engine needs food.

2.3.2 Collocation

Collocation is the lexical pattern within which a word is found. It is a lexical relation in which two words occur next to each other in spoken or written language. It is very helpful in establishing the meanings of words in communication. For example, the collocations of *sensual* describe things that relate to the body as in *They were moved by the sensual movements of the dancer*, whereas the collocations of *sensuous* describe things that relate to the mind as in *They appreciated the sensuous music of the concert*. Thus, one can say that *sensual* is a normal collocate of *movement*, whereas *sensuous* is a normal collocate of *music*. This means that words combine normally with some words and less normally with others. The combination is influenced by what is referred to as the principle of **compatibility**, the tendency of words to co-occur in certain positions due to sharing specific syntactic-semantic features. For instance, the verb *do* is compatible with *exercise* as a direct object, and not with *cake*, which normally takes *make*. The adjective *thick* is compatible with both *fog* and *soup*, but only *dense* is compatible with *fog*.

Constructions are of two types: head-complement and head-modifier. The **head** is that element in the construction which is central because it determines the semantic character of the whole construction. A **complement** is an autonomous element that fills a gap in the semantic structure of the dependent head. It adds intrinsic conceptual substance to the head. Therefore, a complement like *the door* in *close the door* cannot be omitted. A **modifier**, by contrast, is a dependent element that has a gap in its semantic structure which is filled by the head. It adds non-intrinsic specifications to the head. Therefore, a modifier like *dangerous* in *a dangerous road* can be omitted without making the construction ungrammatical. The distinction between complements and modifiers has consequences for lexical selections in that heads select their complements, whereas modifiers select their heads. For example, the head verb *boil* selects complements naming liquids or vegetables such as *beans, carrots, potatoes*, and so on. The modifier *utterly* selects heads of negative connotation such as *appalling, exhausted, miserable, nonsensical*, and so on.

The potential of lexical items to collocate with each other is known as their **collocability or collocational range**. A related term is **semantic prosody**, a term used in corpus-based lexicology to describe a word which typically co-occurs with other words that belong to a particular semantic set. Collocations are, therefore, semantically based. In a collocation, meaning usually extends from one word to another. That is, complements that follow heads must fall within a particular semantic field. For example, the word *cause* usually collocates with words denoting unpleasant things like *difficulty, distress, pain, trouble*, and so on. Therefore, the word *cause* is said to have a negative prosody. Conversely, the word *bring about* collocates with words denoting pleasant things like *cure, improvement, solution, success,* and so on. Therefore, the word *bring about* is said to have a positive prosody. Thus, one can say *a problem is caused*, and *a solution is brought about*.

Exercise 2.9

For each of the following patterns of collocation, write two examples to demonstrate the collocability of the words.

1. verb + noun
2. adverb + adjective
3. adverb + verb
4. verb + adjective
5. verb + adverb

2.3.3 *Colligation*

Colligation is the grammatical patterning within which a word is found. It is a pattern which shows the position of a word in a sentence and/or delimits the types of its complements. In English, adjectives can be used either attributively or predicatively. An **attributive adjective** is one which occurs before a noun. For example, the adjective *main* can only be used attributively, as in *the main road*. A **predicative adjective** is one which occurs after a verb. For example, the adjective *afraid* can only be used predicatively, as in *the child is afraid*. Some adjectives can be used both attributively and predicatively. For example, in *my old friend* the adjective *old* is used attributively. It describes friendship. In *my friend is old* the adjective *old* is used predicatively. It describes age. The same applies to the position of English nouns when they function as modifiers. For example, the noun *paper* can be used attributively as in *a paper cup*, and predicatively as in *a cup made of paper*.

As for verbs, they can take, relative to their semantics, different types of complements. For example, the verb *let* takes the bare infinitive, as in *Let him relax on the beach*. The verb *want* takes the to-infinitive, as in *He wants to relax on the beach*. The verb *enjoy* takes the gerund, as in *He enjoys relaxing on the beach*. Verbs take particular prepositions. For example, the verb *acquit* is in a colligational relation with the preposition *of*, and together they form the phrase *acquit of*, as in *The jury acquitted him of murder*. The same applies to adjectives. For example, the adjective *clever* takes the preposition *at* as in *She's clever at getting what she wants*. Some adjectives take two prepositions but with a difference in use. For example, the adjective *anxious* takes *about* with things as in *He seemed anxious about the exam*, and *for* with people as in *Parents are naturally anxious for their children*.

Exercise 2.10

Write the complement each verb below takes: bare infinitive, to-infinitive or -ing gerund. Then write a sentence containing the verb and complement. Some verbs may take two complements.

1. recall
2. intend
3. make
4. pledge
5. like

2.3.4 Idiomaticity

Idiomaticity is a lexical relation that deals with a group of words whose meaning is different from the meanings of the individual words. For example, *let the cat out of the bag* is an idiom that means 'to tell a secret by mistake'. An **idiom** then is a group of words having a particular meaning which is different from the meanings of each word understood on its own. Unlike the meaning of a collocational phrase which is mainly compositional, the meaning of an idiom is non-compositional. It is non-compositional in the sense that its meaning cannot be derived from the conjoined meanings of the words making it up. Idioms are thus stored in the mental lexicon as ready-made forms. For example, it is not possible to construct the meaning of the idiom *to pull someone's leg* on the basis of the meanings of the words *pull* and *leg*. Idiomatically, it means 'to tell someone something that is not true as a way of joking with them'. Unlike a collocational phrase which is subject to grammatical changes, idioms are grammatically and lexically fixed. No modification or pluralization of any of its words is possible. Idioms often get their meanings from metaphorical interpretations. For example, in *get/have a handle on something* the original meaning is that of 'putting a handle on a physical object which helps to open or carry it', but the metaphorical meaning is that of 'being able to understand somebody or something so that you can deal with it or them later', as in *I can't get a handle on these sales figures.*

Exercise 2.11

The following expressions are considered idioms in English. Can you figure out what each means?

1. keep an eye on
2. bite the bullet
3. ring a bell
4. keep your nose clean
5. by word of mouth

2.4 Paradigmatic-syntagmatic relations

The two types of relation can be simultaneously present in lexical fields. A **lexical field** is a network which subsumes words that are related in meaning, each of which represents a special feature. On this view, the vocabulary of a language is not simply a listing of independent items, but it is organized into fields within which words interrelate and define each other in various ways. The field is divided up among its members, where the meaning of any member is marked by the meanings of the other members in the field. For example, words denoting *kinship* can only be understood by comparing them to each other. A lexical field then is a coherent subset of the vocabulary whose members are interlinked by paradigmatic and syntagmatic relations. For example, an important part of the meaning of the word *close* is its paradigmatic relations with words such as *end, conclude, finish*, and so on, and its syntagmatic relations with words such as *a debate, a case, a meeting*, and so on. Therefore, to know the meaning of any member of a field cannot be achieved without also knowing the meanings of the other members. One does not know fully what *close* means unless one has a grasp of the other members of the field of termination.

Exercise 2.12

Give examples of syntagmatic and paradigmatic relation which the words *hire* and *car* tend to hold in the following sentence.

1. How much would it cost to <u>hire</u> a <u>car</u> for a fortnight?
2.
3.
4.
5.

2.5 Summary

In this chapter, I have presented a broad outline of what lexical semantics is and what it covers. **Lexical semantics** is the branch of semantics which studies the meanings of words. In the outline, I did two things. First, I introduced the notion of **word**, the meaning-bearing unit with which lexical semantics is concerned, and defined **word meaning** as the meaning of a word based on the morphemes it comprises regardless of context of use. Second, I identified the two patterns of lexical relation which words hold and which play a crucial role in explaining their meanings. One is **paradigmatic**, a pattern of language consisting of words that are arranged in vertical order. This includes antonymy, polysemy, synonymy and taxonomy. The other is **syntagmatic**, a pattern of language consisting of words that are arranged in horizontal order. This includes anomaly, collocation, colligation and idiomaticity. The tables below present summaries of the two patterns.

Table 2.1 Paradigmatic relations between words

Lexical relation	Definition	Example
Antonymy	oppositeness in meaning	hot × cold
Polysemy	multiplicity of meaning	foot: of person, bed or mountain
Synonymy	sameness in meaning	begin = commence
Taxonomy	classification into groups	hammer, saw, chisel > tool

Table 2.2 Syntagmatic relations between words

Lexical relation	Definition	Example
Anomaly	odd use of words	kick *with foot
Collocation	lexical co-occurring of words	a hard/*strong frost
Colligation	grammatical patterning of words	busy practising/*to practise
Idiomaticity	peculiar meaning of phrases	to take the bull by the horns = to take charge of a situation

Sentential Semantics

Chapter 3 examines **sentential semantics**, the branch of semantics which deals with the meanings of phrases and sentences. The aim is to show how the lexicon is organized, how the sentences of a language are interrelated and how their meanings are consequently interpreted. The chapter addresses two concerns. One concern relates to terminology. It introduces the terms used in the study of sentential semantics and defines them in a way that is both simple and clear. The other concern pertains to relation. It introduces the meaning relations which exist between sentences. The chapter is organized as follows. Section 3.1 lays emphasis on the issue of what the term **sentence** is and what **sentence meaning** is. Section 3.2 centres on the types of relations which exist between sentences. Section 3.3 concentrates on utterances which require pragmatic inferences. Section 3.4 is concerned with the semantic roles which participants in a sentence fulfil. In all the sections, I pursue three steps. First, I introduce the term. Second, I explain its meaning. Third, I devise an exercise to test its application. Section 3.5 summarizes the main points of the chapter.

3.1 Sentence meaning

The meaning-bearing unit in language with which sentential semantics is concerned is the sentence. A **sentence** is a well-formed string of words put together by the grammatical rules of a language. For example, a string of words like *He won a trophy* is a sentence in English because it conforms to the rule of grammar: subject+verb+object. By contrast, a string of words like *He a trophy won* is not a sentence in English because it consists of subject+object+verb which is a violation of the above rule of grammar. Sentences may be simple, complex or compound. A **simple sentence** is a sentence which consists of only one clause, as in *He was watching a programme on TV*. A **complex sentence** is a sentence which consists of a main clause and at least one subordinate clause linked by a subordinator, as in *He was watching a programme on TV when the bell rang*. A **compound sentence** is a sentence which consists of two or more main clauses linked by a coordinator, as in *He was watching a programme on TV and eating popcorn*. A **clause** is a major

unit of grammar which may contain a subject, verb phrase, object, complement and adverbial, as in *He found the programme on TV very interesting*.

A sentence then is a unit of speech constructed according to the rules of
grammar. **Sentence meaning** is the literal meaning a sentence has by virtue
of the words it contains and their grammatical arrangement, regardless of the
context in which it is used. It is the compositional meaning of a sentence as
constructed out of the meanings of its component words. For example, the
meaning of the sentence *He won a trophy* is the outcome of the meanings
of the words *he*, *win* and *trophy*. When a sentence is used in a context, it
becomes an utterance. **Utterance** is a particular piece of language, be it a
word, phrase or sentence, spoken by a specific speaker on a specific occasion.
For example, the word *trophy*, the phrase *a major trophy*, and the sentence
He won a major trophy are all utterances in English. **Utterance meaning**,
alternatively called **speaker meaning**, is the non-literal meaning a sentence
has when it is used in a specific context on a specific occasion. For example,
the sentence meaning of *I am tied up* is 'I cannot move because my arms and
legs are fastened', but its utterance meaning is 'I am busy', which arises out
of context.

Context is the physical environment in which a linguistic expression is
used. It refers to the location where the discussion takes place. For example,
the context for *The book is now overdue* is a library, and for *We are fully
booked* is a hotel. **Co-text** is the linguistic environment in which a linguistic
expression is used. It refers to that which precedes or follows the linguistic
expression, and so determines its actual meaning. For example, the word
plain has several meanings, but to know which meaning is being used we
need to take into account the meaning of the word next to it. In *a plain dress*,
it means 'simple and undecorated', whereas in *a plain fact* it means 'honest
and direct'. The meaning a linguistic expression has in a context is called
contextual meaning. Every sentence expresses a **proposition,** the semantic
content of an expression which describes a state of affairs in the world. This
notion helps to understand the fact that some sentences may have the same
propositional content but differ in semantic respects. For example, the active
voice in *He won a trophy* and the passive voice in *A trophy was won by him*
have the same propositional content. The difference between them relates to
what is in focus in the mind of the speaker. In the active the action is in focus,
whereas in the passive the result is in focus.

3.2 Sentential relations

One common way of establishing the meanings of sentences is through examining the different types of sentential relation which exist between them. A **sentential relation** is a pattern of association that exists between sentences in a language. Sentences exhibit a number of meaning relations, namely paraphrase, contradiction, entailment, presupposition and implicature. These relations are important in shaping the identity of a sentence within the linguistic system and consequently underlining the dynamic nature of the language as a whole. At the level of a simple sentence, the sentential relations facilitate our understanding of the relations that words hold with each other within a sentence on the basis of their meanings. At the level of a complex sentence, the sentential relations uncover how the clauses in a sentence integrate with each other and how they give a sentence its overall meaning.

3.2.1 Paraphrase

Paraphrase is a semantic relation between a pair of sentences in which the second is an alternative version of the first without changing its propositional meaning. It is the process of expressing something written or spoken using different words or different word order, especially in order to make it easier to understand or bring into focus some parts of it. For example, the sentence *Tom bought a car from Jack* is a paraphrase of *Jack sold a car to Tom*. The two sentences share a common proposition or a single semantic content despite the fact that they differ with respect to focus. In paraphrasing, the semantic roles of the nouns are the same even though their grammatical functions may be different. For example, in *Nancy skimmed the newspaper* the noun *Nancy* is the agent/subject while the noun *newspaper* is the patient/object. In its paraphrase *The newspaper was skimmed by Nancy*, the noun *newspaper* is the patient/subject while the noun *Nancy* is the agent/object of preposition. Paraphrases play useful roles in communication. They provide a variety of stylistic choices, with each choice encoding a different communicative strategy.

A **communicative strategy** is a plan adopted by the speaker to achieve a particular purpose. One such strategy pertains to **foregrounding**, the act of highlighting a part of a sentence, i.e., by making it the main point of attention and consequently emphasizing its importance. The remaining parts of the sentence, which are not the main point of attention, are backgrounded. **Backgrounding** is the act of paying less attention and so less importance to a part of a sentence. There are various linguistic devices for highlighting parts of a sentence. This is illustrated in the sentence *Frank sent the flowers yesterday* and its paraphrases *It was Frank who sent the flowers yesterday, It was the flowers that Frank sent yesterday*, and *It was yesterday that Frank sent the flowers*. The different structures in these examples are called **focusing devices**, methods used to produce a particular result or a wanted effect. The foregrounded part of a sentence is called the **focus**, the central point of a sentence in which speakers are most interested and to which they pay a special attention.

Exercise 3.1

Finish each of the following sentences in such a way that it means exactly the same as the sentence printed before it.

1. She was not only clever but also honest.
   Apart from
2. Staying indoors all the time is unhealthy.
   It
3. It is believed that they knew the answer.
   They
4. I will not leave under any circumstances.
   Under
5. It is a pity they live so far away.
   I wish

3.2.2 Contradiction

Contradiction is a semantic relation between a pair of sentences in which the second is a complete opposite of the first, thus triggering a change in meaning. The two sentences cannot both be true or false at the same time. If one is true, the other must be false. For example, *Cows are mammals and Cows are not mammals* are contradictory sentences. The second sentence is not true by virtue of its meaning. On the basis of truth, sentences can be classified into contradictory, analytic and synthetic. A **contradictory** sentence is one which is necessarily false because of the meanings of certain words in it. A contradictory sentence is usually contrasted with both analytic and synthetic sentences. An **analytic** sentence is one which is necessarily true because of the meanings of the words in it. It is a sentence whose truth is verified by its grammatical form and lexical meaning. For example, *My brother is male* is an analytic sentence because it is true without reference to real world knowledge. A **synthetic** sentence is one which is neither contradictory nor analytic. It is a sentence which may be true or false depending on the way the world is. It is a sentence whose status is determined not by its meaning alone, but rather by the relation between its meaning and the way the world is. For example, *My cousin is female* is a synthetic sentence because its truth can only be confirmed with reference to real world knowledge. This is so because the word *cousin* can be male or female.

Exercise 3.2

Identify each of the following sentences as analytic, synthetic or contradictory. Then, correct the contradictory ones.

1. Cats are fish.
2. Spinsters are unmarried women.
3. A man is a butterfly.
4. A blind person has impaired sight.
5. The spokesperson denied the rumours.

3.2.3 Entailment

Entailment is a semantic relation between a pair of sentences in which the second is the implicit consequence of the first. It is a relation between two propositions in which the second logically follows from the first. For example, *Kim bought pens* entails *Kim bought stationery*. The entailment here is a consequence of the semantic relation between *pens* and *stationery*. This shows that an important part of the meaning of *pens* is contained within the meaning of *stationery*. Accordingly, if the first sentence is true, the second must also be true. If the first sentence is false, the second must also be false. The relation, however, is not reversible. A change of a word in the sentence influences the entailment. *Kim bought stationery* does not entail *Kim bought pens*. The thing bought could be *clips, files* or *folders*. Unlike presupposition, entailment behaves differently under negation. Negating the first sentence causes the entailment in the second sentence to fail. Thus, *Kim didn't buy pens* does not entail *Kim bought stationery*. In presupposition, by contrast, the situation is different. Even if the first sentence is negated, the presupposition holds. For example, both *Kim has stopped working* and *Kim has not stopped working* presuppose *Kim has been working*.

Exercise 3.3

Write in the space provided what entailment each of the following sentences makes.

1. The hunter killed the fox.
2. The man snores so loudly.
3. She decided to take a rest.
4. She bought a nightingale.
5. They were selling tulips.

3.2.4 Presupposition

Presupposition is a semantic relation between a pair of sentences in which the second is the implicit presumption of the first. It is a relation between what the speaker states in saying a particular sentence and what the hearer already knows. For example, when a speaker utters a statement like *David quit his job*, the hearer takes it for granted that *David had been working* although this is not explicitly stated. The presupposition is that the speaker and the hearer know that *David had been working*. Unlike entailment, presupposition behaves differently under negation. Negating the first sentence does not cause the presupposition in the second sentence to fail. The negative version *David did not quit his job* carries the same presupposition as the affirmative version *David quit his job*. In both statements, the presupposition is *David has had a job*. This property of a presupposition remaining true even when it is negated is referred to as **constancy under negation**. Presuppositions are of two types: lexical and structural. They give language users the chance to make their thoughts implicit, and consequently make communication less tedious.

In **lexical presuppositions**, certain words in the first sentence, called **lexical triggers**, presuppose the truth of the information stated in the second sentence.

- Factive verbs like *admit, realize* or *regret*. For example, *Ann regrets breaking the glass* presupposes *Ann broke the glass*. One regrets something one did in the past.

- Non-factive verbs like *dream, imagine* or *pretend*. For example, *She pretends to be happy* presupposes *She is not happy*. One pretends something one does not have.
- Aspectual verbs like *start, continue* or *stop*. For example, *She stopped nagging* presupposes *She used to nag*. One stops something one is doing.
- Implicative verbs like *manage, bother* or *happen*. For example, *He managed to persuade her* presupposes *He persuaded her*. When one manages something, one succeeds in doing it.

In certain cases, presuppositions depend on the speaker's knowledge of the world. For example, *She finally signed the contract* presupposes *She hesitated before signing the contract*. When one finally does something, one does it after a long time.

In **structural presuppositions**, certain sentence structures, namely wh-words, presuppose the truth of the stated information. For example, the interrogative sentence in *When did he resign?* presupposes the sentence *He resigned*.

Exercise 3.4

Write what presupposition each of the following sentences gives rise to.

1. The furniture was covered in dust.
2. The children are complaining again.
3. If I weren't ill, I would have come.
4. The board of inquiry is continuing its investigation.
5. She admitted having driven the car without insurance.

3.2.5 Implicature

Implicature is a semantic relation between a pair of sentences in which the second is the implied meaning of the first. It is a relationship between two propositions in which the first is said but the second is meant. For example, the implicature from *The tree branches are getting long* is *The tree needs pruning*. Implicatures result from the process of **implication**, suggesting something without saying it directly, on which speakers and hearers agree in the course of communication. Two basic sorts of implicature can be distinguished in language.

One is **conventional implicature**, where the message is expressed explicitly in the first sentence. It is usually made irrespective of context. It is associated with discourse markers which help to arrive at the additional meanings such as *after all, actually, all in all, and, besides, but, even, furthermore, like, so, still, too, yet, well,* and so on. For example, the use of *and* carries the conventional implicature of addition when it joins static information as in *He was genial and affable*, and of sequence when it joins dynamic information as in *She came in and took her coat off.* The use of *but* in the utterance *The student worked hard, but he failed* is normally taken to convey the conventional implicature of contrast. The use of *even* in the utterance *Even a child can understand it* carries the conventional implicature of contrary to expectation. The use of *so* in the utterance *It was still painful, so I went to see a doctor* carries the conventional implicature of result. The use of *yet* in the utterance *Bill hasn't come yet* carries the conventional implicature of expected to happen at a later time.

The other is **conversational implicature**, where the message is expressed implicitly in the first sentence. It is usually made with respect to context. In some conversational implicatures, the additional meaning is deduced from particular knowledge where the implicature is entirely context dependent. For example, the answer *A relative is coming for a visit* to the question *Do you want to go out tonight?* is definitely no. The answer *Is the earth round?* to the question *Do you like ice-cream?* is clearly yes. In other conversational implicatures, the additional meaning is inferred from general knowledge where the implicature is more predictable and less context dependent. For example, in *I was sitting in a car* the indefinite article *a* shows that the car is not the speaker's. In further conversational implicatures, the additional meaning is derived from scalar knowledge where the implicature is scale dependent. For example, the utterance *Some players are injured* is interpreted as implicating *not all*. The utterance *You should see a consultant* is interpreted as implicating *not must*.

Finally, there exists a kind of expression in which you repeat the same word twice. This is called **tautology**. A tautology is analytically and logically true. The expression conveys an additional meaning which goes beyond what the words mean. For example, in the expression *Business is business* the implicature conveyed is that in business it is financial and commercial considerations which matter, and not friendship. Examples of other tautologies include *A hamburger is a hamburger, Boys will be boys, War is war, When you are dead, you are dead*, and so on.

Exercise 3.5

Each of the following situations gives rise to a conversational implicature. Say what the implicature would be?

1. Do you love me? I am fond of you.
2. The campaigners went to the school.
3. The talk show we saw on TV was okay.
4. Some of my friends like playing dominos.
5. Can I speak to Frank? He is in the shower.

Implicatures are then implicit messages that are inferable in a particular or general context. In order to make them work, speakers and hearers have to comply with a basic **co-operative principle**. This principle demands that participants should make an important contribution to the success of the conversation. Compliance with this principle helps to reduce misunderstanding in conversation and achieve rational interaction in communication. This principle is divided into four sub-principles, referred to as **maxims**, basic rules which participants should adhere to in any ordinary conversation.

1. Maxim of **quantity**. Speakers should be economical and informative; should say neither too little nor too much. For example, when asked about one's age, one should simply give the years. It is a violation of the maxim of quantity to give further details like the months, days or minutes. The reason is that the answer is too much.
2. Maxim of **quality**. Speakers should be truthful; they should not say what they believe to be false or for which they lack adequate evidence. For example, when asked about one's financial state, one should tell the truth and say *penniless*. It is a violation of the maxim of quality to say *millionaire*. The reason is that the answer is untrue.
3. Maxim of **relevance**. Speakers should be relevant; what they say must connect suitably with the rest of the conversation. For example, when asked about somebody's *hairstyle*, one's response should be on it. It is a violation of the maxim of relevance to say *What is on TV tonight?* The reason is that the answer is irrelevant.
4. Maxim of **manner**. Speakers should be brief, clear and orderly. For example, it is a violation of the maxim of manner to utter the sentence *He left her in tears*. The reason is that the sentence is not clear. It means either 'He was in tears when he left her', or 'She was in tears when he left her'.

Exercise 3.6

In the following conversations, the answers violate the co-operative principle. Decide which maxim is violated, and then explain why.

1. What should I do to get rid of this headache, Doctor? Take some medicine.
2. When am I going to get back the money I lent you? Boy, it's very hot here!
3. Mr. Murphy got his Ph.D. in 1986, his BA in 1982, and his MA in 1980.
4. How many hours do you work a week? 80 with no vacation.

3.3 Inference

Another common way of establishing the meanings of sentences is through **inference**, a conclusion which a hearer draws about something unsaid based on existing evidence or general knowledge. Inference is crucial to interpretation because a great deal of what speakers communicate is implicit. From the utterance *There is smoke* the inference is *There is fire*. This type of inference is based on evidence as there can be no smoke without fire. From the utterance *The tourists enjoyed being on the beach* the inference is *The sun was shining and the sea was calm*. This type of inference is based on general knowledge as people enjoy the beach when the weather is nice. The word *infer* should be distinguished from the word *imply*. Both words can describe the same event, but they do so from different points of view. The word *imply* means 'to communicate an idea or feeling without saying it directly'. In *She asked him if he would help her and he nodded,* the implication is that he agreed to help her. The word *infer* means 'to arrive at a conclusion by relying on evidence'. In *She is looking pale*, the inference is that she is ill.

Inference is required particularly in the analysis of utterances such as ambiguity, deixis and speech acts.

3.3.1 Ambiguity

Ambiguity is a phenomenon whereby an expression form has more than one meaning, and may therefore cause confusion. If the ambiguity is in a single word, it is lexical ambiguity. In *She could not bear children*, the word *bear* means either 'could not give birth to children', or 'could not put up with children'. If the ambiguity is in a sentence, it is sentential ambiguity. In *The host met the guest with a smile*, the prepositional phrase *with a smile* can be grouped either with the word *host* or with the word *guest*. Typically, the speaker intends just one of the alternative meanings and expects the hearer to attend to that meaning. The process of establishing a single interpretation for an ambiguous word or sentence is known as **disambiguation**. Ambiguity, which is about one form having two or more meanings, is different from other phenomena which characterize linguistic expressions, namely vagueness and indeterminacy.

Vagueness is about lack of referential clarity, which results from giving little information about something. This occurs when the referent in the world is not clear for the hearer. For example, in *They have a house near the flow of water* the phrase *the flow of water* is vague as it is difficult to decide whether it is a *brook, stream* or *river*. A *brook* is smaller than a *stream* and a *stream* is smaller than a *river* in size. Likewise, in *She walked in an area of trees*, the phrase *an area of trees* is vague as it is difficult to decide whether it is a *grove, wood* or *forest*. A *grove* is smaller than a *wood* and a *wood* is smaller than a *forest* in size. **Indeterminacy** is about difficulty of referent identification. This occurs when it is difficult to identify exactly, without reference to real world knowledge, the referent of an expression. For example, there is indeterminacy in the use of the word *friend* in *I will bring a friend*. The word *friend* could be male or female. Likewise, there is indeterminacy in the expression *Alice's book is interesting*. It could refer either to the book she wrote, or the book she bought.

3.3.1.1 Lexical ambiguity

This type of ambiguity arises when a sentence contains a word which has more than one meaning. For example, the word *organizer* in *What an excellent organizer!* is ambiguous because it may be interpreted as 'a person who plans things carefully', or 'a device for storing information'.

Exercise 3.7

Study each of the following sentences carefully and underline the word that makes the sentence ambiguous. Then, give the two possible meanings for each.

1.   She waited near the bank.
2.   The boy looks backward.
3.   Jim took me to the court.
4.   She broke the glasses.
5.   It must be a new record.

3.3.1.2   Sentential ambiguity

This type of ambiguity, alternatively called **structural** or **grammatical**, arises when the structure of a sentence has two or more meanings. Sentential ambiguity is of two subtypes. The first subtype is called **grouping ambiguity**. This occurs when a phrase in a sentence can be arranged in two ways, and so can have two readings, as in *She invited young boys and girls*. In the first reading, the word *young* is grouped with boys and girls, resulting in 'young boys and young girls'. In the second reading, the word *young* is grouped with boys alone, resulting in 'young boys and girls'.

Exercise 3.8

Study each of the following utterances carefully and underline the structure that causes the sentence to be ambiguous. Then, give the two possible interpretations for each.

1.   We talked about the party last night.
2.   Small boys and girls are easily frightened.
3.   The chicken is ready to eat.
4.   That is just a crazy lawyer's idea.
5.   There is a café in the district which I like.

The second subtype is **function ambiguity**. This occurs when a phrase in a sentence fulfils two or more grammatical functions, as in *the ringing of the bells*. This is a noun phrase which could mean either *the bells are ringing* or *someone is ringing the bells*. In the first reading, the word *bell* functions as subject. In the second reading, the word *bell* functions as object.

Exercise 3.9

Study each of the following utterances carefully and underline the phrase that has double grammatical functions. Then, give the two possible interpretations for each.

1. Visiting relatives can be boring.
2. The shooting of the hunters was appalling.
3. Flying planes can be dangerous.
4. I like ice-cream and cake.
5. She likes pets more than him.

3.3.2 Deixis

The word *deixis* is derived from the Greek word meaning 'to point to' via language. **Deixis** is the mechanism which encodes the personal, spatial and temporal dimensions of language by means of linguistic forms relative to the speaker's standpoint. Like pointers, the linguistic forms are contextually bound, i.e., they rely on context in order to be correctly interpreted. They are called **deictic expressions**, alternatively called **indexicals**. Deixis is, therefore, the process of referring that is tied to the speaker's location, as the deictic centre, from which a scene is described. In terms of location, deictic forms can be proximal or distal. A **proximal** form is one that is near the speaker like *this*, *here* or *now*. A **distal** form is one that is away from the speaker like *that*, *there* or *then*. In *Can you pass me that pen?*, for example, the referent *pen* is relatively distant from the speaker, and so the appropriate deictic form used to point to it is *that*. In linguistics, three sub-types of deictic forms exist: person, space and time.

Person deixis

Person deixis refers to forms used to point to people. It is concerned with identifying the roles of the participants in an utterance: the current speaker, the addressee and others. Linguistically, person deixis is expressed by means of (a) personal pronouns, and (b) vocatives. Personal pronouns comprise three main forms. The first person singular pronoun, *I*, points to the speaker. The plural is expressed by *we*. The second person singular pronoun, *you*, points to the addressee. The plural is expressed by *you*. The third person singular pronouns, *he/she/it*, point to others, neither the speaker nor the addressee.

The plural is expressed by *they*. The coding of gender is expressed by *he/she*, while neutrality is expressed by *it*. **Vocatives** are forms which point to the social status of the addressee. The choice of one form rather than another is governed by the status of the person addressed, which is expressed in turn by the use of politeness markers like *please* and *thank you* as in *Please sit down* and *Would you like some help with that? Oh, thank you*, and **honorific markers** like *Doctor* and *Sir* as in *Good morning, Doctor Staples* and *Are you ready to order, sir?* Such forms of address come under the rubric of **social deixis**, the social relationship between speaker and hearer which is encoded by certain linguistic forms.

Sometimes, the speaker uses a word or phrase, either earlier or later in the discourse, to enable the hearer to identify an entity. This act is known as **reference**, and the word or phrase used is known as a **referring expression**. Referring expressions can be nouns like *Steve*, noun phrases like *a/the man*, and pronouns like *he/him*, etc. When the reference is to a word or phrase that is mentioned earlier, the relationship is called **anaphora**, the use of a word that refers to or replaces another word which comes earlier in the discourse. The word, typically a pronoun, which maintains reference to an entity that is mentioned earlier is called **anaphor**. The word which gives anaphor its meaning is called **antecedent**. For example, in *He grabbed the ball and threw it in the air*, the anaphor *it* refers to the word *ball*, which is the antecedent. By contrast, when the reference is to a word or phrase that is mentioned later in the discourse, the relationship is called **cataphora**, the use of a word that refers to or replaces another word which comes later in the discourse. The word, typically a pronoun, which maintains reference to an entity that is mentioned later is called **cataphor**. For example, in *When he saw the accident, Steve went into shock*, the cataphor *he* refers to the word *Steve*. Anaphoric and cataphoric references are used in discourse to achieve **cohesion**, the act of connecting one piece of language to another.

Space deixis

Space deixis refers to forms used to point to location. It is concerned with specifying the location of an entity relative to the speaker's location and his/her distance from it. Generally, there are three frames which express location: (a) intrinsic; (b) relative; and (c) absolute. The intrinsic frame is object-based as in *The bank is behind/in front of the station*. The relative frame is viewpoint-based as in *The bank is on the right/left of the station*. The absolute frame is compass-based as in *The bank lies to the north/south of the station*. Linguistically, space deixis is expressed by (a) demonstratives and

(b) adverbs of place. The demonstratives *this/these* and *that/those* pick out things according to their proximity to or distance from the speaker. The first two locate things near the speaker, whereas the last two locate things far from the speaker. For example, in *This book is interesting* and *That book is interesting*, the demonstratives *this/that* change relative to the distance of the book from the speaker. The adverbs of place *here* and *there* work in a similar fashion. The first points to location near the speaker, whereas the second points to location away from the speaker. For example, in *It is quiet here* and *It is quiet over there*, the adverbs *here/there* change relative to the speaker's location. Finally, some verbs of motion mark things relative to the location of the speaker, as in *come to bed* or *bring the books with you* which mark motion towards the speaker, and *go to bed* or *take the books with you* which mark motion away from the speaker.

Time deixis

Time deixis refers to forms used to point to time. It is concerned with designating the time of an event relative to the speaker's time of speaking. Linguistically, time deixis is expressed by means of (a) adverbs of time and (b) tense. Adverbs of time include *now*, and *then*. *Now* designates proximal time or the time of speaking as in *Most people now own a laptop*. *Then* designates distal time, either in the past or in the future as in *I was working in the city then*, and *I've been invited too, so I'll see you then*. Tense locates an utterance in the three main temporal points: past, present and future. Linguistically, tense is expressed by means of verbal inflection and temporal adverbs. The past simple tense is the distal form used to describe events which are deictically distant from the speaker's current situation. It is indicated by such adverbs as *yesterday, formerly, ago, last*, etc. as in *They arrived yesterday*. It also describes events that are extremely unlikely, as in *If I had a lot of money, I would buy a car*. The present simple tense is the proximal form used to describe events which are deictically close to the speaker's current situation. It is indicated by such adverbs as *today, always, often, usually*, etc. as in *I have got a piano lesson today*. The future simple tense is the distal form used to describe events which are deictically distant from the speaker's current situation. It is indicated by such adverbs as *tomorrow, later, next, soon*, etc. as in *She will finish the job tomorrow*. Finally, some verbs of motion can be used temporally to describe events that move towards the speaker from the future as in *The coming week will be really busy at work*, or away from the speaker to the past as in *The past week was really busy at work*.

Exercise 3.10

In the following sentences, point out the deictic expressions and indicate their types.

1. He is not here. He is there in the garden.
2. She agreed to visit them next summer.
3. Would you like to see the menu, sir?
4. There's a car park in front of the hotel.
5. Is Jim coming to tomorrow's meeting?

3.3.3   Speech acts

A **speech act** is an act which a speaker performs by using an utterance to communicate. An utterance usually names three acts. A **locutionary act** is the act of simply producing an utterance which follows the grammatical rules of language. It is the literal meaning of an utterance which is expressed by the particular words and structures which it contains. An **illocutionary act** is the act of producing an utterance which serves to communicate information such as advising, promising, stating, thanking, warning, and so on. A **perlocutionary act** is the act of producing an utterance which serves to make something happen such as convincing, deterring, misleading, persuading, surprising, and so on. Let us take an example. In *I am hungry*, the locution resides in the words being uttered in a grammatical sequence. The illocution resides in what the utterance says about the speaker's physical state. It is uttered to make a statement. The perlocution resides in the effect which the utterance has on the hearer. It is uttered to make a request for something to eat. Speech acts are classified into:

1. **Assertives**. An assertive, or representative, is a speech act which commits the speaker to the truth of the expressed proposition. Paradigm cases are asserting, claiming, concluding, reporting, stating, and so on. For example, in *He is my colleague* the act is that of making a statement.

2. **Directives**. A directive is a speech act in which the speaker attempts to get the hearer to do something. Paradigm cases are advising, commanding, ordering, requesting, warning, and so on. For example, in *She implored him to stay* the act is that of making a request.

3. **Commissives**. A commissive is a speech act which commits the speaker to performing some action in the future. Paradigm cases are offering, pledging, promising, refusing, threatening, and so on. For example, in *I will buy you a present* the act is that of making a promise.

4. **Expressives**. An expressive is a speech act in which the speaker expresses feelings or attitudes about something. Paradigm cases are apologising, blaming, congratulating, praising, thanking, and so on. For example, *Mary thanked her mother for the present* the act is that of expressing gratitude.

5. **Declaratives**. A declarative is a speech act which causes a change of some sort in the world. Paradigm cases are appointing, bidding, declaring, nominating, sacking, and so on. For example, in *They appointed him captain of the team* the act is that of making an appointment.

The speech acts mentioned so far can be described as **direct speech acts**, where an explicit relationship exists between the linguistic form and the communicative function of an utterance. That is, the form of the utterance coincides with the meaning which the speaker conveys. This is realized by the use of saying verbs, as in *She warned him not to be late again, I promise I'll see you tonight, I invite you to come and see me sometime*, and so on. However, much of what we say is not so direct. This is called **indirect speech acts,** where an implicit relationship exists between the linguistic form and the communicative function of an utterance. The utterance lacks a saying verb, but assumes the presence of one. The use of indirect speech acts helps the participants to sound more polite in communication, as in *Don't be late again* (indirect warning), *I'll see you tonight* (indirect promise), *Come and see me sometime* (indirect invitation), and so on. Sometimes, the hearer can detect from an utterance both direct and indirect meaning. In *It is cold in here*, for example, the direct meaning is a statement about the degree of temperature, whereas the indirect meaning is a request asking the hearer to close the window.

For an utterance to count as a speech act, it should meet **felicity conditions,** certain criteria which must be met if the speech act is to achieve its purpose. If these conditions are not met, the speech act misfires, i.e., fails to have the effect that is intended. Felicity conditions can be grouped under three headings. The first is the **preparatory condition**, which obliges the speaker not to exceed his/her authority in the performance of an act. In making a promise, the speaker must have the capacity for making the promise. The second is the **sincerity condition**, which requires the speaker to be sincere in the performance of an act. In making a promise, the speaker must genuinely intend to perform the act. The third is the **essential condition**, which compels the speaker to perform an act. In making a promise, the speaker must know the promise puts him under an obligation to perform the act.

Exercise 3.11

Study the following utterances and then write the type of speech act which each represents.

1. They apologized for the late departure of the flight.
2. The police warned the visitors against pickpockets.
3. The house was reported as being in good condition.
4. They were sacked for refusing to work on Sundays.
5. The attackers threatened the passengers with guns.

3.4 Semantic roles

A further common way of establishing the meanings of sentences is through defining the semantic roles, also called **functional roles, thematic roles** or **participant roles**, of their components or through examining the semantic relations that link a verb to its arguments, i.e., nouns, in the description of a situation. For example, in the sentence *The boy oiled his bike* the entities are related by the action described by the verb *oil*: the noun *boy* is often termed the agent and the noun *bike* is the patient. Usually, a particular semantic role can be represented only once in a sentence, and a particular noun can fulfil only one role. However, some verbs are so flexible that they can be used in two different patterns, and so fulfill two semantic roles but only one role at a time. The verb *ripen*, for example, can be used grammatically either with or without an object. In the sentence *The summer sunshine ripened the melons*, the verb *ripen* is transitive and so the word *melons* takes the role of patient. In the sentence *The melons are ripening nicely*, the verb *ripen* is intransitive and so the word *melons* takes the role of agent.

The following are the most common semantic roles, which may generally be recognized in all languages:

1. agent   the entity performing the action expressed by the verb
                   Bill cleaned the board.

2. patient   the entity undergoing the action expressed by the verb Bill cleaned **the board.**

3. experiencer   the entity psychologically affected by an action **Bill** was happy.

4. causer   the thing that makes something happen **The bad weather** caused traffic chaos.

5. benefactive   the entity benefiting from an action Bill bought flowers **for Kim.**

6. location   the place where an action happens Bill cleaned the board **in the classroom.**

7. time   the time when an action happens Bill cleaned the board **in the morning.**

8. instrument   the means by which something is done Bill cleaned the board **with a duster.**

9. goal   the entity towards which something moves Bill sent a postcard **to Kim.**

10. source   the entity from which something moves Kim received a postcard **from Bill.**

Exercise 3.12

In the sentence below, try to assign a semantic role to each of the underlined expressions in relation to the verb.

The boy inflated the ball with a pump for his brother in the garage yesterday.

3.5 Summary

In this chapter, I have presented a broad outline of what sentential semantics is and what it covers. **Sentential semantics** is the branch of semantics which studies the meanings of sentences. In the outline, I did three things. First, I introduced the notion of **sentence**, the meaning-bearing unit with which sentential semantics is concerned, and defined **sentence meaning** as the meaning of a sentence based on the words which it contains regardless of the context in which it is used. Second, I identified the three ways of establishing the meanings of sentences. The first is through the patterns of relation which sentences hold. This includes such relations as paraphrase, contradiction, entailment, presupposition, and implicature. The last three are means of expressing **implicit meaning**: what can be communicated beyond what is explicitly said. The second is through the use of pragmatic knowledge. This includes such phenomena as ambiguity, deixis and speech acts. The third is through the semantic roles which participants in an utterance play. This includes the semantic links which a verb has with its arguments in the utterance. The table given below presents a summary of the sentential relations.

Table 3.1 Semantic relation between sentences

Sentential relation	Definition	Example
Paraphrase	restatement	She sprayed perfume on her wrists. She sprayed her wrists with perfume.
Contradiction	oppositeness	The cat is on the table. The cat is under the table.
Entailment	implication	She drives recklessly. She is prone to accidents.
Presupposition	assumption	When did you buy the book? You bought the book.
Implicature	suggestion	She is complaining again. She has complained before.

Part II

Underpinnings

As a reaction to Generative Linguistics, a new approach to the study of language known as **Cognitive Linguistics** began to emerge in the 1970s. A number of basic tenets underlie this new approach. Cognitive Linguistics makes a strong case for the pervasiveness of these tenets in language. **Non-modularity** implies that there is no autonomous portion of the brain which is specialized for language. Linguistic abilities are inseparable from other cognitive abilities. Accordingly, no distinction can be drawn between linguistic meaning and general knowledge. **Symbolism** means that language is a set of symbols or conventional means that are available to language users for representing ideas or communicating thought. **Usage based** suggests that language patterns emerge as a result of generalizations made from actual instances of language use. **Meaningfulness** reveals that language is a means of conveying meaning; therefore all its resources serve to carry out this function. **Creativity** means that language production represents the capacity of language users to conceptualize a given situation in multiple ways and choose the linguistic forms to stand for them in communication.

One essential part of the Cognitive Linguistics movement is **Cognitive Semantics**, the study of the cognitive aspects of linguistic meaning. It is an approach to meaning which is built on five central assumptions. These assumptions are all-pervasive, applying to all areas of language. They help to provide a unified account of lexical and grammatical structures rather than viewing them as distinct subsystems. **Embodiment** denotes that the meaning of a linguistic expression is determined in large measure by the nature of our bodies. **Motivation** shows that the meaning of a linguistic expression arises as the outcome of stimulation to achieve a desired goal. **Dynamism** demonstrates that the meaning of a linguistic expression is flexible in the sense of extending its scope to express new experiences. **Encyclopaedia** indicates that the meaning of a linguistic expression subsumes vast repositories of knowledge, both linguistic and non-linguistic. **Conceptualization** signifies that the meaning of a linguistic expression serves as a prompt for an array of mental processes. This shows that the scope of Cognitive Semantics deals equally with areas related to both semantics and pragmatics. Cognitive Semantics takes a **maximalist** approach to meaning, one in which differences between semantics and pragmatics are not recognized.

Outline

4

Guiding Assumptions

Chapter 4 presents the general approach to language study, known as **Cognitive Linguistics**, and the specific approach to linguistic meaning, known as **Cognitive Semantics**. The chapter begins by outlining the guiding assumptions that characterize the two approaches to language description. The aim is to show how adept the assumptions are in analysing linguistic data and capturing semantic phenomena. The chapter is organized as follows. Section 4.1 introduces the assumptions of **Cognitive Linguistics** that characterize language as being non-modular, symbolic, usage based, meaningful and creative. Section 4.2 presents the assumptions of **Cognitive Semantics** that characterize linguistic meaning as being embodied, motivated, dynamic, encyclopaedic and conceptualized. In all the sections, I pursue three steps. First, I present the assumption. Second, I elaborate on its essence. Third, I devise an exercise to validate its application. Section 4.3 summarizes the main points of the chapter.

4.1 Cognitive Linguistics

Cognitive Linguistics is a modern school of linguistics which has developed since the 1970s. It includes a variety of approaches which are, however, unified by a number of common assumptions. The general aim is to provide insights into aspects of the human mind and offer glimpses into patterns of thought. Cognitive Linguistics has emerged as a reaction against some of the theoretical assumptions developed within Generative Linguistics. One of the distinctive assumptions of Cognitive Linguistics pertains to the position of meaning in language analysis. In Generative Linguistics, the structure of language is determined by a system of formal rules that is largely independent of meaning. In Cognitive Linguistics, the structure of language is a direct reflection of cognition in the sense that the structure of a particular linguistic expression reflects a particular way of conceptualizing a given situation. This leads to the view that the structure of language is explained not only in terms of language-internal principles, as assumed in Generative Linguistics, but also in terms of language-external ones. The meaning associated with linguistic structures is based on human perception and human cognition.

Linguistic structures code different ways of perceiving a given scene, and differ relative to communicative demands.

In order to give an adequate account of linguistic structure, Cognitive Linguistics is founded on some fundamental assumptions. Below is a discussion of each assumption.

4.1.1 Language is non-modular

Generative Linguistics takes a modular approach to language. It claims that the human mind consists of a number of different modules, one of which is language. Each module has its own distinctive property and functions separately from the others. This has two implications. Externally, language is treated as an autonomous module. As a result, it is studied without reference to other modules. Internally, aspects like morphology, phonology, pragmatics, syntax and semantics are treated as sub-modules of the language module. As a result, they are investigated without reference to each other. Cognitive Linguistics rejects this claim. Instead, it assumes a non-modular approach to language. There is an external and internal link between language and other modules. Externally, linguistic structures embody general mental faculties like attention, memory, reasoning, etc. Internally, linguistic explanation must cross boundaries between aspects of language. Linguistic structures are explained by simultaneously taking into account other aspects of language. Accordingly, language is not a self-contained system that is independent of other mental faculties and aspects of language do not form independent modules. This is a reflection of the **cognitive commitment** of Cognitive Linguistics, where the characterization of linguistic structures should reflect principles from other cognitive sciences like philosophy, psychology and neuroscience. In the same vein, this is a reflection of the **generalization commitment** of Cognitive Linguistics, where the characterization of linguistic structures should reflect principles from other aspects of human language like morphology, phonology, pragmatics, syntax and semantics.

Let us take an example to illuminate this assumption. Semantically, the adjective-forming suffix *-able* has a passive interpretation, meaning 'capable of undergoing the action stated in the root'. *A washable shirt* is a shirt that can be washed. However, the passive interpretation of the suffix does not always work, and so the suffix needs the help of other language aspects, namely pragmatics, for its interpretation. Pragmatically, the suffix has additional meanings which can be understood from the context in which it is used.

In this case, the context is the root to which it is attached. In some formations, it is the substance trait of the inanimate entity that is focused. *Eatable fungus* does not mean fungus that can be eaten, but fungus that is safe to eat. Presumably, poisonous fungus can be eaten, but it is not eatable. In other formations, it is the character trait of the animate entity that is focused. For example, *an adorable child* does not necessarily mean a child who can be adored, but a child who is extremely attractive. Presumably, every child can be adored, but not every one is attractive.

For the nature of meaning, the cognitive assumption of non-modularity has three significant consequences.

- Cognitive Linguistics rejects the internal distinction between morphology and phonology or morphology and syntax, which are traditionally deemed as separate modules of language. Let us cite an example. Under certain conditions of occurrence, the past tense morpheme *-ed* has three phonological variants, as in *stopped* [stopt], *played* [pleid] and *waited* [weitid]. Number contrasts in nouns require syntactic definition (singular subject requiring a singular verb) and morphological definition (adding -s for plural).

- Cognitive Linguistics rejects the internal division between syntax and semantics, which are traditionally treated as independent subsystems of language. Aspects of both interact in shaping the meaning of an expression. Let us offer an example. In *She wants to buy a house*, the main verb *want* describes an action that happens later, and so takes the *to*-infinitive complement clause *to buy a house* which refers to an action that has not yet taken place.

- Cognitive Linguistics rejects the internal separation between semantics and pragmatics, which are traditionally considered as autonomous components of language. Aspects of both can be incorporated into the meaning of an expression. Let us consider an example. In *She is buzzing around like a honey-bee*, the non-literal meaning of the expression is not the same as the literal meanings of the words. The non-literal meaning is 'She is busy'.

Exercise 4.1

In explaining the meaning of the following expressions, the language aspects of semantics and pragmatics interact. Show how.

1. loveable child
2. watchable film
3. agreeable deal
4. readable book
5. drinkable water

4.1.2   *Language is symbolic*

Generative Linguistics claims that there is no direct link between the form of language and the meaning it expresses. As a consequence, forms of linguistic expressions are studied separately from their meanings. Linguistic expressions that are seemingly similar have the same deep structure, which determines their meaning. Since they are related by the same deep structure, they are semantically equivalent. Cognitive Linguistics rejects this claim. Instead, it assumes that language is inherently symbolic in nature. **Language** is a structured inventory of linguistic units defined as form-meaning pairings. A **unit** is any simple or composite expression which is frequently used and thoroughly mastered, thus acquiring the status of a habit. **Inventory** is a detailed list of all the linguistic resources which speakers exploit in constructing units. **Structured** means the units are related to one another in organized ways. A **linguistic unit**, also called a **symbolic structure**, consists of a semantic structure, a phonological structure and a symbolic relationship between them. The phonological structure refers to form, which can be spoken or written. The semantic structure refers to meaning, which is related to a concept. A **concept** is a mental representation which is associated with a symbol in a person's mind. It is the abstract meaning which a linguistic expression represents. There is a direct association between the phonological and semantic structures of language. The association is motivated by the manner in which speakers interact with the world. Accordingly, form cannot be investigated independently of meaning. This entails that form and meaning are seen as mutually interdependent. As a symbolic system, language provides speakers with the means to communicate the contents of their thoughts to others, as well as to themselves.

Let us examine an example to illustrate this assumption. The prefixes *de-* and *un-* are symbols used with the intention of symbolizing concepts. Although they are attached to the same root *couple* meaning 'to connect or combine two things', each prefix symbolizes a particular meaning and so gives the derived word a different meaning. In *The revenues had been decoupled from the sales*, the verb *to decouple* means 'to disengage one thing from another'. To decouple two things is to end the relationship between them. The verb *decouple* is regarded as an association between the phonological structure /diːˈkʌpl/ and the semantic structure [DECOUPLE], which is realized by the graphic symbols. The use of the prefix *de-* is motivated by the idea of ending an abstract relationship. In *The carriages had been uncoupled from the train*, the verb *to uncouple* means 'to disconnect one thing from another'. To uncouple two things is to separate two things that are joined together, by undoing a fastening that connects them. The verb *uncouple* is regarded as an association between the phonological structure /ʌnˈkʌpl/ and the semantic structure [UNCOUPLE], which is realized by the graphic symbols. The use of the prefix *un-* is motivated by the idea of ending a physical relationship.

For the nature of meaning, the cognitive assumption of symbolism has three important ramifications.

- Linguistic expressions, be they morphemes, words, phrases or sentences, are bipolar. They have two poles: phonological and semantic. The act of mating the phonological and semantic poles is referred to as **pairing**. The pairing is motivated by discourse demands or communicative purposes. The form and meaning equally contribute to the make-up of an expression. The two poles are thus inseparable. See, for example, the bound morpheme *-ity*. It is a symbolic structure linking the phonological structure /iti/ with the semantic structure [ITY], which expresses a state. In *civility*, it means the state of being civil.
- Linguistic expressions have semantic values which motivate their linguistic forms. The semantic value of a linguistic expression is a reflection of a particular concept. A **concept** is a mental representation which is associated with a symbol in the mind of the language user. Take, for example, the bound morpheme *crypto-*. It means 'hidden or secret'. It is used by the language user to describe an entity as being not openly avowed or declared. In *a crypto-coalition*, it means a coalition which is made in secret.
- Linguistic expressions are neither integrated at random nor conditioned by formal rules. The integration of their subparts is governed

by valence determinants. **Valence** is the capacity of two structures to combine to form a composite structure. One significant determinant resides in the phonological and semantic compatibility between the subparts of an expression. Consider, for example, a free morpheme like *red*. To mean fairly or slightly red in colour, it needs to be combined with the bound morpheme *-ish*, which denotes approximation.

Exercise 4.2

Identify the phonological and semantic structures of the following derivational morphemes and the ideas that they express.

1. iso-
2. eco-
3. -itis
4. hydro-
5. -ology

4.1.3 *Language is usage based*

Generative Linguistics draws a distinction between knowledge of language and use of language. Every human is equipped with a language faculty, an innate cognitive subsystem, which gives rise to competence, unconscious knowledge of language. Knowledge of language arises from what is innate in the mind at birth. According to this view, which is referred to as **nativism**, language knowledge (competence) determines language use (performance). Cognitive Linguistics rejects this distinction. Instead, it assumes that language is **usage based**, the quality of linguistic units being authentic. Knowledge of language is derived from the environment or experience. Knowledge of language is knowledge of how language is used. According to this view, which is referred to as **empiricism**, language use determines language knowledge. Knowledge of language, i.e., the mental grammar, is based on and grounded in **usage events**. A usage event is an actual instance of language use. It includes an **utterance**, which can be thought of as a symbolic expression performed on a particular occasion for a particular purpose. In terms of structure, an utterance may consist of a single word like *disbelief*, a phrase like *utter disbelief*, or a sentence like *She shook her head in disbelief*. Usage events have a double import. First, the linguistic system is built up from them. General patterns, often called **schemas**, arise from their repeated use. A **schema** is a cognitive representation with a general meaning, whose full details are reflected in its specific instances of usage. The instances elaborate the schema in contrasting ways. Second, they are used to coin and understand novel expressions. Through repeated usage, these novel expressions become entrenched in the lexicon.

Let us take an example to exemplify this assumption. The words *sensual, sensuous, sensible* and *sensitive* are all derived from *sense*, but they are connected with different meanings of it as revealed by their actual instances. The word *sensual* describes something as appealing to the body, as in *They were impressed by the sensual movements of the dancer*. The word *sensuous* describes something as appealing to the mind as in *They appreciated the sensuous music of the concert*. The word *sensible* describes the ability to make good judgements, as in *She adopted a sensible approach to the problem*. The word *sensitive* describes the ability to understand other people and be aware of their needs, as in *She is very sensitive to other people's feelings*. All this shows that the actual instances of a linguistic expression help one to make accurate observations about the real state of language. They can thus help one to work out meaning differences between lexical expressions.

For the nature of meaning, the cognitive assumption of authenticity has three crucial effects.

- Linguistic expressions have overt manifestations. They do not conceal deep structures. They embody the conventional means a language employs for the symbolization of semantic content. A good example is offered by the utterances *The museum was swarming with tourists* and *Tourists were swarming in the museum*. The two utterances share the same content, but they have different conceptualizations. In the first, the subject is conceptualized as a container. The content is marked with the preposition *with* after the verb. In the second, the subject is conceptualized as content. The container is marked with the spatial preposition *in*.

- Linguistic expressions represent utterances. An **utterance** is an actual spoken or written sequence produced in a specific situation. An utterance has substance and use. The **substance** consists of two parts, form and meaning. The **form** is the phonological representation. The **meaning** is the idea conventionally associated with it. The **use** is the way the language user construes the content. The substance is activated as a response to language use. A clear example is afforded by the sentential pair *He threw a ball to the boy* and *He threw a ball at the* *boy.* Although they are similar in content, they are dissimilar in use. In the first, the action of catching is meant. In the second, the action of hitting is meant.

- Linguistic expressions can be semantically distinguished by analysing their surroundings, which significantly affect their meaning. One such surrounding is **collocation**, the case when two or more words go together and form a common expression. A simple example is supplied by the pair *fake* and *false*. The adjective *fake* describes concrete entities, and so collocates with words such as *passport, gun, painting, fur, signature*, and so on. The adjective *false* describes abstract entities, and so collocates with words such as *name, identity, evidence, impression, statement*, and so on.

Exercise 4.3

The semantic value of a word can be identified by the collocation that it takes. Which word collocates best in the following examples?

1.	fast/quick	___ meal	___ food
2.	dangerous/perilous	___ mission	___ road
3.	powerful/strong	___ evidence	___ drug
4.	large/big	___ occasion	___ salary
5.	right/correct	___ decision	___ answer

4.1.4 Language is meaningful

Generative Linguistics claims that there are elements in language that are semantically empty. Their presence in linguistic expressions serves only syntactic or morphological functions. Following this claim, an affix is assumed to be a meaningless element, which is summoned simply to derive a new word. The presence of rival affixes is a matter of coincidence, and the existence of the resulting alternatives is an instance of synonymy. Cognitive Linguistics rejects this claim. Instead, it assumes that all language elements have semantic values. Linguistic expressions, be they closed-class or open-class, are inherently meaningful. The meaning of a linguistic expression can be derived from the context in which it occurs. **Context** is the environment in which an expression is used. Context accounts for two phenomena. One is **ambiguity**, the case when one and the same expression can be interpreted in more than one way. The expression *killer* has two interpretations. It can refer to a person as in *They found the killer*, or a thing as in *Cancer is a killer*. Another is **rivalry**, the case when two or more affixes or lexical expressions occur in the same environment but convey different messages. Both adjectival suffixes *-ish* and *-y* attach to the root *freak*, but each has a different meaning. *Freakish* describes strange character as in *She dislikes freakish visitors*, whereas *freaky* describes strange appearance as in *She dislikes freaky clothes*.

Let us analyse an example to demonstrate this assumption. The adjective *sharp* displays multiple meanings. Each meaning arises from the particular context in which *sharp* is used. In *She used a sharp knife*, it means having a thin edge. In *There was a sharp drop in prices*, it means sudden and rapid. In *This TV gives a very sharp picture*, it means clear and definite. In *She is a girl of sharp intelligence*, it means quick to notice, understand or react to things. In *He was very sharp with me when I was late*, it means critical and severe. In *There was a sharp knock on the door*, it means loud and high in tone. In *The cheese has a distinctively sharp taste*, it means strong and slightly bitter. In *Tony is a very sharp dresser*, it means fashionable and new. In *His lawyer is a sharp operator*, it means clever but dishonest. In *He had a sharp pain in his chest*, it means strong and sudden. All this shows that any linguistic expression conveys new meanings or communicates new ideas depending on the different contexts in which it is employed.

For the nature of meaning, the cognitive assumption of semanticity has three essential corollaries.

- Linguistic expressions are attributed semantic import. Not only sentences have meanings. Articles, affixes and prepositions, which are considered by some theories to be empty of information, contribute something specific to the meanings of utterances in which they occur and can thus be legitimately considered as having meanings in their own right. Speakers always speak or write in order to express a meaning of one kind or another. A striking example is the sentential pair *I like fish* and *I like the fish*, in which the article *the* causes a difference in meaning. It serves to convert the concept of a general fish into a concept of a particular fish, identifiable to both the speaker and hearer.
- Linguistic expressions which are ambiguous are analysable in context. **Context** is the environment in which an utterance is used. It refers to the circumstances which determine, specify or clarify the meaning of an utterance. It is the best evidence available in accounting for the multiple meanings of an expression. It shows that the meaning of an expression is not fixed, but changes relative to the demands of

discourse. A telling example is the expression *cleaner*, which has two contextual meanings. In *He works as an office cleaner,* the expression *cleaner* refers to a person whose job is to clean places. In *We ran out of floor cleaner*, the expression *cleaner* refers to a substance used for cleaning objects.

• Linguistic expressions, be they words or sentences, sharing a common content are different in meaning. They exhibit **rivalry**, where two or more alternatives describe the same situation but profile distinct aspects of its meaning. The alternatives are phonologically distinct and semantically dissimilar. Any alternation in form spells an alternation in meaning. A revealing example is the sentential pair *A tiger hunts by night* and *The tiger hunts by night*. The first denotes a generic reference. It describes class as a whole. The second denotes a specific or individuative reference. It describes one single element. It applies to an instance which is accessible to both the speaker and hearer.

Exercise 4.4

The adjective *clean* displays numerous meanings which arise from the different contexts in which it is used. Can you identify what the meaning of *clean* in each of the following sentences is?

1. They need clean air
2. The wine has a clean taste.
3. Keep the jokes clean please!
4. The house was extremely clean.
5. The plane made a clean take-off.
6. He has a clean driving record.
7. It was a tough but clean game.
8. She used a clean sheet of paper.
9. A sharp knife makes a clean cut.
10. He is expected to make a clean sweep.

4.1.5 Language is creative

In Generative Linguistics, creativity refers to the ability of humans to generate and understand an infinite number of sentences in a language by means of a finite set of rules. The task of the generative linguist then is to explain the rules which are capable of generating well-formed sentences. In Cognitive Linguistics, creativity refers to the ability of speakers to coin a novel expression from a conventional expression, or construe the same situation in alternate ways using different linguistic expressions. The task of the cognitive linguist then is to describe the mental processes responsible for producing and understanding such expressions. A **conventional** expression is a linguistic unit that is established in the lexicon through repeated usage. The use of a novel expression involves creativity because the speaker has to find an already existing pattern in the language on the basis of which it can be produced. The pattern is referred to as **schema**, a mental representation with a general meaning, whose specifics are elaborated by its instances in contrasting ways. Traditionally, this is referred to as **analogy**, the formation of a new word on the basis of a unique expression or pattern. A schema is extracted from actual **instances**, specific units which represent situations or events. They are regarded as the basis on which schemas are built. The use of a novel expression involves creativity because the speaker has the capacity to construe the same situation in alternate ways using different linguistic expressions. Meaning reflects not only the content of a situation, but also how the speaker describes that content in alternative ways.

Let us consider an example to clarify this assumption. On the basis of such instances as *enable, enfeeble, enrich,* and so on, the schema [EN-] can be formed. Once it is formed, the schema acts as a pattern for deriving new words in the language such as *encamp, enforce, engulf,* etc. In the first set of instances, *-en* is added to adjectival roots to form verbs, whereas in the second it is added to nominal roots to form verbs. Likewise, on the basis of such instances as *classmate, flatmate, roommate,* and so on, the schema [-MATE], can be formed. Once it is formed, the schema acts as a pattern for deriving new words in the language such as *playmate, team-mate, workmate,* and so on. In the first set of instances, *-mate* is added to nouns to derive words which refer to a person you share an accommodation with. In the second set of instances, *-mate* is added to nouns to derive words which refer to a person you share an activity with. Accordingly, knowledge about language derives from generalizations made over specific instances of use.

For the nature of meaning, the assumption of creativity has three pivotal repercussions.

- Linguistic expressions are not grounded in formalism or mathematical rules, but in cognitive capacities. They are the outcome of **cognitive operations**, processes which reflect capabilities of the mind or functions of the brain in producing and interpreting linguistic expressions. Mental abilities include general operations like derivation and compounding within which particular ones like categorization, configuration and conceptualization take place. To take a concrete example, from a word like *neo-baroque*, in which *neo-* means 'new' or 'recent', expressions such as *neo-classical, neo-colonialism, neo-fascist, neo-populism, neo-realist*, and so on have been derived.

- Linguistic expressions embody different construals which speakers employ to describe situations. **Construal** is the ability to conceive and express a situation in different ways. Linguistic expressions differ in meaning depending not only on the entities they designate but also on the construals employed to describe the scenes. Construal allows the speaker to describe the same content in different ways. To offer a concrete example, consider the sentential pair *The hungry boy ate for 15 minutes* and *The hungry boy ate in 15 minutes*. In each sentence, the scene is construed differently. The first sentence construes an action which continues for the length of the time specified. The second sentence construes an action which is finished by the time specified.

- Linguistic expressions are not synonymous even if they share the same source. **Synonymy** is the case where two expressions have more or less the same meaning. Rather than being regarded as substitutes, linguistic expressions are attributed distinct meanings. Each linguistic expression is a vehicle of a certain message. To give a concrete example, consider the sentential pair *Many people did not attend the meeting* and *Not many people attended the meeting*. Even though the sentences share the same proposition, they are different in meaning. The difference resides in the scope of negation. The first means many people stayed away, whereas the second means few people came.

Exercise 4.5

The following pairs of sentences are not synonymous. The structure of each sentence represents a distinct construal. What is it?

1. a. She lives in London.
   b. She is living in London.
2. a. She has drunk my coffee.
   b. She has been drinking my coffee.
3. a. I have been on the island for a month.
   b. I have gone to the island for a month.
4. a. They will attend the film festival.
   b. They are going to attend the film festival.
5. a. The saleswoman is very friendly.
   b. The saleswoman is being very friendly.

4.2 Cognitive Semantics

Cognitive Semantics, which is part of the Cognitive Linguistics movement, is an approach to meaning which has developed since the 1970s. It is an approach based on a collection of ideas drawn from other theories like cognitive psychology, cognitive anthropology, etc. Cognitive Semantics has emerged as a reaction against some of the assumptions developed by pre-cognitive accounts of meaning. One of the distinguishing assumptions of Cognitive Semantics pertains to the role of speaker in characterizing scenes and determining meanings, employing the conventional means of language. In pre-cognitive accounts of meaning, the emphasis is laid on **objectivism**, the doctrine that the role of language is to describe states of affairs in the world. The meaning of a linguistic expression is seen as an objective reflection of the external world. In this view, there is no place for the speaker in shaping the language. In Cognitive Semantics, the emphasis is laid on **subjectivism**, the doctrine that language does not refer to an objective reality, but to concepts in the mind of the speaker. The meaning of a linguistic expression is seen as relating to a concept derived from bodily experience. In this view, the emphasis is very much on the role of the speaker in shaping the language.

In order to conduct a fruitful discussion of linguistic meaning, Cognitive Semantics is founded on fundamental assumptions. Below is a delineation of each assumption.

4.2.1   Meaning is embodied

In the pre-cognitive accounts of meaning, there is a correspondence between language and the state of the world it describes. On the basis of such a correspondence, a statement can be judged as true or false. For example, *His hair is grey* is true if and only if his hair is in fact grey. In terms of the **correspondence** theory, figurative uses of language are seen as anomalous. As a reaction to this claim, Cognitive Semantics assumes that the structure of reality, as reflected in language, is a product of the human mind and human embodiment. People can only talk about what they perceive and conceive, which in turn is derived from embodied experience. The nature of concepts and the way they are organized is constrained by the nature of embodied experience. In terms of the **embodiment** theory, figurative uses of language are seen as essential. Accordingly, Cognitive Semantics explores the ways in which conceptual structure arises from bodily experience, or the ways in which our species-specific bodies interact with the environment we inhabit. If language reflects conceptual structure, it follows that language reflects embodied experience.

An example of the way in which bodily experience gives rise to meaning concepts is the concept of **containment**, the act of keeping an entity in an enclosed space and consequently restricting its movement. The concept arises as a result of the properties of both the enclosed space and the human body. The concept reflects a physical relationship in which embodied experience interacts with enclosed spaces. The concept associated with containment is an instance of what cognitive semanticists call an **image schema,** a conceptual representation which emerges from human bodily interaction with the world. It is a dynamic pattern which is grounded in human bodily movements through space. The containment schema gives rise to abstract states conceived as a container, which is shown by the use of the prepositions *in, out of* and *into*, as in *He is in debt*, *He is out of work* and *He fell into decay*. These bodily experiences give rise to the conceptual structure, or the image schema, of containment, which in turn projects the conceptual domain of STATES, to which concepts like *debt, work* and *decay* belong. The process derives the conceptual metaphor STATES ARE CONTAINERS. This topic will be taken up and discussed in greater detail in Chapter 5.

Exercise 4.6

The FORCE schema emerges when a force acts on an entity. It includes such related image schemas as ATTRACTION, BLOCKAGE, COMPULSION, DIVERSION and ENABLEMENT. Match each of the following sentences with the appropriate related schema.

1. They were coerced into negotiating a settlement.
2. An injury was hindering him from playing his best.
3. The war distracted attention from the economic situation.
4. This ticket does not entitle you to travel first class.
5. The city has magnetized thousands of young people.

4.2.2   *Meaning is motivated*

In the pre-cognitive accounts of meaning, a linguistic expression has both form and meaning, but the connection between the two is arbitrary or unmotivated. There is no natural reason why a particular linguistic form should be associated with a particular meaning. **Arbitrariness** is the phenomenon where the form of a sign bears no resemblance to its referent. There is no way of predicting the meaning of a linguistic expression by relying on its form. In response to this claim, Cognitive Semantics assumes that the relationship between the form and meaning of a linguistic expression is often motivated or inseparable. **Motivation** is the psychological incentive which influences the choice of the speaker. The choice of the form of a linguistic expression is largely motivated by the meaning which the speaker plans to convey, which in turn is motivated by the communicative purpose. This entails that form is produced with the intention of symbolizing meaning. The choice between two linguistic expressions is not random. Linguistic distinctions are motivated by semantic considerations. Every linguistic structure is a vehicle of a certain semantic structure.

An example of the way in which the form of a linguistic expression is motivated by meaning is the concept of **iconicity**, the phenomenon where the form of a sign bears some resemblance to its meaning, or where the structure of language bears similarity to conceived reality. According to Generative Linguistics, the two grammatical sentences *He smeared the wall with paint* and *He smeared paint on the wall* are derived from the same underlying structure, and so are regarded as syntactic paraphrases. According to Cognitive

Linguistics, the two grammatical sentences are neither derived from the same underlying structure nor regarded as syntactic paraphrases. They have different syntactic structures, and so are attributed different semantic values. The two sentences share the same semantic content, but that content is construed differently by the speaker. In the first sentence, the implication drawn is that the whole wall is painted. This is reflected by the fact that the wall, being a direct object, is close to the verb. In the second sentence, the implication drawn is that only part of the wall is painted. This is reflected by the fact that the wall is separated from the verb by a preposition.

Exercise 4.7

On the basis of formal criteria, the following pairs of sentences are freely interchangeable. On the basis of cognitive criteria, they are semantically distinctive. Point out how.

1. a. He sent his family a letter.
    b. He sent a letter to his family.
2. a. He helped her carry the trunk.
    b. He helped her to carry the trunk.
3. a. He saved the boy drowning in the canal.
    b. He saved the boy from drowning in the canal.
4. a. He arranged to attend the baby.
    b. He arranged for a babysitter to attend the baby.
5. a. She pleaded for the offender to confess his offence.
    b. She pleaded that the offender should confess his offence.

4.2.3 Meaning is dynamic

In the pre-cognitive accounts of meaning, the meaning of a linguistic expression is more or less stable or inflexible, namely it cannot be changed to suit new experiences. It adopts the **classical** or **check-list** theory of linguistic meaning. According to this theory, humans categorize concepts by means of necessary and sufficient conditions. Contrary to this claim, Cognitive Semantics assumes that the meaning of a linguistic expression is dynamic and flexible, namely it is able to change to suit new experiences. One good reason for this is the expression of new meanings. This has to do with creativity, the ability of language to permit the expression of new meanings. Creativity is shown in two ways. One is the ability of language users to create new forms to express new ideas. Because societies change, there is always a need to express new meanings in language. The other is the ability of language users to extend the existing forms to encompass new meanings. As a means of expressing needs, language extends to cope with the constant changes in the circumstances language users live through, and deal with the new experiences they encounter in life. The semantic structure of any linguistic expression is thus not rigid; it takes on new meanings and is continuously extending.

An example of the way in which a linguistic unit demonstrates flexibility is manifested by the concept of **polysemy**, the phenomenon where a linguistic expression acquires multiple meanings. The preposition *on* is dynamic in the sense that it can conceive a spatial relation differently. In *The camera is on the table*, the two objects are in physical contact, with the *camera* placed above the *table*. In *The fly is on the ceiling*, the two objects are in physical contact but the relationship between them is unusual because the *fly* is placed beneath the *ceiling*. In *The painting is on the wall*, the two objects are in physical contact, with the *wall* placed behind the *painting*. In *The leaves are on the tree*, the two objects are in physical contact, with the leaves covering the tree. In *The writing on the paper is clear*, the *paper* is construed as a background against which the *writing* is displayed, which is foregrounded. In all the examples mentioned so far, the relationship between the two objects is one of physical support. In *The house is on fire*, the schema metaphorically extends to an abstract domain, where fire is conceived as a place. I take up the **prototype** theory in Chapter 7, where I examine more closely its theses, advantages and consequences.

Exercise 4.8

The modal auxiliary *would* is so dynamic that it can express different meanings in different contexts. Can you identify them?

1. I'd rather have a beer.
2. I wouldn't worry about it, if I were you.
3. Would you have dinner with me on Friday?
4. I would imagine the job will take about two days.
5. Would you mind leaving us alone for a few minutes?

4.2.4   *Meaning is encyclopaedic*

In the pre-cognitive accounts of meaning, the semantic content of a linguistic expression represents a neatly packaged bundle of meaning, a claim referred to as **definitional** or **dictionary view**. The meanings of linguistic expressions stored in our minds can be defined, much as they appear in a dictionary. In the semantic decomposition approach, which is one version of this view, meaning is encoded in terms of semantic features or primitives. The core meaning of a word is the information contained in the word's definition, excluding the non-contextual knowledge. Contrary to this claim, Cognitive Semantics assumes that the semantic content of a linguistic expression is broad in scope, a claim referred to as **encyclopaedic view**. The meaning of a linguistic expression cannot be understood independently of the vast repository of encyclopaedic knowledge to which it is linked. **Encyclopaedic knowledge** refers to the structured body of non-linguistic knowledge to which a linguistic expression such as a word potentially provides access. In the description of a word, it is not just the general definition that counts, but also the actual circumstance in which it is used and the complete information which it contains. Encyclopaedic knowledge is modelled in terms of a number of constructs such as the domain, the cognitive model and the idealized cognitive model.

An example of the way in which linguistic expressions differ relying on encyclopaedic knowledge is shown by the concept of **domain**, a coherent body of conceptual content which serves as an essential background for some individual concepts. The verbs *boo, cheer, groan, scream* and *sob* gather under the domain of noise, but they manifest specific differences. The verb *boo* means 'to give a loud shout of disapproval', as in *The crowd booed when the player was sent off the field*. The verb *cheer* means 'to give a loud shout of approval', as in *The supporters cheered the president at the end of the speech*. The verb *groan* means 'to make a long deep sound showing great pain or unhappiness', as in *He lay on the floor groaning with pain*. The verb *scream* means 'to give a loud high cry showing fear, excitement or anger', as in *The girl screamed for help when the thief pulled out a knife*. Finally, the verb *sob* means 'to cry noisily taking in deep breaths', as in *I found her sobbing in the bedroom because she'd broken her doll*. I take up the **domain** theory in Chapter 8, where I examine more closely its premises, advantages and repercussions.

Exercise 4.9

The nouns listed below are similar in their definitional meaning, but in their encyclopaedic meaning they are distinct and associated with specific uses. What are the uses?

1. rim
2. edge
3. fringe
4. frame
5. border

4.2.5 Meaning is conceptualized

In the pre-cognitive accounts of meaning, the meaning of a linguist expression is equated with **truth conditions**, whereby the meaning is just an objective reflection of the outside world. For example, to know the meaning of a sentence like *It is cloudy* one has to look at the sky to check whether the statement is true or not. In that light, if two sentences express the same state of affairs in the world, or have the same content, they are considered equal. Contrary to this claim, Cognitive Semantics assumes that the meaning of a linguistic expression is equated with **conceptualization**, whereby the meaning is a reflection of concepts, and not directly of things. Conceptualization refers to the ability to form concepts and explain language structure with reference to human experience, be they social, linguistic or cultural. Concepts are basic expressions of mental representation, and mirror the existing properties of the world. They are not arbitrary creations of language, but constitute part of our understanding of what the world is like. Language is the product of our interaction with the world around us. Language structure is an immediate reflection of thought, of the way the mind works. The way we build discourses and develop linguistic categories are derived from the way we experience our environment. The semantic structure of a linguistic expression, therefore, includes both conceptual content and a particular way of construing that content. Two expressions may invoke the same conceptual content, yet differ semantically by encoding different conceptualizations of experience. Making use of the symbolic resources made available by language, these conceptualizations are mapped onto different linguistic realizations. Each linguistic realization describes the same scene, but does so in its own way. In fact, it is these linguistic realizations that make the mental experiences of the conceptualizer visible.

An example of the way in which linguistic expressions differ relative to the ways in which the speaker describes a scene is shown by the concept of **construal**, the act of conceiving and expressing experiences in different ways. In terms of truth conditions, the two linguistic expressions *The faculty agrees*, and *The faculty agree* refer to the same state of affairs in the world and so they are semantically equal. They share the same truth conditions: they can both be true of the same state of affairs. In terms of cognitive criteria, they have distinct semantic values. They convey different conceptualizations of the same content. In the first expression, the speaker conceptualizes the faculty as a unified body agreeing with an external proposal. In the second expression, the speaker conceptualizes the faculty as a collection of individuals agreeing with one another. The linguistic differences between the two expressions, therefore, reflect conceptual differences which in turn reflect different experiences. I take up the **construal** theory in Chapter 9, where I examine more closely its axioms, advantages and ramifications.

Exercises 4.10

The following pairs are not free alternatives, but rather semantic variants. The preposition in each represents a different conceptualization of the speaker. Say what it is.

1. a. He jumped on the table.
    b. He jumped over the table.
2. a. He crawled in the garden.
    b. He crawled into the garden.
3. a. The guests arrived on time.
    b. The guests arrived in time.
4. a. She walked across the grass.
    b. She walked through the grass.
5. a. There is a street behind the station.
    b. There is a street beyond the station.

4.3 Summary

In this chapter, I have introduced details of the cognitive approach to meaning. In Generative Linguistics, the word **cognitive** means language is seen as an autonomous component of the mind. Knowledge of language is innate. The mind has a blueprint for language. In Cognitive Linguistics, the word **cognitive** means language is seen as an integral facet of cognition. Knowledge of language is based on experience. The mind is initially a blank slate and cognitive development is a matter of learning. First, I have explained what Cognitive Linguistics is and what its fundamental assumptions are. A distinctive feature of the approach is the slogan that linguistic knowledge is part of general cognition. Language reflects patterns of thought; therefore, the study of language resides in studying patterns of conceptualization. Second, I explained what Cognitive Semantics is and what its fundamental assumptions are. A defining characteristic of the approach is its focus on the subjectivist basis of meaning. Language is experientially-based; therefore, the study of meaning is the study of the basic conceptual structures which are grounded in bodily, physical, social and cultural experiences.

Table 4.1 Guiding assumptions of Cognitive Linguistics

Assumption	Gist
Language is non-modular	There is no autonomous portion of the brain which is specialized for language.
Language is symbolic	There is a direct association between the form and meaning of language.
Language is usage based	Knowledge of language is derived from actual instances of language use.
Language is creative	Language allows speakers to produce new linguistic expressions from conventional ones and describe the same situation in discrete ways.
Language is meaningful	All language expressions are attributed semantic values and assigned significant roles in language.

Table 4.2 The guiding assumptions of Cognitive Semantics

Assumption	Gist
Meaning is embodied	The nature of conceptual organization arises from bodily experience.
Meaning is motivated	The choice of a linguistic form is motivated by the meaning which the speaker intends to convey.
Meaning is dynamic	The meaning of any linguistic expression changes or extends to cope with new experiences speakers encounter in life.
Meaning is encyclopaedic	The semantic content of a linguistic expression is broad in scope, and includes both linguistic and non-linguistic knowledge.
Meaning is conceptualized	The semantic structure of a linguistic expression includes both conceptual content and a particular way of conceptualizing that content.

Conceptual Structures

Chapter 5 discuses the central roles in language assigned to conceptual structures, namely knowledge representations which pertain to the organization of
concepts in the human conceptual system. The chapter includes three sections.
Section 5.1 defines the conceptual system and highlights its role in reflecting
language. Section 2 enumerates forms of conceptual structure. Section 5.2.1
covers **metaphor**, whereby something is compared to something else which
has the same characteristics. Section 5.2.2 concerns **metonymy**, whereby
something is substituted by something else which is closely connected with
it. Section 5.2.3 pertains to **image schemas**, abstract patterns which derive
from our everyday interaction in the world and provide the basis for more
richly detailed lexical concepts. Section 5.2.4 relates to **mental spaces**,
knowledge patterns containing specific kinds of information and constructed
for interpretive purposes. Section 5.2.5 explains **blending**, whereby selected
elements from two mental spaces are incorporated in a third space, the **blend**.
In all the sections, I pursue three steps. First, I elaborate on the essence of
the conceptual structure. Second, I touch upon its properties. Third, I present
its patterns. For each conceptual structure, I devise exercises to validate its
application. Section 5.3 summarizes the main points of the chapter.

5.1 Conceptual system

In Cognitive Semantics, **language** refers to concepts in the mind of the
speaker rather than, directly, to entities which exist in the external world.
Language reflects the human **conceptual system**, the repository of concepts
available to a human being. In the conceptual system, a concept takes the
form of a **conceptual structure**, knowledge representation assembled for
purposes of meaning construction. In order to be encoded in language, a conceptual structure takes the form of a **semantic structure**, the meaning that
is conventionally associated with linguistic expressions. The meanings associated with words are referred to as **lexical concepts**: the conventional form
which conceptual structure assumes when encoded in language. Accordingly,
one important thesis that characterizes the cognitive approach to semantics is
that semantic structure reflects conceptual structure. Consequently, Cognitive

Semantics has two tasks. The general task is to employ language as a lens to investigate the human conceptual system. The specific task is to investigate the relationship between experience, the conceptual structure and the semantic structure.

5.2 Forms of conceptual structure

Cognitive Semantics studies the relationship between the mind and experience. It employs language as a tool for uncovering conceptual structure: knowledge representation of concepts in the human conceptual system. In Cognitive Semantics, linguistic meaning is seen as a manifestation of conceptual structure. Conceptual structure is modelled in terms of mappings such as metaphor and metonymy, establishment of image schemas, formation of mental spaces and blending of spaces. There are some general properties which the different types of conceptual structure share. (a) Conceptual structures are aspects of meaning construction in language; they are central to human thought. (b) They are grounded in experience; they are activated through human interaction with the socio-physical world. (c) They are inherently meaningful; they reveal fundamental information about the nature of meaning. (d) They serve to conceptualize the world; they serve to shape the forms of our linguistic expressions. (e) They are pervasive in everyday language; they are aspects of ongoing language processing.

What follows is a description of each conceptual structure, which includes its architecture, properties and patterns.

5.2.1 Metaphor

Metaphor is a form of conceptual structure that involves mapping between two things from distinct areas of knowledge, where one is compared with the other. In the mapping, aspects of a more familiar area of knowledge, called the **source**, are placed in comparison with aspects of a less familiar area of knowledge, called the **target**. Typically, the source is concrete, whereas the target is abstract. The purpose of the comparison is to portray the target in a way that makes it more accessible to human understanding. In *The ship ploughs through the sea*, the metaphor consists of comparing the act of farming with the act of sailing which it resembles in some respect. The sentence means 'The ship moves through water like a plough through soil'. The target area being described is sailing, whereas the source area being used for the comparison is farming. In literary studies, the source area of knowledge is referred to as *vehicle*, the target area of knowledge as *tenor*, and the mapping operation as *ground*.

A good example of metaphor is LOVE IS A JOURNEY. Here, the abstract domain of love is understood in terms of the concrete domain of journey. This metaphor is made up of a number of conventional mappings: journey is mapped into love, travellers into lovers, vehicle into love relationship, the distance covered into the progress made, the obstacles encountered into the difficulties experienced, decisions about which way to go into choices about what to do, destination of the journey into goals of the relationship, and so on. Linguistically, this metaphor motivates a wide range of utterances of which the following are illustrative: *Look how far they've come, They can't turn back now, They are at a crossroads, They may have to go their separate ways, Their marriage has been a long bumpy road,* and so on. As can be seen, the structure of the source domain is imposed onto the target domain, and so helps to shape its structure.

5.2.1.1   Properties

1. Metaphor is a tactic used to conceptualize one area of experience in terms of another. Any given metaphor has, thus, a source domain and a target domain. The source domain tends to be concrete, whereas the target domain tends to be abstract. For example, In *I see what you mean*, the source domain is the physical act of seeing, while the target domain is the mental act of understanding. In *He has a high reputation in the department*, the source domain is the vertical dimension of physical space, while the target domain is social status. As the examples show, metaphor serves to supply a tangible conceptual structure for abstract concepts. That is, there is a shift from concrete to abstract areas of experience.

2. Metaphor is a device employed to explain the nature of complex issues or hard-to-understand ideas. Unlike the classical view which sees metaphor as a literary feature of language or a figurative use of language, Cognitive Semantics views it as a process which helps to conceptualize a particular concept in different ways. For example, the concept of intimacy can be thought of sometimes in terms of heat, as in *Alan is such a cold person*, and sometimes in terms of distance as in *Alan is quite unapproachable*. As the examples show, metaphor serves to highlight individual aspects of the target concept, which are realized differently in language.

3.   Metaphor is a means applied to create new senses or extend the meanings of the existing ones. It is the key to understanding the phenomenon of polysemy. An example illustrating the process of metaphorical extension comes from human body parts, where human characteristics are mapped onto non-human objects, as in *the head of a department/ state/page, the face of a mountain/building/watch, the eye of a needle/ potato/hurricane, the mouth of a hole/tunnel/cave, the lips of a cup/ jug/crater, the nose of an aircraft/tool/gun, the neck of a land/shirt/ bottle, the shoulder of a hill/road/jacket, the arm of a chair/coat/company*, and so on. These metaphors are referred to as **conventionalized** because their meanings have been so deeply entrenched in the speech community through repeated usage that they become automatic.

5.2.1.2   Patterns

Cognitive semanticists have identified three patterns of metaphor. Below is a description of each pattern.

1. Structural metaphors

In a structural metaphor, an abstract concept is fathomed in terms of a concrete concept. It is a metaphor which arises from comparing one thing with another. This is illustrated by the structural metaphor ARGUMENT IS WAR, which allows us to think and talk about argument in terms of war. Here, speakers conceptualize the abstract concept of argument, which is the target domain, in terms of the concrete language of war, which is the source domain. This is shown by such everyday expressions as *He got into an argument, He defended his argument, He won/lost the argument, He attacked their argument, He demolished their argument*, and so on.

Below is a sample list of structural metaphors with their representative linguistic expressions.

LIFE IS A JOURNEY

She has embarked on a new career.
He has reached a career crossroads.
He is very talented and should go far.

TIME IS MONEY

You'll save time if you take the car.
She wasted no time in rejecting the offer.
I spend too much time watching television.

IDEAS ARE PLANTS

None of his ideas came to fruition.
She planted bright ideas in their minds.
The benefit scheme withered on the vine.

ARGUMENT IS BUILDING

You must learn how to construct a logical argument.
These arguments are completely without foundation.
Her arguments over the war are a little shaky.

SOCIAL ORGANIZATIONS ARE PLANTS

They have pruned the staff numbers back to 175.
They are reaping the rewards of their hard work.
The bank has branches all over the country.

Exercise 5.1

Give example sentences of ordinary language in English for the structural metaphors listed below.

1. IDEAS ARE OBJECTS
2. TIME IS MOTION
3. LOVE IS MADNESS
4. BELIEFS ARE POSSESSIONS
5. ARGUMENT IS CONTAINER

---

2. Orientational metaphors

In an orientational metaphor, an abstract knowledge area is couched in terms of spatial experience. It is a metaphor that arises from awareness of the orientation of our own bodies in physical space. This is illustrated by the orientational metaphor MORE IS UP, LESS IS DOWN, where speakers relate the abstract notion of more with the physically UP position and less with the physically DOWN position. This is illustrated by such everyday expressions as *The price of cigarettes keeps going up, Her income rose last year, Temperatures rarely rise above freezing, The standard of his work has fallen during the year, The discount applies only to children under 14, Prices have gone down recently,* and so on.

Below is a sample list of orientational metaphors with examples of linguistic expressions relating to each.

HAPPY IS UP

He is feeling up today.
He has been in high spirits lately.
Her spirits rose as she read the letter.

SAD IS DOWN

He is feeling down today.
He has been in low spirits lately.
Her spirits sank as she read the letter.

HAVING CONTROL OR FORCE IS UP

She is still at the height of her powers.
She has control over the pupils.
A captain ranks above a lieutenant.

BEING SUBJECT TO CONTROL OR FORCE IS DOWN

The party has fallen from power.
A soldier is inferior to an officer.
The disease is now under control.

GOOD IS UP

The situation is looking up at last.
She is at the peak of her career.
They sell high-quality goods.

Exercise 5.2

Identify the orientational metaphor which each of the following every-day linguistic expressions manifests.

1. He woke up to find himself alone in the house.
2. The patient has once more sunk into a coma.
3. They maintain high standards of patient care.
4. I have rather a low opinion of the head teacher.
5. The children at school are at the peak of health.

---

3. Ontological metaphors

Ontology is derived from the Greek root *onta* 'the things which exist' and the suffix *logy* 'the science of'. In an ontological metaphor, an abstract concept is figured out in terms of physical objects in the real world. It is a metaphor in which abstract concepts are conceptualized as though they were physical entities. Three subtypes of ontological metaphors exist. These allow us to extend entity status to a wide range of experiences.

- In the entity metaphor, an abstract concept is conceptualized as though it were a physical entity. This is illustrated by the metaphor INFLATION IS AN ENTITY, where the abstract notion of inflation is talked about as though it were a physical entity, as in *Inflation is lowering our standard of living, Inflation is nibbling away at spending power, Inflation is the government's main bugbear, The government is determined to fight inflation. Inflation is currently running at 3%.*, and so on.

- In the container metaphor, a land area is conceptualized as though it were a physical container with overt boundaries. This is illustrated by the metaphor VISION IS CONTAINER, where speakers often treat what they see within their visual field as though it were a kind of bounded container, as in *The lake soon came into view, There was nobody in view, There was no one in sight, Leave any valuables in your car out of sight,* and so on.

- In the personification metaphor, various kinds of human qualities are attributed to non-human entities. This is illustrated by the metaphor IDEAS ARE ANIMATE BEINGS OR PERSONS, in which abstract non-human entities like ideas are conceived as though they were human entities, and so attributed human characteristics, as in *The school has decided to adopt the idea, They find it hard to conceive the idea, They are intent on combating the idea,* and so on.

Exercise 5.3

Show how the ontological metaphor in each of the following sentences treats the abstract concept.

1. They fell in love with each other.
2. Violence is a cancer in our society.
3. The law finally caught up with him.
4. The country was in an economic depression.
5. The government took measures to combat unemployment.

5.2.2 Metonymy

Metonymy is a form of conceptual structure which involves mapping between two things within the same area of knowledge, where the name of one is substituted for the name of the other with which it is connected in some respect. In the mapping, the thing, called the **target**, is not called by its own name, but by the name of the thing, called the **source**, with which it is intimately associated. Typically, the source is more salient than the target. The purpose of the substitution is to depict the target in a way that makes it intelligible to human understanding. In *Hollywood protested against censorship*, the metonymy resides in using the name *Hollywood* instead of the name *American film industry*, with which it is associated. The sentence means 'The American film industry protested against censorship'. Clearly, the literal interpretation of the sentence does not work because a place cannot protest against censorship. Such an interpretation results in anomaly. The metonymic interpretation works quite well, where the word *Hollywood* refers to the *American film industry*. Normally, we refer to people by the place where they live or work.

A clear example of metonymy is INSTITUTION FOR PEOPLE. Here, the abstract domain of institution is understood in terms of the concrete domain of people. Linguistically, this metonymy motivates a wide range of utterances of which the following are illustrative: *The Army was called out to enforce the curfew, The company is unable to absorb such huge losses, The university can be justifiably proud of its record, The hospital is trying to raise funds for a new kidney machine, The law has no chance of being passed by the Senate,* and so on. As is clear, the metonymic mapping provides a suitable context for the interpretation of the examples by linking the entities through a contiguity relation, where the entities substituted are conceptually close.

5.2.2.1   Properties

Metonymy establishes a connection of association between two entities within a single domain. By contrast, metaphor establishes a connection of similarity between two entities in two different domains. In *a crocodile handbag*, there is an animal domain with the focus being laid on the leather produced from the animal skin rather than on the animal as a whole. There is a natural association between the skin and the animal, which belong to a single domain. In *a crocodile opponent*, there is a metaphorical mapping from the animal domain onto the human domain. There is similarity between the opponent and crocodile, which belong to two different domains.

1. Metonymy is a strategy for establishing reference. Its goal is to refer to an entity, prototypically a person, denoted by the target domain by means of the source domain. The referential function is represented by the stand-for notion. In *The land is owned by the Crown*, the word *crown* is used to refer indirectly to the monarch. This is a part-whole relationship, in which the part *crown* serves as a reference point for accessing the whole *monarch*. In *The Times hasn't arrived at the Press Conference yet*, the word *Times* is used to represent the reporter who works for the newspaper. This is a whole-part relationship, in which the whole *Times* serves as a reference point for accessing the part *reporter*. The process of using a part of something to represent the whole or vice versa is often referred to as **synecdoche**.

2. Metonymy is a medium for linguistic processes. One process is compounding. One metonymy is SALIENT FEATURE FOR PERSON/ OBJECT. A *paperback* stands for a book, in which the feature *paper* stands for the object *book*. Another metonymy is BODILY FEATURE FOR SPECIES. A *redbreast* stands for robin, in which the feature *red breast* stands for *bird*. The other process is conversion, especially noun-verb. One such general metonymy is PARTICIPANT FOR ACTION, which takes the following subtypes: AGENT FOR ACTION as in *to tutor a student, to author a book*; INSTRUMENT FOR ACTION as in *to hammer the nail, to saw off a branch*; OBJECT FOR ACTION as in *to dust the room, to pepper the dish*, BODY PART FOR ACTION as in *to tiptoe into the room, to elbow someone out of the way*, and so on.

3. Metonymy is a vehicle for expressing emotions. In emotional expressions, the bodily symptoms are the outcome of the expressed emotions. This type of metonymy is based on cause-effect relationships. One such general metonymy is THE PHYSIOLOGICAL EFFECTS OF AN EMOTION STANDS FOR THE EMOTION. In *She was paralysed with fear*, the effect is inability to move, whereas the cause is fear. In *She was shaking with anger*, the effect is agitation, whereas the cause is anger. In *He swelled with pride*, the effect is erect posture or chest out, whereas the cause is pride. In *He was jumping for joy*, the effect is jumping up and down, whereas the cause is joy.

5.2.2.2 Patterns

Cognitive semanticists have distinguished different patterns of metonymy. Below is a sample list of the patterns with their linguistic realizations.

WHOLE FOR PART

France won the tournament.
I filled the car up with petrol.
I have to go to the bathroom.

PART FOR WHOLE

She saw some new faces at the meeting.
At long last George had his own wheels.
They need extra hands for the harvest.

PLACE FOR EVENT

Vietnam witnessed great atrocities.
Watergate involved abuses of office.
Hiroshima changed our view of war.

PRODUCER FOR PRODUCT

They bought a second-hand Ford.
She received a Picasso as a reward.
I got a Parker for a birthday present.

OBJECT FOR USER

The piano is playing a new melody.
The BMW drove off without paying.
The sirloin steak is waiting for the bill.

Exercise 5.4

Discuss the types of metonymic relationships involved in the use of the italicized words in the examples below.

1   The *kettle* is boiling.
2.   It was two years after the *Wall*.
3.   They enjoy watching *Hitchcock*.
4.   They keep all their *glass* in a dresser.
5.   Rumours are circulating about *Westminster*.

5.2.3 Image schemas

An image schema is a form of conceptual structure or a conceptual representation which arises from repeated instances of embodied experience.

Embodiment is the way in which human psychology arises from the body's physiology. It explains how our bodies influence the ways we think and speak. Accordingly, an image schema is a recurring dynamic pattern which emerges from our interaction with the environment or observation of the world around us. An image schema is a representation of sensory and perceptual experience and includes such mechanisms as visual (vision), haptic (touch), auditory (hearing) and vestibular (movement). An image schema is thus an aspect of general cognition or a mental pattern that helps to advance our understanding of various experiences. An image schema serves to organize our experience, and so gives it coherence. In metaphor, in particular, it is used as a source domain to provide an understanding of the target domain, which represents experience.

An obvious example of image schema is the **CONTAINER**. This image schema is derived from the experience of having something inside something else or including something as a part of something else, as in *The bottle contains two litres of water*. The schema can be applied, however, to other areas of experience by a process of metaphorical extension from physical into abstract domains. Conversely, our experience of non-physical phenomena can be described in terms of physical phenomena. To see how this works, let us look at some examples. In *There was a ship in sight, The ship was out of sight*, etc., the visual field is conceived as a container. In *The runner was in the race, The runner was out of the race*, etc., activities are viewed as containers. In *The patient was in a coma, The patient came out of a coma*, etc., states can be viewed as containers.

5.2.3.1   Properties

1. Image schemas are inherently meaningful. They serve as conceptual representations that underpin lexical items. They are grounded in our socio-physical experiences. To illustrate this point, consider the image schema for FORCE. This image schema arises from our experience of acting upon or being acted upon by other entities, resulting in the transfer of motion energy. The properties of the FORCE image schema show up in linguistic meaning, as illustrated by the meanings of the English modal auxiliary verbs. In *You must be home by 11 o'clock*, the basic meaning of the modal *must*, which is obligation, derives from the COMPULSION schema. In *He can fix the computer*, the basic meaning of the modal *can*, which is ability, derives from the ENABLEMENT schema. In *You may come in if you wish*, the

basic meaning of the modal *may*, which is permission, derives from the REMOVAL OF RESTRAINT schema. As the examples show, the meanings associated with the modal verbs are grounded in embodied experience.

2.   Image schemas are internally complex. The complexity resides in the fact that they are made up of numerous components. To clarify this point, consider the image schema PATH, which derives from our experience of moving in the world or experiencing the movements of other entities. The PATH image schema has a beginning (source), a destination (goal), and a sequence of contiguous locations in between them. In a concrete context, this is shown in *She walked from the castle through the countryside to the mansion*, where the different components of the path are profiled by the use of different lexical items. The PATH image schema can be extended from concrete into abstract domains. We talk, for example, about achieving purposes as paths. This is illustrated by such examples as *He is composing a poem for his wife, and he is nearly there*, and *I was supposed to be writing a letter, but I am afraid I got sidetracked*.

3.   Image schemas are used in metaphor as source domains for target domains. Image schemas are important in the sense that they help to understand new experiences. Consider the image schema OBJECT. This image schema is based on our everyday interaction with concrete objects which have physical properties such as colour, weight, shape, and so on. This image schema can also be mapped onto an abstract entity like obligation. The metaphoric mapping facilitates understanding the abstract entity in terms of a physical object. This is illustrated by examples such as the following: *He has got a heavy teaching load this term, The government shouldered the task of restructuring the entire health service, They have a pressing obligation to protect the environment, She bore the responsibility for most of the changes, He was weighed down with family commitments*, and so on.

5.2.3.2 Patterns

Cognitive semanticists have identified different patterns of image schemas. Below is a list of the main image schemas with their sub-schemas.

SPACE	UP-DOWN, FRONT-BACK, LEFT-RIGHT, NEAR-FAR, CENTRE-PERIPHERY

CONTAINMENT	CONTAINER, IN-OUT, SURFACE, FULL-EMPTY, CONTENT
LOCOMOTION	MOMENTUM, SOURCE-PATH-GOAL
BALANCE	AXIS BALANCE, TWIN-PAN BALANCE, POINT BALANCE, EQUILIBRIUM
FORCE	COMPULSION, BLOCKAGE, COUNTERFORCE, DIVERSION, REMOVAL OF CONSTRAINT, ENABLEMENT, ATTRACTION, RESISTENCE
MULTIPLICITY	MERGING, COLLECTION, SPLITTING, ITERA-TION, PART-WHOLE, COUNT-MASS, LINK
IDENTITY	MATCHING, SUPERIMPOSITION
EXISTENCE	REMOVAL, BOUNDED SPACE, CYCLE, OBJECT, PROCESS

Exercise 5.5

Identify the image schemas that serve as source domains to describe abstract entities in the following sentences.

1. He is at a crossroads in his life.
2. The boy is close to the girl in age.
3. The price of cigarettes is going up.
4. Both parties are hungry for power.
5. They reached the end of the project.

5.2.4 Mental spaces

A mental space is a form of conceptual structure in which a particular mental construct is set up on the basis of a general scenario to understand a message. It is a temporary package of knowledge structure, which is built up through ongoing discourse for interpretive purposes. Its construction in communication involves two spaces. The first is the **base space**: the real space that serves as the starting point for a particular stage in discourse. The second is the **space builders**: the linguistic elements that serve as triggers for opening new mental spaces or shifting focus to existing ones. The word *maybe* in *Maybe she is in love with him*, for example, is a space builder; it sets up a possibility space relative to the discourse base space at that point. The interpretation of mental spaces draws not only on the hints given by the linguistic expression but also on the speech situation and encyclopaedic knowledge of the discourse participants. As talk unfolds and thought proceeds, new mental spaces are formed relative to others. This gives rise to a mental spaces **lattice**.

An often-cited example of mental spaces is the sentence *The girl with green eyes has blue eyes*. In terms of its compositional meaning, the sentence expresses a contradiction. Yet, we can easily make sense of the sentence by assuming two mental spaces. Each mental space contains three entities: the girl, the eyes and the eye colour. In the mental space of reality, the girl has green eyes. In the mental space of the portrait, the girl has blue eyes. The girl in the two mental spaces is identical. The eyes in the two mental spaces are identical. The colours of the eyes in the two mental spaces do not correspond. Neither the mental spaces nor the correspondence relations between the spaces are overtly encoded in the linguistic expression. These aspects of the interpretation are beyond the scope of strict compositionality. That is, the meaning of a linguistic expression can go beyond the meanings that are contributed by its component parts.

5.2.4.1 Properties

1. Mental spaces serve to show that the interpretation of a complex expression cannot be attributed to the contributions of its component parts, but to different space-connecting strategies. Mental spaces serve to account for ambiguities that arise from the use of space builders. In the expression *In 1966, my wife was a model*, the prepositional phrase *in 1966* is a space builder denoting time. It triggers two spaces: the *now* space of the speaker and the time space of 1966. The nominal *my wife* is open to two interpretations. The first is that the wife established in the 1966 time space is either the same wife in the *now* space or not. The second is that the wife established in the *now* space was not his wife in 1966, but is referred to as *my wife* by a shift linking the mental spaces.

2. Mental spaces are evoked by certain linguistic expressions called **space builders**, which motivate the hearer to set up a scenario to understand the intended message. Expressions like *I think, may*, etc. build a potentiality space. Expressions like *last week, recently*, etc. open a time space. Expressions like *If you were here* create a counterfactual space. Expressions like *just imagine* set up an imagination space. Expressions like *I would like* open a desire space. Expressions like *What if* open a hypotheticality space. Some adjectives specifically have the function of introducing non-veridical mental spaces. An *imaginary illness* exists only in the mental space of the sufferer's

imagination. A *would-be actor* is an actor only in the mental space of the person who is hoping to become an actor.

3. Mental spaces are used to account for a counterfactual conceptualization; a mental space is set up that runs counter to a presupposed reality. The utterance *If I were your father, I'd smack you*, can prompt a number of different interpretations, each of which arises from different mappings between reality and the counterfactual scenario that is constructed. The counterfactual scenario entails consequences for how we view the father and his parenthood in reality. In the first, the father is lenient, while the speaker is strict. In the second, the father is strict, whereas the speaker is lenient. In the third, the speaker is not allowed to smack the child. All this show that context directs the mapping between a situation that is grounded in reality and a situation that is based on a counterfactual scenario.

5.2.4.2 Patterns

Mental spaces are used to explain a range of semantic phenomena mostly connected with reference: the issue of how speakers and hearers keep track of the entities referred to in the language.

1. Indefinite reference

An indefinite noun phrase introduced by *a* merely designates an entity in some mental space, as in the well-known case of *Jane wants to marry a millionaire*. Here, we can set up a wish space and a reality space. In the wish space, Jane marries a millionaire. In the reality space, the sentence has two distinct interpretations. The first is called the specific interpretation. Here, a specific millionaire exists and Jane wants to marry him. The second is called the non-specific interpretation. Here, a specific millionaire does not exist. Jane merely has the desire to marry him. These interpretations may be distinguished by the manner in which the millionaire is referred to in subsequent discourse. On the specific interpretation, the millionaire can be referred to by personal pronouns such as *he* or *him*. *Jane wants to marry a millionaire. She met him at the Casino.* On the non-specific interpretation, the millionaire can be referred to by indefinite pronouns such as *one*. *Jane wants to marry a millionaire. She hopes to meet one at the Casino.*

2. Definite reference

A definite noun phrase introduced by *the* merely designates an entity in some mental space. The sentence *The minister changes every four years* relates to

potential ambiguity. The sentence contains a noun phrase with definite interpretation, but with an open reference. This means the noun phrase may or
may not refer to a unique referent. The sentence has two interpretations. The
first is that every four years the person who is minister changes in some way,
either physiologically or psychologically. The second is that every four years
the person who serves as minister changes. The two interpretations come
about because of the possibility of setting up two mental spaces. One relates
to value, while the other relates to role. The value reading relates to the individual who is the minister. This mental space fits the first interpretation of the
sentence. The role reading relates to the position of the minister, regardless of
who fills it. This mental space fits the second interpretation of the sentence.

This and other examples illustrate the fact that meaning construction is a
dynamic process; it is inseparable from context. Meaning is not solely found
in the words which an utterance contains, but relies on the conceptual processes that make connections between spaces.

Exercise 5.6

Using the theory of mental spaces, explain the referential opacity in
each of the following italicized items.

1.   In the film, *Catherine* is a *psycho*.
2.   *Nancy* wants to marry *a film star*.
3.   If *I* were *you*, *I* would accept the offer.
4.   In 1985, *my wife* was a sportswoman.
5.   Your father's *car* is always *different*.

5.2.5 Blending

Blending, also known as **Conceptual Integration**, is a form of conceptual
structure in which two mental spaces are blended to create a new space. The
two spaces, known as **input spaces**, represent relevant aspects of the concepts being combined. They correspond to the source and target domains
of conceptual metaphor. The created space, known as the **blended space**
or **blend**, is the result of the interaction of the input spaces. The blend has
emergent meaning of its own that is not contained in either of the inputs. In
other words, the blend takes information from both inputs, but goes further
in providing additional information that cannot be attributed to either of its
inputs. There is also a generic space, which facilitates the identification of

counterparts in the input spaces, and so serves as a basis for shared information. The conceptual blending theory derives from two traditions within Cognitive Semantics: Conceptual Metaphor Theory and Mental Spaces Theory.

An often-cited example of blending is the expression *That surgeon is a butcher*. In this expression, there are two input spaces, the surgeon and the butcher. In the generic space, the speaker identifies the surgeon with the butcher. The blend space links features from the input spaces to create a new blend. The emergent feature of the blend is that the surgeon in question is incompetent, although this feature is not revealed in any of the input spaces because it is not characteristic of surgeons or butchers. This emergent feature of incompetence represents the additional meaning provided by the blend. The incompetence is inferred by comparing the surgeon operating on a human body with a butcher tackling a carcass. By conceptualizing a surgeon as a butcher, we are evaluating the surgeon as incompetent. This example is metaphorical in nature, yet it cannot be accounted for by the Conceptual Metaphor Theory. This is so because the negative evaluation cannot be derived from the source domain 'butcher' as butchery is a highly skilled profession.

5.2.5.1 Properties

1. Blending provides speakers with a way of describing new experiences. It focuses on how information from two spaces is combined to produce a novel blend. The creation of a blend is an imaginative action that involves the interaction of source and target domains, containing features that belong to neither of the input domains. The expression *the grim reaper* is an imaginary figure representing death. The expression has death as a target domain, and involves two source domains: that of the reaper and that of a killer. Death is personified as a reaper. The word *reaper* refers to a person who cuts and collects crops on a farm, and so has positive connotation. However, in the expression it means a killer, and so takes on negative connotation. The meaning of the blend does not reside in the input domain of harvesting because grim features do not fit there.

2. Blending offers an insight into some complex areas of language use like compounding. As a productive means of word formation in English, **compounding** is the process of putting together two free morphemes, be they nouns, adjectives or verbs, to make a compound word, a brand-new word. A **compound** is a blend formed by integrating two substructures, free morphemes. A standard example of a

blend is the expression *landyacht*. This novel noun-noun compound consists of two input spaces. One relates to *land*. The other relates to *yacht*. In the blend, these linguistic forms are projected into the blend. However, only selected aspects of their meanings are integrated into the blend. As a result, the integration gives rise to the new form *landyacht* with a distinct meaning: a large expensive luxury car.

3. Blending is a cognitive operation that proves crucial in describing the semantics of counterfactual statements. An often-cited example is *In France, Bill Clinton wouldn't have been harmed by his relationship with Monica Lewinsky*. The expression includes two input spaces. One input space is about American politics and contains Clinton, Lewinsky and their relationship. In this frame, marital infidelity causes political harm. The other input space is about French politics, which contains French president, his mistress and their relationship. In this frame, marital infidelity does not result in political harm. The generic space establishes cross-space counterparts between the two frames. In the blended space, the emergent meaning which does not exist in either of the inputs is that Clinton is not politically harmed by his marital infidelity.

5.2.5.2   Patterns

Cognitive semanticists have used blending in a variety of linguistic processes, covering a wide range of cognitive phenomena from the formation of morphological structures to the creation of grammatical constructions.

1. Morphological blends

Blending is well-known as a word formation process. Morphological blends are words formed by combining parts of other words. They can be understood as a special kind of compound, including in particular nominal compounds based on adjective plus noun and noun plus noun combinations. For example, the word *wheelchair* is morphologically composed of the two input spaces *wheel* and *chair*. Semantically, certain core information from the input spaces is projected into the blended space *wheelchair*. The additional meaning, which goes beyond the meanings inherent in the two input spaces, is that of hospital or invalid or both. This and other blends have been so deeply established or entrenched that the language user no longer recognizes the blending background.

Exercise 5.7

Discuss the conceptual blends in each of the following morphological expressions.

1. motel
2. brunch
3. moped
4. breathalyser
5. infotainment

---

2. Grammatical blends

In the area of grammar, grammatical blends are represented by proverbs. The blends are the result of undergoing a process of conceptual projection and composition of material from input spaces into a blended space. For example, the proverb *Children are poor men's riches* contains two input spaces. One input space contains the elements rich men and riches. The other input space contains the elements poor men and children. The generic space contains the schematic information men and possessions, and sets up cross-space connections between counterparts in the input spaces. In the blend, certain elements from the input spaces are integrated into the blended space and results in an emergent structure. In neither of the input spaces does there exist a connection between children of poor men and riches of rich men.

Exercise 5.8

Discuss the conceptual blends in each of the following grammatical constructions which are proverbs.

1. Brevity is the soul of wit.
2. Money is the root of all evil.
3. Vanity is the quicksand of beauty.
4. Speech is the mirror of the mind.
5. Necessity is the mother of invention.

5.3 Summary

In this chapter, I have demonstrated the distinctive feature of **Cognitive Semantics**, its attempt to ground meaning in conceptual structures. The crucial insight of Cognitive Semantics is that the meaning of an expression derives from structure that is apparently unavailable in its linguistic realization. **Conceptual structures** are knowledge representations which are rooted in physical and social experiences. That is, meaning is experientially based. In Cognitive Semantics, language functions as a recipe for constructing meaning and linguistic structure triggers a series of cognitive processes. These processes mediate between the world of concepts and their linguistic realizations in language. Human thought and its expression in language are intimately interrelated. Five important forms of conceptual structure, which serve to construct meaning, have been identified. These are so important because they allow language users to conceptualize experiences, create new linguistic expressions, and account for their interpretations.

Table 5.1 Forms of conceptual structure

Conceptual structure	Definition
Metaphor	A conceptual structure in which one domain, the source, is employed to describe another domain, the target, with which it shares some characteristics. It involves a relation of resemblance or analogy and represents the relation 'X is understood in terms of Y'. It involves a mapping between two domains.
Metonymy	A conceptual structure in which one element, the source, is employed to identify another element, the target, with which it is associated within the same domain. It involves a relation of association and represents the relation 'X stands for Y'. It involves a mapping within a single domain.
Image Schema	A conceptual structure which arises directly from our physical and perceptual interaction with and observation of the world. Accordingly, it derives from embodied experience. It contributes to the interpretation of a complex situation. An example is the up-down schema, as in *Prices are up five per cent*.
Mental Space	A mental pattern which contain one or more of the following sorts of information: an element, a property and a relation. In ongoing discourse, distinct mental spaces are established. An element in one mental space is linked to its counterpart element in another on the basis of co-reference or identity.
Blending	A conceptual structure in which selected elements from input spaces are integrated to create a novel space, the blend. The blend may have a feature that is not found in either of the input spaces. An example is the blend *transistor* which is a combination of the inputs transfer and resistor.

Cognitive Mechanisms

Chapter 6 discusses the cognitive mechanisms which account for the relationship between the component parts of a linguistic expression, whether at the word or phrase level. The aim is to introduce the tools of the cognitive framework and explore how they account for intricacies of linguistic expressions. The chapter consists of two sections. Section 6.1 relates to **integration**: the way the subparts are combined to form a composite structure. In four subsections, four pivotal factors are presented: correspondence, determinacy, elaboration and constituency. These concern the ways in which lexical items are combined with each other to make meaningful expressions. Section 6.2 relates to **interpretation**: the way the meaning of the resulting composite structure is explained. This concerns the fact that the meaning of a composite structure is derived not only from the meanings of its subparts but also from the pragmatic knowledge behind its use. In two subsections, two essential principles are presented. These are compositionality and analysability. In both sections, I pursue three steps. First, I present the factor. Second, I spell out its nature. Third, I test its application.

6.1 Integration

Integration is the combination of the component subparts of a composite symbolic structure into a linear sequence. A composite symbolic structure is a construction, which could be a complex word, a phrase or a sentence. Integration resides in the notion of **valence**, the mechanism whereby two grammatical expressions combine to form a composite expression. More generally, the notion can be used to encompass all instances of what is traditionally described as the head-dependent relation. For example, the composite structure *behind the counter* is comprised of the component subparts *behind*, *the* and *counter*, which are related by valence or the head-dependent relation. The integration of the component subparts in a construction depends on the sharing of some features between them. The presence versus absence of these features often has striking consequences for the semantic value of the construction. The component subparts are not the building blocks out of which a composite structure is assembled, but they function instead to motivate selected facets of its meaning. The integration of the participating subparts in a composite structure is affected by the following four factors.

6.1.1 Correspondence

This factor relates to how the component subparts of a composite structure fit together and form a coherent assembly. Two subparts can be integrated to form a composite structure only if they have certain elements in common at both semantic and phonological levels. A **composite structure** is formed by unifying corresponding subparts which overlap conceptually. Typically, one subpart corresponds to, and serves to elaborate a semantic entity within the other. The composite structure *observer*, for example, is composed of the two component subparts *observe* and *-er*. The integration of the two subparts is affected by correspondences established between them. Phonologically, the subpart *-er*, when used agentively, makes schematic reference to a process, which is elaborated by *observe*. Semantically, the subpart *-er* denotes an agent which becomes meaningful only when added to the process designated by the subpart *observe*. By unifying the two corresponding processes, one obtains the composite structure *observer*. As a noun, *observer* refers to a person who watches an event.

Consider the prepositional phrase *behind the counter*. The preposition *behind* is a relational predication, whereas the noun phrase *the counter* is a nominal predication. The preposition becomes meaningful only when it relates two entities which are represented as part of its meaning. The correspondence is understood in terms of **trajector-landmark organization**, which relates to the relative prominence of participants in a linguistically encoded scene and reflects the more general perceptual phenomenon of figure-ground organization. The **trajector** is the focal, or most prominent, participant in a relationship. The **landmark** is the secondary participant in a relationship. The grammatical functions subject and object are reflections of trajector-landmark organization. There is a correspondence between the landmark of *behind* and the profile of *the counter*. The landmark of *behind* is a schematic representation of some thing in space. Unless this facet of *behind* is overtly expressed, the phrase cannot be conceptualized. The correspondence arises from the ways in which the trajector-landmark organization of the component subparts interacts.

Exercise 6.1

Account for the phonological and semantic correspondences between each of the following expressions.

1.   red carpet
2.   vandalism
3.   under the bed
4.   our friend, James Joyce
5.   her husband, the lawyer

6.1.2 Determinacy

This factor relates to which of the component subparts determines the profile of the composite structure as a whole. A composite structure consists of two or more subparts. Of the two or more subparts, one lends its profile to the entire composite structure. This subpart is called the **profile determinant,** traditionally known as the **head**. It is that part in a construction which is central because it determines its categorial status, establishes its core meaning, and selects its dependents. In the composite structure *observer*, for instance, the free morpheme *observe* signifies an action, whereas the bound morpheme *-er* signifies a thing. The composite structure as a whole signifies a thing in the sense that it describes an entity, referring to a person who observes something. This is so because the bound morpheme *-er* is the key subpart in that it lends its profile to the entire composite structure. The free morpheme *observe* is describable as one whose profile is overridden by that of the profile determinant *-er*. Both the free and bound morphemes are crucial to the meaning of *observer*, but the bound morpheme which acts as profile determinant is much more prominent.

Consider the prepositional phrase *behind the counter.* This construction contains the preposition *behind*, which profiles a relation, and the noun phrase *the counter*, which profiles a thing. However, the prepositional phrase as a whole profiles a relation rather than a thing in the sense that it describes a property of some entity in terms of its location in space. The composite structure acquires this meaning because the preposition *behind* is the profile determinant of the construction. Phrased differently, the complex concept has inherited the relational profile of *behind*. In *the woman behind the counter*, by contrast, the prepositional phrase *behind the counter* modifies the noun *woman*, which is the profile determinant of the whole construction.

Therefore, the construction as a whole is a noun phrase, a construction that profiles a thing.

In traditional terms, dependents divide into two main categories: complements and modifiers. A **complement** is the subpart that elaborates a schematic entity in the semantic structure of the dependent head. It adds intrinsic conceptual substance to the head. In the derived expression *observer*, for instance, the subpart *-er* is the profile determinant, whereas the subpart *observe* is its complement. In the prepositional phrase *behind the counter* the preposition *behind* is the profile determinant, while the noun phrase *the counter* is its complement. The complement is conceptually autonomous, whereas the profile determinant is conceptually dependent because it relies upon the complement to complete its meaning. A **modifier**, by contrast, is the subpart that has a schematic entity in its semantic structure which is elaborated by the head. It adds non-intrinsic or additional information to the head. In the compound expression *football*, the noun *ball* elaborates a thing and functions as a profile determinant, whereas *foot* qualifies a thing and functions as a dependent modifier, hence it is extrinsic to the meaning of *ball*. The composite structure profiles a thing, a kind of ball designed to be kicked with the foot. In *the woman behind the counter*, the phrase *behind the counter* modifies the noun *woman*.

Exercise 6.2

Identify the subpart which serves as the profile determinant in each of the following composite expressions.

1. jar lid
2. boredom
3. inessential
4. in the drawer
5. send the letter

6.1.3 Elaboration

This factor relates to how one component subpart contains a schematic hole which the other component subpart serves to elaborate. This amounts to saying that the profile of a particular subpart fills in the hole in the structure or completes the meaning of another combining subpart via the elaboration process. The component subpart that provides the elaboration is conceptually **autonomous** (A), whereas the subpart that is elaborated is conceptually **dependent** (D). The dependent subpart requires elaboration in order to become fully meaningful. A exists on its own without need of D to complete its meaning, whereas D is dependent on A to complete its meaning to the extent that A constitutes a salient subpart within D, or fills the hole that D has. The hole in the D subpart is called an **elaboration site**, or briefly **e-site**. The A subpart elaborates the e-site, which is a salient subpart within the semantic structure of the D subpart.

As a noun, *observer*, for example, shows an A/D pattern. The free morpheme *observe* represents the A subpart. Phonologically, it can exist as a fully autonomous form. Semantically, it can exist as a fully acceptable expression. It is possible to conceptualize it without making any necessary reference to anything outside the concept itself. By contrast, the bound morpheme *-er* represents the D subpart. Phonologically, it cannot exist as an autonomous form. Semantically, it cannot exist as a fully acceptable expression. It has to attach itself to a host of an appropriate kind, which elaborates a salient subpart within its semantic structure and adds specifications to it. In *behind the counter*, the subpart *the counter* is conceptually autonomous, while the subpart *behind* is dependent because it requires elaboration in order to become fully meaningful. Nominal concepts, those designated by nouns, are relatively autonomous, whereas relational concepts, those designated by prepositions, adjectives, adverbs and verbs, are conceptually dependent.

Exercise 6.3

Separate the autonomous (A) and dependent (D) subparts in the following composite expressions.

1. leakage
2. leisurely
3. disqualify
4. besprinkle
5. budgetary

6.1.4 Constituency

This factor relates to the construction of progressively more complex composite structures. A composite structure consists of two or more subparts. The order in which the subparts are successively integrated to yield a composite structure is referred to as **Constituency**. In the integration process, the subparts can be arranged at different levels of constituency, such that subparts at one level integrate to form a composite structure that functions as a unitary entity at the next higher level, and so on. Constituency tends to be variable. An expression which has the same composite structure and the same grammatical relations can have alternate orders of composition. In *gentlemanly*, for example, at the first or lower level of constituency, the subpart *gentle* is integrated with the subpart *man* to form the composite structure *gentleman*. At the second or higher level, *gentleman* combines with *-ly* deriving the overall expression. The expression *the woman behind the counter* is built in two stages. At the first stage, the subpart *behind* combines with the subpart *the counter*. At the second stage, the subpart *behind the counter* combines with the subpart *the woman*.

Some composite structures allow only one manner of integration. As an illustration of this, let us examine the formation of the word *impersonal*. At the first level, the nominal root *person* and the adjectival suffix *-al* are integrated to produce the adjective *personal*. At the second level, *personal* is integrated with the negative prefix *im-* to produce the adjective *impersonal*. If we combine *person* and *im-* first, we get *imperson* which is incorrect as there is no such word in English. The analysis can be diagrammed as follows:

impersonal

Other composite structures, by contrast, allow alternate manners of integration. As an illustration of this, let us examine the formation of the word *unlockable*. The first layer of structure is as follows. At the first level, the root *lock* and the adjectival suffix *-able* are integrated to produce *lockable*. At the second level, *lockable* is integrated with the negative prefix *un-* to produce the adjective *unlockable*. The second layer of structure is as follows. At the first level, the negative prefix *un-* is integrated with the root *lock* to produce the verb *unlock*. At the second level, *unlock* is integrated with the adjectival suffix *-able* to produce the adjective *unlockable*. The analysis can be diagrammed as follows:

1	2

Exercise 6.4

Diagram the following expressions to show their layers of structure. Note that two of them allow alternate orders of composition.

1. unlawful
2. disgraceful
3. enlargement
4. coauthorship
5. insupportable

6.2 Interpretation

Interpretation is the explanation of the meaning of the resulting composite structure. It resides in the two principles of compositionality and analysability. The principle of **compositionality** refers to the degree to which the meaning of a composite expression is thought of as being assembled from the meanings of its component parts. For example, the semantics of the expression *behind the counter* involves the meanings of its subparts: *behind*, *the* and *counter*. However, in some cases the semantics of a complex expression resides in the background information provided by its contextual use, the speaker's conceptualization or the world knowledge. For example, *to be in seventh heaven* does not mean that somebody is really in heaven, but rather somebody who is extremely happy. The principle of **analysability** refers to the extent to which the component parts of a composite expression match up phonologically and semantically. The analysis of the composite structure *behind the counter*, for example, is carried out on the basis of both the phonological and semantic contributions made by its subparts. Below is a description of each principle responsible for the interpretation of a composite structure.

6.2.1 Compositionality

The principle of compositionality, which is adopted by formal semanticists, refers to the process of deriving the meaning of a composite structure from the meanings of its subparts. The meaning of a complex word arises from the meanings of the morphemes out of which it is composed, together with the way in which the morphemes are arranged by morphology. According to this view, then, the meaning of a complex word is reconstructed from the meanings of its individual elements and their morphological relationship to one another. The meaning of the word *eventful* is determined by the meanings of *event* and *-ful*: full of events. The meaning of a sentence is built up from the meanings of the words it contains, together with the way in which the words are syntactically arranged. According to this view, then, the meaning of a sentence is the output of the context-independent meanings of individual words and of the properties of the grammar. The meaning of the sentence *We had an eventful journey* is based on the meanings of its individual words: We had a journey full of interesting or important events.

Cognitive semanticists have a different say on the question. The idea that word meaning is built straightforwardly out of morpheme meanings is totally unfounded. The idea that sentence meaning is built simply out of word meanings is largely vacuous. While the principle of compositionality might work well enough for compositional expressions, it fails to account for non-compositional expressions: those expressions whose meaning cannot be predicted from the meanings of the subparts. That is, not all expressions of a language conform to this principle. Those that do not are described as non-compositional or semantically opaque. Non-compositional expressions are not the exception as argued by formal semanticists, but rather the norm. Figurative language is in fact central to our way of thinking as well as to the way language works. The meaning associated with a word or sentence is subject to change depending on the context of use.

Linguistic expressions exhibit two types of compositionality. One is full, where the meaning of a composite structure is a function of the meanings of its subparts. The other is partial, where the meaning of a composite structure is symbolized by not only the meanings of its subparts but also the contextual knowledge surrounding its use. These show that the semantic value of an expression, as we will see, cannot just be limited to conventional means but enriched by encyclopaedic knowledge.

6.2.1.1   Full compositionality

Under full compositionality, the meaning of a composite structure is fully determined by the meanings of its subparts and the manner in which they are combined or the grammatical pattern in which they coexist. Full compositionality works for a large number of linguistic expressions in language. In derivation, for example, the meaning of *mendable* in *a mendable fault* is a combination of the root and the suffix: a fault that can be mended. In compounding, full compositionality represents a case of **endocentricity**, where the meaning of a compound is a specialization of the meaning of its head. Endocentric compounds are those whose meaning can be figured out by analysing their parts. In such compounds, the second substructure functions as the head, whereas the first substructure functions as its modifier, attributing a property to the head. In *hair pin*, for example, *pin* is the head, whereas *hair* is the modifier. The meaning of the compound is a combination of the meanings of the modifier and the head: a pin used to keep the hair back off the face. It is a compound that denotes a hyponym of the head. A *hair pin* is a type of pin. The meaning of the phrase *the woman behind the counter* is obtained by adding together the meanings of the individual items: *the, woman, behind, the* and *counter*.

Exercise 6.5

The following compounds are fully compositional. Write what the meaning of each compound is.

1. day care
2. heartfelt
3. manhunt
4. silver plate
5. sugar bowl

6.2.1.2   Partial compositionality

Under partial compositionality, the meaning of a composite structure is determined by both the semantic contribution of its subparts and the pragmatic knowledge behind what is actually symbolized. For example, the meaning of the word *questionable* in *questionable theory* is not only a function of the meanings of the root and the suffix, a theory that can be questioned, but rather a theory that is dubious. Presumably, every theory can be questioned.

The meaning of the phrase *be riding high* in *They are riding high in the polls*, cannot be worked out on the basis of the meanings of the individual words which it contains, but rather on the basis of pragmatic considerations. The phrase means 'very successful'. Partial compositionality or semantic opacity, which is a matter of degree, is a prototypical characteristic of compounds, idioms, proverbs and clichés.

Compounds

A compound is a structure formed by integrating two substructures, namely two free morphemes. As a productive means of word formation in English, compounding is the process of putting together two free morphemes, be they nouns, adjectives or verbs, to make a compound word, a brand-new word. In compounding, partial compositionality represents a case of **exocentricity**, where the meaning of a compound is not a specialization of the meaning of its head as it lacks a head. Since the head is not explicitly expressed, the meaning of the compound is accounted for by means of encyclopaedic knowledge. For example, the compound *birdbrain* does not denote a hyponym of the head. Its meaning is not only a function of the meanings of the modifier and head: a brain that belongs to a bird, but rather a type of person: a person who is stupid. The compound *redbreast* does not mean a breast that is red but rather a robin. As it is obvious, the meaning of the compound is different from the meanings of the individual words which it contains.

Exercise 6.6

The meanings of the following compounds are non-compositional. Account for the meaning of each.

1. skinflint
2. hardback
3. walkman
4. greenhorn
5. hammerhead

Full compositionality fails when the meanings of composite structures cannot be worked out on the basis of the meanings of their parts. Their interpretation goes beyond the information that is linguistically encoded. This is so because of two reasons. First, lexical items do not have fixed meanings. Their meanings tend to vary according to different contexts. Second, lexical items need, when they integrate, to adjust to each other in certain details. This requires shifting in their values relative to the intended conceptualization. This process is referred to as **accommodation,** the phenomenon in which a component substructure adjusts itself when integrated with another to form a composite structure. For example, the meaning of the word *child* can have positive and negative qualities. The nature of the quality is highlighted by the type of derivational morpheme used. In *childish*, the root *child* accommodates itself to the meaning of the suffix *-ish* to denote immaturity. Prototypically the word *house* means a place for people to live in. In *a warehouse*, however, the meaning of *house* accommodates itself to the meaning of *ware* to refer to a place where things are stored.

Exercise 6.7

In the following expressions, the head *box* accommodates itself to the meaning of the modifier. Write the resulting meaning.

1. jury box
2. deed box
3. press box
4. phone box
5. music box

Idioms

An idiom is a group of words that functions as a single expression and has a particular meaning that is different from the meanings of the individual words. Idioms are linguistic expressions which are not predictable simply by knowing the rules of a grammar and the vocabulary of a language. Idioms have two principal characteristics. From a semantic viewpoint, the meaning of the idiom as a whole cannot be constructed from the meanings of its individual words. From a syntactic viewpoint, the idiom does not allow the substitution or modification of any of its words. For this reason, idiomatic expressions are described as non-compositional and have to be learned as a whole. Idioms have two readings: compositional (literal) and non-compositional (idiomatic). An example of an idiom is *to beat around the bush*. First, it is not possible to derive the meaning of this expression on the basis of the standard readings of *beat* and *bush*. The non-compositional reading of the expression is that to talk about something for a long time without coming to the main point. Second, it is not possible to modify the verb *beat* by an adverb nor is it possible to make the word *bush* plural.

Exercise 6.8

The meanings of the following idioms are non-compositional. Specify what the meaning of each is.

1. a brain box
2. a high-flier
3. a misery guts
4. a tissue of lies
5. a money-spinner

Proverbs

A proverb is a popular short saying, meant as advice or warning. Two qualities characterize proverbs. One is popularity. A proverb is popular for it contains enduring wisdom. The other is pithiness. A proverb is short in form but full of meaning. Proverbs cover a wide range of human experience, gained through doing, seeing or feelings things. Proverbs have two interpretations: Compositional (literal) and non-literal (metaphorical). The compositional interpretation is the basic or usual meaning of a proverb. The non-compositional interpretation is the symbolic meaning of a proverb when it is applied to a new real-life situation. That is, their literal meanings are extended to other situations or given new applications. Let us examine a proverbial saying like *The bull must be taken by the horns*. The literal meaning of the proverb is that in moments of danger during a bullfight, a strong expert will grasp the bull by the horns and so prevent it from tossing him. The metaphorical meaning of the proverb is that when faced by difficulties or perils one should meet them fearlessly or boldly, not try to evade them.

Exercise 6.9

The meanings of the following proverbs are non-compositional. Assign a metaphorical meaning to each.

1. A stitch in time saves nine.
2. All that glitters is not gold.
3. As you sow, so shall you reap.
4. Make hay while the sun shines.
5. Birds of a feather flock together.

Clichés

A cliché is a commonly occurring utterance that is used schematically. A dictionary definition of a cliché is that it is a comment that is very often used and no longer has any real meaning. By contrast, a linguistic definition of a cliché is that it is an expression, usually used by people, that has the purpose of giving advice or expressing feelings. It is an expression which is apparently compositional, but in reality it is not. It has a particular meaning that is different from the meanings of the individual words which it contains. Let us take as an example the expression *play with fire*. In so far as its propositional meaning is concerned, this expression would have to be described as fully compositional. As a whole phrase, however, it would not. It does have meaning of a more subtle kind. That is, the meaning of the expression is not calculated on the basis of its literal content. The meaning conveyed is to act in a way that is very dangerous or risky. Because clichés are too often used, they are stored as complete units in the minds of speech participants. They are easy to retrieve for the speaker and easy to decode for the hearer. Like an idiom, a cliché is stored in the mental lexicon in a ready-made form.

Exercise 6.10

The meanings of the following clichés are non-compositional. Specify what the meaning of each is.

1.   She was in a fix.
2.   That was easy as pie.
3.   She is as fit as a fiddle.
4.   It made my blood boil.
5.   The story is hard to swallow.

6.2.2 Analysability

The principle of analysability refers to the process of matching up the subparts of a composite structure phonologically and semantically. Precisely, it refers to the ability of the speaker to recognize the phonological and semantic contributions made by the component subparts to the composite structure s/he is choosing. Analysability is a matter of awareness, i.e., of the presence and contribution of the subparts of a composite structure. Analysability is an essential feature of language and of linguistic meaning. It helps speakers to see if each substructure, which has an identifiable semantic and phonetic content, can contribute to the meaning of the composite structure. Linguistic expressions exhibit two types of analysability. One is full, where there is an accord between the subparts at the phonological and semantic levels. The other is partial, where there is a clash between the subparts at the phonological and semantic levels.

6.2.2.1 Full analysability

Full analysability is the case when the phonological subparts of a composite structure match up, one to one, with their semantic subparts. In such expressions, the speaker is aware of how the subparts contribute to the semantic make-up of the composite structure, and so enrich its interpretation. A word like *farmer*, for example, is considered fully analysable at both phonological and semantic levels. At the phonological level, it is analysable. The speaker is aware of its two subparts *farm* and *-er*. At the semantic level, it is analysable. The speaker is aware of the semantic contributions of its subparts. A *farmer* is a person who operates a farm. Likewise, a compound structure like *homework* is considered fully analysable. At the phonological level, the speaker can divide it into its component subparts *home* and *work*. At the semantic level, the speaker can identify the contribution made by each substructure. That is, the semantics of the compound derives from its subparts. *Homework* is work that is given by teachers for students to do at home. The same analysis applies to the phrase *the woman behind the counter*, which is analysable at both phonological and semantic levels.

Exercise 6.11

The following compounds are fully analysable. Write what the meaning of each compound is.

1. hay fever
2. coffee pot
3. fruit market
4. wheat bread
5. college staff

6.2.2.2 Partial analysability

Partial analysability is the case when the phonological subparts of a composite structure fail to correspond with their semantic contributions. In such expressions, the composite structure is only phonologically, not semantically, analysable. A word like *reminder*, for example, is considered partially analysable. Phonologically, it is analysable, but semantically it is not. It does not mean a person who reminds others, but something that makes one think about or remember somebody or something. Likewise, a compound structure like *highbrow* is considered partially analysable. At the phonological level, it is quite analysable. The speaker is aware of the fact that it consists of the two phonological subparts *high* and *brow*. At the semantic level, however, it is not analysable. The speaker is not aware of the contributions made by the subparts. It is not easy to recognize the meanings of the parts in the resulting structure. The speaker has to go beyond the information that is linguistically encoded by its subparts. The meaning becomes clear when the speaker takes into account clues from context and encyclopaedic knowledge. *Highbrow* refers to an intellectual who is interested in cultural ideas. Likewise, the idiom *keep in touch* is phonologically analysable but semantically it is not. The meaning is 'remain informed through writing or telephoning'.

Partial analysability is a prototypical characteristic of compounds, idioms, proverbs and clichés.

Compounds

Phonologically, a compound is analysable into its subparts. Semantically, it is not analysable. The meaning cannot be predicted from its linguistic form. Rather, it requires pragmatic knowledge, which involves general inferences together with non-linguistic contextual factors. For example, the compound *blockhead* is semantically not analysable. It means a very stupid person.

Exercise 6.12

The following compounds are partially analysable. Solicit encyclopaedic knowledge to write what each means.

1. low life
2. spoilsport
3. paperback
4. featherbrain
5. copperhead

Idioms

At the phonological level, the subparts of an idiom can be demarcated. At the semantic level, however, the subparts cannot provide the particular meaning of the idiom. The meaning conveyed is different from the meaning of each subpart understood on its own. For example, the idiom *a big shot* does not mean a shot that is big, but rather an important or powerful person in a group or organization.

Exercise 6.13

The following idioms are partially analysable. Disclose the meaning which each idiom expresses.

1. be all ears
2. call it a day
3. run the show
4. lead the field
5. be lost for words

Proverbs

A proverb lends itself to phonological analysis by allowing the division of its subparts. A proverb, however, falls short of a semantic analysis. This is because the meaning drawn from the proverb goes beyond the meanings of the subparts taken in isolation. For example, the proverb *There is no rose without a thorn* is semantically not analysable. The meaning is that however happy we are there is always some little touch of sadness or disappointment.

Exercise 6.14

The following proverbs are partially analysable. Disclose the resulting meaning which each proverb expresses.

1. It never rains but it pours.
2. Clothes do not make the man.
3. A rolling stone gathers no moss.
4. Do not make a mountain out of a molehill.
5. A bird in the hand is worth two in the bush.

Clichés

At the phonological level, the subparts of a cliché can be separated. At the semantic level, however, the subparts cannot provide its specific meaning. The overall meaning of the cliché is different from its literal meaning conveyed by the subparts in isolation. The meaning becomes clear if one knows the context. For example, the cliché *I shall be there in a twinkling* has a hidden meaning. The cliché is used to mean in a very short time.

Exercise 6.15

The following clichés are partially analysable. Disclose the meaning which each cliché expresses.

1. I was at a pinch.
2. It was a waste of time.
3. It made her skin crawl.
4. The ball is in your court.
5. We didn't see eye to eye.

6.3 Summary

In this chapter, I considered the cognitive mechanisms which govern the composition and interpretation of composite words. The aim was to introduce the tools of the cognitive framework and show how they account for intricacies of linguistic expressions. Two sorts of mechanism were presented. One mechanism is **integration**, the combination of subparts into a linear sequence. Four factors were shown to affect linguistic integration. They are correspondence, dependence, determinacy and constituency. The other mechanism is **interpretation**, the assignment of meaning to a linguistic expression. Two principles were shown to affect linguistic interpretation. They are compositionality and analysability.

Table 6.1 presents a summary of the cognitive mechanisms and their application to linguistic expressions.

Table 6.1 Cognitive mechanisms

Integration	Interpretation
1. Correspondence, which refers to the compatibility between two subparts in forming a composite structure. 2. Determinacy, which refers to the tendency of one subpart to lend its character to the entire composite structure. 3. Elaboration, which refers to the semantic hole which one subpart has and which the other subpart fills. 4. Constituency, which refers to the order in which the subparts are successively integrated to yield a composite structure.	1. Compositionality, whereby the meaning of a composite structure is either derived from the meanings of its subparts and/or includes knowledge outside its limits. 2. Analysability, whereby the subparts of a composite structure either match up phonologically and semantically or not. In the latter case, the speaker has to go beyond the linguistic information that is encoded by its subparts.

Part III

Operations

One significant task which Cognitive Semantics attempts to carry out is the explanation of linguistic structures with reference to human mental abilities, i.e., the cognitive operations which language users perform in the course of producing and interpreting linguistic expressions. Three crucial aspects of mental function are underlined in Cognitive Semantics. These are categorization, configuration and conceptualization.

Categorization is the mental ability to group the multiple senses of a linguistic item in a category. In view of the **Category** theory, a lexical item forms a complex category of interrelated senses. The category contains peripheral zones situated around a conceptual centre. The conceptual centre of a category, termed the **prototype**, is the most representative or most salient example of the category. The **periphery** of a category includes the remaining examples which are derived from the centre via semantic extensions. The senses gain membership in the category based on similarity rather than identity. The peripheral zones need not conform rigidly to the conceptual centre. For instance, a *kitchen chair* is regarded as the prototype of the *chair* category because it possesses almost all of its features: a piece of furniture for one person to sit on, which has a back, a seat and four legs. By contrast, *rocking chair, swivel chair, armchair, wheelchair* and *highchair* are regarded as being on the periphery because they possess only some of those features.

Configuration is the mental ability to group linguistic items into domains, in which each item occupies a specific facet. In the light of the **Domain** theory, the meaning of a lexical item cannot be understood independently of the domain with which it is associated. A **domain** is a knowledge structure with respect to which the meaning of a lexical item can be described. A **facet** is a portion of a domain which is associated with a particular experience. For example, the exact meanings of the words *incident, happening, occurrence* and *episode* cannot be identified unless one activates the domain of *event* as the background knowledge for their description. *Event* implies something interesting, as in *a sports event. Incident* implies something unpleasant, as in *a road incident. Happening* implies something unusual, as in *strange happenings in the town. Occurrence* implies something repeated, as in *a frequent* *occurrence. Episode* implies something memorable within a particular period, as in *the depressive episode in his life.*

Conceptualization is the mental ability to construe a given situation in alternative ways and to express them in language by using different linguistic expressions. By virtue of the **construal** theory, the meaning of a linguistic expression is identified in terms of the way its content is construed. **Construal** is the ability of the speaker to conceptualize a situation differently and use different linguistic expressions to represent them in discourse. Two linguistic expressions may share the same content, but differ in terms of the alternate ways the speaker construes their common content. The expressions *Even Chris knows the answer* and *Chris even knows the answer* have the same words, but they differ in meaning. They differ in how the speaker construes the situation. The first means Chris knows the answer although he's stupid. The second means Chris knows the answer among the many things he knows. The speaker's capacity for making alternative conceptual choices results in different structural realizations.

Outline

7

Categorization

Chapter 7 explores the role of **categorization** in the semantic description of single linguistic items. The aim is to find out what the significant elements of a single linguistic item are. The chapter is organized as follows. Section 7.1 delineates the phenomenon of categorization and underlines its significance. **Categorization** refers to the mental act of grouping together the multiple senses of a linguistic item, be it lexical or grammatical, into a category. A **category** then is a network of distinct but related senses of a given linguistic item. Section 7.2 discusses the two theories of categorization: **classical** and **prototype**. In the classical theory, categorization is carried out in terms of defining features. In the prototype theory, which is advocated in Cognitive Semantics, categorization is carried out in terms of degrees of similarity to a prominent example. In the discussion, I pursue three steps. First, I underline the essence of each theory. Second, I disclose its theses and implications. Third, I provide examples to confirm its application. Section 7.3 makes a summary of the main points of the chapter.

7.1 Introduction

An interesting aspect of the lexicon is **polysemy**, the tendency of a linguistic item, lexical or grammatical, to have a range of different meanings that are related in some way. The term **polysemy** comes from Greek *poly* (many) and *semy* (meaning). A **polyseme** is a word or phrase that has multiple meanings. The noun *play*, for instance, shows polysemy when used in different contexts: enjoyment as in *We watched the children at play in the park*, drama as in *The play was written by Shakespeare*, a game as in *We've seen some very untidy play from both teams*, free movement as in *They enjoyed the play of moonlight across the water*, use or effect as in *All resources were brought into play to cope with the crisis*, and so on. In the literature, there has been a great deal of discussion of this aspect. Most theories agree on the multiplicity of senses of a given item, but they differ with reference to two questions. The first is: Does a linguistic item exhibit multiple senses, and if so, on what basis are its senses organized? The second is: Do the senses derive from a primary sense, and if so, how is the primary sense identified?

7.2 Theories of categorization

To answer the questions raised above, linguists with different theoretical backgrounds have developed two theories: classical and prototype. Both theories consider categories a pivotal means of making sense of experience. Yet, they stand in stark contrast to each other regarding how people categorize and on what grounds they do so. The different views of the two theories follow from their underlying assumptions. The classical theory has an affinity to philosophy and logic. It relates meaning to truth conditions and describes the meanings associated with an entity in terms of features. The prototype theory has an affinity to psychology. It relates meaning to mental representations or bodily experiences, and describes the meanings associated with an entity in terms of networks. The classical theory places the regular senses in the category, and leaves the irregular ones outside the category, whereas the prototype theory places all regular and irregular senses in the category. In what follows, I elaborate on the stances held by the two theories of categorization.

7.2.1 The classical theory

This theory was the most widely accepted account of categorization from the time of Aristotle until the early 1970s. According to this theory, every concept is associated with a definition and the category it forms has a definitional structure. An entity that satisfies the definition is included in the category. An entity that fails to satisfy the definition is excluded from the category. Definitions typically take the form of a set of features which are individually necessary and collectively sufficient for membership in the category. To illustrate, consider the category *fruit*. In most dictionaries, the concept *fruit* is defined as the usually sweet-tasting part of a plant, tree or bush which holds seeds and which can be eaten. For an entity to belong to this category, it must have the following features: [sweet], [soft], [having seeds]. These features are the **necessary and sufficient conditions** for inclusion in the category. They are individually necessary in that an entity which has them qualifies as fruit, and so becomes a member of the category. They are collectively sufficient in that an entity which has all of them qualifies as fruit, and so becomes a member of the category. On the basis of these conditions, some fruits, e.g. apples, pears and apricots, would be in the category. They fulfil the conditions. Other fruits, e.g. lemons, avocados and bananas, would be outside the category. Lemons are excluded because they are not sweet. Avocados are excluded because they are not soft. Bananas are excluded because they do not have seeds.

7.2.1.1 Theses

The classical theory of categorization hinges on key theses, which can be summarized as follows:

1. Categories are defined conjunctively. They are defined in terms of a conjunction of necessary and sufficient features. The features are singly necessary but only jointly sufficient for an entity to gain membership in a category. If an entity exhibits all of the features, it is included in the category. If an entity does not have one or more of the features, it is excluded from the category. Let us examine the category *bird*. For an entity to belong to this category, it must have the following features: [feathers], [wings], [legs], [ability to lay eggs], [ability to build a nest], [ability to fly], [ability to sing], and so on. On this basis, a sparrow, falcon and robin would be in the category for having most of the features. A penguin, ostrich and chicken would be outside the category for lacking some of the features such as the ability to fly.

2. Categories display equal degrees of salience. Members of a category have equal status. Members of a category share the same set of definitional features. There are no entities which are better members of a category than others. Entities that are more salient are not better examples than entities that are less salient. Continuing with the category *bird*, because a sparrow, falcon and robin share the same set of definitional features, they have equal status in the category. The features are individually necessary in that every member of the category *bird* must possess them. The features are jointly sufficient in that every member of the category *bird* must possess all of them.

3. Categories have sharp boundaries. The boundaries are clearly defined, so inclusion in any category is clear-cut or unequivocal. A category, once established, divides the universe into two sets of entities: those that are included, and those that are not. There are no middle cases, where some entities in some way belong to the category but in another way do not. Proceeding with the category *bird*, because the boundaries of the category are clearly defined, a sparrow, falcon and robin would be included in the category for having the ability to fly. By contrast, a penguin, ostrich and chicken would be excluded from the category because they do not have the ability to fly.

4. Categories are rigid. There are no degrees of membership in a category. Category membership is an either-or matter. An entity either is or is not a member of a category. There is a distinction between

members and non-members. Features are either present or absent; they cannot apply only to some degree. A feature is either involved in the definition of a category, or it is not. A member either possesses a feature or it does not. Remaining with the category *bird*, because they possess all the features, a sparrow, falcon and robin would be members of the category. Because they lack some of the features, a penguin, ostrich and chicken would not be members of the category.

7.2.1.2   Consequences

The adoption of the classical model of categorization in the description of linguistic items has the following consequences.

1. Linguistic meaning is objective. The meaning of a linguistic item is primarily about propositions that are either true or false. This view is inspired by the theory of **objectivism**, which stipulates that symbols used in language get their meaning via correspondence with things in the external world. The meaning of a linguistic item is objective in the sense that it is not influenced by the subjective viewpoints of a language user. Physical or emotional feelings play no role in shaping the nature of categories. To take an example, the preposition *off* is used to denote concrete entities with different senses such as *He fell off his bike* (away from), *Take the lid off the jar* (remove), *He lives just off the main road* (near to), and so on. However, the preposition *off* is used to denote abstract entities, as in *He is off the medicine now* (not taking), *I am taking the day off tomorrow* (not working), and so. Unfortunately, the classical theory fails to include these abstract uses in the semantic network of the preposition.

2. Polysemy is understood as the case in which a linguistic item has a wide range of discrete senses that happen to share the same phonological form. The different senses of a linguistic item are separated from one another. The construction of a category for any linguistic item includes only its regular senses. In this way, the irregular senses are considered a list of exceptions and transferred to the lexicon. To offer an example, an adjective is a word which describes a noun. Prototypically, an adjective occurs before a noun (attributive) as in *the smart student*, or after the verb *be* (predicative) as in *the student is smart*. Many adjectives, however, fail to match one or more of these criteria: *asleep* cannot be used before a noun as in *The baby is asleep*, and *sole* cannot be used after the verb *be* as in *the sole runner*.

Unfortunately, the classical theory names these marginal uses exceptions. Thus, it overlooks the fact that they are part of the semantic nature of adjectives in English.

3. Linguistic meaning is disembodied, i.e., separated from the body. The category of a linguistic item is defined in terms of features, which are not represented within the sensory and motor system. Linguistic items are studied as a part of an autonomous linguistic structure. This implies that semantics is an autonomous discipline. In this way, semantic phenomena are studied apart from the physical or cultural experiences of a language user. To give an example, the word *eye* refers to the organ of seeing, as in *She's got beautiful green eyes*. However, the word *eye* is used in other ways which went unnoticed by the classical theory. In *We were all eyes as the Princess emerged from the car*, it means watching. In *I'm up to my eyes in school reports this week*, it means busy. In *She has an eye for detail*, it means good at noticing. In *In my eyes she was the most beautiful child in the class*, it means in my opinion. In *You have no need to be jealous. I only have eyes for you*, it means interested in.

To remedy the shortcomings of the classical theory, a new theory about the nature and structure of concepts, named prototype, has been proposed.

7.2.2 The prototype theory

This theory of categorization has gained prevalence since the advent of Rosch's works during the 1970s. According to this theory, a concept is centred round an ideal or central member called **prototype**. It assembles the key attributes of a given category. The remaining members that contain some, not all, of the attributes are called the **periphery**. The different members of a category are, therefore, not equal. The inclusion of an entity in a category is determined by its degree of resemblance to the prototype. The members conflict in some ways with the attributes of the prototype, but are included in the category on the basis of some perceived similarity to the prototype. To illustrate, consider the category *fruit*. In terms of the prototype theory, this category does not reflect objective assemblies of features. Rather, it involves approximations which consist of prototypical as well as peripheral members. Prototypical members are represented by examples like apples, pears, apricots, etc. These have all the attributes of the category, which are sweet, soft and having seeds. Peripheral or less central members are represented by examples like lemons, avocados, bananas, etc. These have some of the attributes of the category. Lemons are considered peripheral because they are not sweet. Avocados are considered peripheral because they are not soft. Bananas are considered peripheral because they do not have seeds. Although these do not have all the attributes, they are included in the category. This shows that members of a category do not have equal status, category boundaries are not always determinate, and some members of a category are better examples than others. That is why it is difficult to find a single definition which covers the category.

7.2.2.1 Theses

The prototypical view of categorization is based on key theses, which can be summarized as follows:

1. Categories are defined disjunctively. They are not defined by a set of essential attributes which members of a category are expected to manifest. Some of the allegedly essential attributes of the central exemplar of a category may appear to be optional at the periphery. Within a prototypically organized category, membership is based on similarity rather than identity. Let us examine the category *bird*. All types of bird are included in the category. The order of the types hinges on the degree of resemblance of a type to the prototype. The more attributes a type shares with the prototype, the less distant it is. The fewer attributes a type shares with the prototype, the more distant it is.

2. Categories display different degrees of salience. Members of a category have different status. Attributes not shared by all the members of a category are less important than attributes that appear in all or most of the members. Members of a category which carry more weight are considered better exemplars than members which are less salient. Continuing with the category *bird*, both a sparrow and an ostrich are types of bird. However, there is a difference in status. A sparrow would be a more typical example of bird, whereas an ostrich would not because of its inability to fly. In spite of this atypical attribute, an ostrich would be included as a member in the category.

3. Categories have vague boundaries. Categories contain peripheral zones round clear centres. Categories may have marginal instantiations that do not conform rigidly to the central cases. A category is structured in terms of similarity and distance. The more similar a sense to the centre is, the closer in distance it is. The less similar

a sense to the centre is, the farther in distance it is. Proceeding with the category *bird*, because the boundaries of the category are vague, all types of bird are included in the category. Because the category is not defined by a single set of attributes, the kind of birdiness that is relevant for sparrow is different from the one for ostrich. Being able to fly is not part of the birdiness of ostrich.

4.   Categories are flexible. Category membership is defined by similarity rather than identity. The distinction between essential and accidental attributes is not rigid. There need not be a set of attributes that is applicable to all the members of a category. Category membership is not a question of either-or, but a matter of degree. Therefore, not every member is equally representative of a category. Remaining with the category *bird*, a sparrow and an ostrich are both types of bird. Because a sparrow is able to fly, it is prototypical. Because an ostrich, by contrast, is unable to fly, it is not prototypical. Accordingly, both are members of the category but in different degrees.

7.2.2.2   Consequences

The adoption of the prototype model of categorization in the description of linguistic items has the following pivotal consequences.

1.   Linguistic meaning is subjective. The meaning of a linguistic item is derived from the different ways a language user construes a situation and the different structures chosen to encode them. This view is influenced by the theory of **subjectivism**, or alternatively **experientialism**, which stipulates that symbols used in language get their meaning via correspondence with conceptualizations of the world. The meaning of a linguistic item is subjective in the sense that it grows out of real-world scenarios and user-specific background data. A clear example is afforded by **mood**, the form of a verb in a sentence which expresses the speaker's attitude towards the content of an utterance. Three moods can be distinguished: (a) Indicative mood, which is used to express a statement or question, as in *He went away*; (b) Imperative mood, which is used to express commands, as in *Go away*!; and (c) Subjunctive mood, which is used to express uncertainty or wishes, as in *I insist that he go away*.

2.   Polysemy is understood as the case in which a linguistic item has a wide range of discrete senses that are subsumed under one phonological form. In this approach, the different senses of a linguistic item

are related. They are treated like members of a large family. They do not share defining features, but rather family resemblances which overlap. The construction of a category for any linguistic item should include both its regular and irregular senses. A simple example is supplied by a type of sentence termed **question**. The prototypical meaning of a question is requesting information, as in *When did he go?* The information is the time at which the stated event occurred. There are, however, other types of questions which have marginal functions: (a) Statement, as in *Why do these things always happen to me?*; (b) Repetition, as in *The newcomer is a psycho. The newcomer is what?*; (c) Comment, as in *Are you blind?*; (d) Request, as in *Could you please close the door?*; and (e) Confirmation, as in *They are happy, aren't they?*

3. Linguistic meaning is embodied. The category of a linguistic item is constructed in terms of networks. The meaning of a linguistic item is defined in terms of the actual experiences gained by the human encountering a physical or social world. Linguistic items can be described against the realities of life. Accordingly, semantics is not an autonomous discipline. Semantic studies should take notice of the experiential and cultural background of the language user. A good example is offered by **declarative** sentences. The prototypical meaning of a declarative sentence is in making a statement or some assertion about reality, as in *They are making noises*. However, based on the speaker's experiences, a declarative sentence can have other functions: (a) Order, as in *You must stop making noises*; (b) Question, as in *You do not stop making noises?*; and (c) Command, as in *You stop making noises!*

7.2.2.3 Advantages

The adoption of the prototype model of categorization in the description of linguistic items has some practical advantages.

One advantage is that it embodies the notion of gradation in the characterization of a linguistic item. The parameters along which the senses of a linguistic item vary are scalar or gradual, rather than binary, plus-or-minus qualities. The differences along such parameters are relative rather than absolute. This view shows that there is no place for absolute predictability. Rather, the use of a given linguistic item is influenced by context. To demonstrate this case, let us consider an example. In the classical model, the derivative force of the suffix *-able* is restricted to the formation of adjectives from verbal roots with a passive meaning as in *eatable goods*, meaning goods that can be eaten. In the prototype model, the derivative force of the suffix is extended to cover an active meaning as in *perishable stuff*, meaning stuff that can perish, or both meanings as in *changeable*, meaning can be changed or is able to change. Thus, the prototype model of categorization facilitates the description of a scenario in various ways, which differ in relative degrees.

Another advantage is that it is all-encompassing, including the conforming as well as the non-conforming senses in the characterization of a linguistic item. Thus, it permits the study of more phenomena, whereas in pre-cognitive accounts only those exhibiting absolute commonality were deemed amenable to semantic investigation. In doing so, it helps to delineate all the specific senses of a linguistic item, showing the points where they converge and the points where they diverge. To clarify the point, let us take an example. In the classical model, the suffix *-ish* is used mainly to denote disapproval. It picks out an undesirable quality of the thing specified by the nominal root as in *foolish behaviour*, meaning behaviour that is unwise. In the prototype model, the suffix is used additionally, though rarely, to stand for a desirable quality of the thing specified by the nominal root as in *a stylish dress*, meaning a dress that is fashionable. Hence, the prototype model of categorization allows for generality by including uses that have hitherto been treated as exceptions to the rule or left outside the category.

A further advantage is that it is experiential, involving the role of the human in structuring the world and allowing for the mental capacities to shape language. Categories should be defined in terms of the peculiarities of human understanding or human capacity of conceptualization, and not in terms of the shared properties of their members. If the members share the properties, then no members should be better examples than others. To see how this works, let us look at an example. In the classical model, the suffix *-less* is simply employed to construe the absence of something undesirable as in *a noiseless flight*, meaning a flight that is without noise. In the prototype model, the suffix is used also to construe the absence of something desirable as in *a powerless person*, meaning a person who is without power. In this way, the prototype model of categorization helps to describe new phenomena reflecting experiences which the language user encounters in life.

7.2.2.4   Applications

The prototype theory of categorization can be applied to different areas of language with equal effect. To construct a category for a given linguistic item, the following steps should be taken:

1. Determining the prototypical sense of a linguistic item. There are some crucial factors which help to select the prototypical sense of a linguistic item. It is the sense that comes to mind first. It is the sense that occurs most frequently in our experience. It is the sense that stands out as the most salient among the category senses. It is the sense that is most basic in its capacity to clarify the other senses. It is the sense that serves as a reference-point for the less salient ones.
2. Identifying the peripheral senses of a linguistic item. There are some key principles which assist in establishing the peripheral senses in the semantic network of a linguistic item. They are the senses that have additional meanings that are not apparent in the other senses. They are the senses that are derived from context or inferred from other senses. They are the senses that display certain structural properties. They are the senses which are rated according to how similar they are to the prototype.
3. Laying down the itinerary which links the senses. There are some pivotal means which help to clarify the relations between the different senses of a linguistic item. The linkage is motivated by semantic rather than syntactic considerations. Such considerations make the transition possible from one sense to another. Any linguistic item has a core sense; the other senses arise because they satisfy different semantic conditions. This process helps to uphold the unity of the linguistic item.

A number of objectives lie behind drawing the semantic network of a linguistic item, the most important of which are:

1. Meanings are structured. The multiple senses associated with a linguistic item are not represented in the mind as single entities, but rather as a network of distinct but related senses. The multiple senses associated with a linguistic item are structured round a centre. The senses are not related to one another in equal ways. Some may be directly related to the centre; others may be indirectly related to the centre. The gist of the argument is that the semantic network of a linguistic item has a clear centre, and its fuzzy boundaries embrace overlap.
2. Meanings motivate meanings. New senses are derived from the existing ones. The senses are related to one another by semantic principles in the human mind. Semantic principles defining nouns are concrete/abstract, human/non-human and common/proper.

Semantic principles defining adjectives are qualitative/quantitative or gradable/non-gradable. Semantic principles defining verbs are transitive/intransitive. The thrust of the argument is that there exist semantic principles which help to yield new senses.

3. When the perceptual system experiences an entity in the environment, the conceptual system places the entity into a category. Categories mirror human sensory modalities (sight, sound, smell, taste and touch) and reflect the particular way in which something exists or is experienced. In addition, they reflect emotions and thoughts. Language helps speakers to categorize their experiences of the world. The import of the argument is that the conceptual system is organized in terms of categories, which relate to entities experienced in the world.

Morphology

An affix, prefix or suffix, is argued to form a complex category made up of distinct senses which are structured in the shape of a network. The senses are organized with respect to a central, prototypical, sense. The prototypical sense is the one that comes to mind first when thinking about the affix, occurs most frequently and is the most basic in its capacity to clarify the other senses. The remaining senses range over a continuum from less prototypical to peripheral. They are arranged relative to their distance from the central sense. Accordingly, the more peripheral senses are less related to the central sense than the less peripheral ones. The borders between the senses within the network are extremely fuzzy, and so the senses tend to overlap with one another in meaning.

An example of a morphological item is the suffix *-ary*. The prototype of the suffix *-ary* signals relation. It consists of two senses. **(a)** 'relating closely to the thing named by the root'. This sense succeeds when the nominal roots are abstract and the adjectives formed apply to inanimate entities. For example, *a budgetary policy* is a policy that relates to the budget. A handful of other adjectives includes *customary, dietary, disciplinary, elementary*, etc. **(b)** 'serving to do the thing named by the root'. This sense succeeds when the nominal roots are abstract and the adjectives formed name inanimate characteristics. For example, *a complementary list* is a list that serves to complete another. A handful of other adjectives includes *complimentary, exemplary, inflationary, precautionary, supplementary*, etc. The periphery of the suffix *-ary* consists of the sense 'embodying the characteristics of the entity referred to by the root'. This sense succeeds when the nominal roots are abstract and the adjectives formed name animate characteristics. For example, *a legendary broadcaster* is a broadcaster who embodies a legend in being famous and admired. A handful of other adjectives includes *honorary, visionary*, etc.

Figure 7.1 presents a graphical representation which captures the multiple uses of the suffix *-ary*. Note that the solid arrow represents the prototypical sense, whereas the dashed arrows represent the semantic extensions.

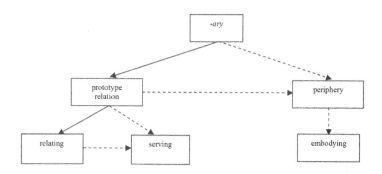

Figure 7.1: The semantic network of the suffix *-ary*

Exercise 7.1

The prefixes in A and suffixes in B exhibit multiplicity of meaning. Sketch out the semantic network for each.

	A		B
1.	un-	1.	-ure
2.	non	2.	-ness
3.	fore-	3.	-ment
4.	ultra-	4.	-hood
5.	under-	5.	-some

Syntax

A grammatical item forms a category of distinct but related senses. The distinct senses, which are related by virtue of a semantic network, are the result of dynamic processes of meaning extensions. The extensions are built by semantic principles which bring about the senses. The sense that has the common attributes of the category is described as prototypical. The prototype is the sense that comes to mind first or is the easiest to recall. The remaining senses that contain some, not all, of the attributes are described as peripheral. The peripheral senses inherit the specifications_of the category, but flesh out the category in contrasting ways. The senses of a category are related to each other like the members of a family, where they share some general attributes but differ in specific details.

An example of a grammatical item is the complementizer *to-*. Prototypically, *to-* conveys the idea of subsequence. This meaning can be paraphrased in two ways. The first is subsequent potentiality, where the realization of the event expressed by the complement verb is futurized with respect to that of the main verb. This occurs especially after verbs of desire, intention and endeavour, as in *They hoped/planned/attempted to climb Mount Everest*. With these verbs, the *to*-infinitive evokes an event as non-realized or yet to be realized. The second is subsequent actualization, where the event expressed by the complement verb is realized as a consequence of a previous event bringing it into being. This occurs especially after verbs expressing achievement as in *They managed to climb Mount Everest*, and some verbs expressing causation as in *She forced him to reconsider his position*. With these verbs, the *to*-infinitive evokes an event as realized. Peripherally, *to-* conveys the idea of sameness of time. After cognitive verbs, *to* does not refer to actions but to states that occur at the same time as the event expressed by the main verb. In *I believe him to be honest*, both my belief and his honesty coincide in time. This serves as evidence that a network includes not only regular but also irregular meanings.

Figure 7.2 presents a graphical representation which captures the multiple uses of the complementizer *to-*.

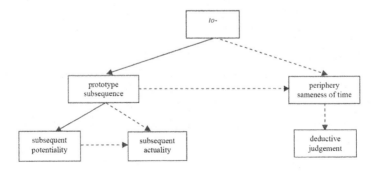

Figure 7.2: The semantic network of the complementizer *to-*

Exercise 7.2

The grammatical elements listed below exhibit multiplicity of meaning. Sketch out the semantic network for each.

1. anticipatory *it*
2. preposition *by*
3. complementizer *-ing*
4. complementizer *for-to*
5. modal auxiliary *should*

Lexicology

A lexical item is polysemous in nature. It is associated with a range of distinct
senses which form a complex category. Some senses are regarded as better
examples of the category than others. The sense that is the best example of
the category is the prototype, whereas the other senses are the periphery. The
prototype is the sense that has the common attributes of the category. It is the
sense that comes to mind first or is the most salient. The peripheral senses
are linked to the prototype by a set of semantic principles. That is, the prototype gives rise to a variety of peripheral senses. The peripheral senses have
some, not all, of the attributes of the category. Like members of a family, the
peripheral senses share the general attributes of the category, but they differ
in specific details.

An example of a lexical item is the word *strong*. The prototypical zone
of the adjective *strong* signifies strength. It has different shades of meaning;
(a) 'having physical strength', as in *a strong swimmer*; **(b)** 'having moral
strength', as in *a strong woman*, one has the potential to endure hardship;
(c) 'having a lot of influence', as in *a strong leader*; **(d)** 'likely to succeed
or happen', as in *a strong candidate for the job*; and **(e)** 'not easily upset
or frightened', as in *a strong personality*. The peripheral zone of the adjective *strong* signifies other meanings: **(a)** 'having a lot of taste', as in *strong
cheese*; **(b)** 'containing a lot of substance', as in *a strong coffee*; **(c)** 'firmly
established', as in *a strong marriage*; **(d)** 'difficult to attack or criticize', as
in *a strong argument*; **(e)** 'having a lot of force, often causing offence to people', as in *The movie has been criticized for strong language*. (= swearing);
and **(f)** 'great in number', as in *There was a strong police presence at the
demonstration*.

Figure 7.3 presents a graphical representation which captures the multiple
uses of the word *strong*.

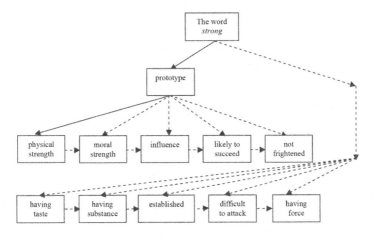

Figure 7.3: The semantic network of the word *strong*

Exercise 7.3

The verbs in A, adjectives in B and nouns in C exhibit multiplicity of meaning. Sketch out the semantic network for each.

	A		B		C
1.	cut	1.	safe	1.	wave
2.	run	2.	cool	2.	table
3.	take	3.	light	3.	work
4.	close	4.	clear	4.	flower
5.	drive	5.	bright	5.	wheel

7.3 Summary

In this chapter, I have explored **categorization**, the mental act of arranging things into categories. It is the process of grouping together the numerous senses of a linguistic item into a category. A **category** is a network of the senses of a linguistic item which is structured in terms of prototype and periphery. A linguistic item is **polysemous** and so displays a network of inter-related senses. It forms a network of senses subsumed under a **schema**, a pattern which represents an outline of the item. The **prototype** is the most salient example. It is the central sense that comes to mind first and is the most frequent in the category. It is the sense on the basis of which the other senses are arranged. The **periphery** includes the remaining senses which are derived from the prototype by semantic extensions. They are defined by their resemblance to the prototype, and so arranged in terms of distance from it. They are the boundary senses surrounding the prototype.

Table 7.1 presents a comparison between the classical theory and the prototype theory.

Table 7.1 Theories of classification

Classical theory	Prototype theory
1. Categorization is a matter of necessary conditions, in which the members must satisfy all conditions.	1. Categorization is a matter of family resemblance, in which the members share general attributes but exhibit incidental nuances.
2. Category membership is determined by identity. It is considered a binary issue, i.e., a yes-or-no issue.	2. Category membership is determined by similarity. It is a matter of degree.
3. Because membership is binary, members enjoy equal status.	3. Because membership is graded, members differ in status. Some are considered better examples than others.
4. A sharp or clear boundary separates members from non-members.	4. A fuzzy or unclear boundary separates the members.

Configuration

Chapter 8 inspects the role of **configuration** in the semantic description of linguistic items as groups. The aim is to discover the distinctive meaning of each linguistic item in a field. The chapter is organized as follows. Section 8.1 considers the phenomenon of configuration and underlines its significance. **Configuration** refers to the mental act of grouping together a number of linguistic items, be they lexical or grammatical, into a cognitive domain. A **domain** then is a knowledge background with respect to which the meanings of lexical items can be properly described. Section 8.2 presents the two theories of configuration: **Lexical Field** and **Cognitive Domain**. In the Lexical Field theory, which is advocated in Structural Semantics, configuration represents a model which focuses only on linguistic meaning. In the Cognitive Domain theory, which is advocated in Cognitive Semantics, configuration represents a model which focuses on both linguistic and non-linguistic meanings. In both sections, I pursue three steps. First, I underscore the essence of each theory. Second, I reveal its premises and repercussions. Third, I give examples to verify its application. Section 8.3 makes a summary of the main points of the chapter.

8.1 Introduction

A striking aspect of the lexicon is **lexical relationship**, the tendency of linguistic items, lexical or grammatical, to form a set of relations. In studying the lexicon of English, for example, we find that most items group together in a way that they define each other. The words *cry, lament, moan, weep* and *wail* all express audible sorrow. This indicates that the lexis of a language is not merely a list of independent items, but is rather organized into areas on the basis of some principles. Within each area, the words interrelate and define each other in various ways. That is, the lexis is not regarded as an inventory of independent items, but rather as a collection of interrelating networks of relations between items. In the literature, there have been many attempts to explore this aspect. While there is a sort of agreement on the aspect, there is a debate over its analysis. The debate has to do with two central questions. The first is: Do linguistic items form semantic sets, and if so, on what basis are they grouped together? The second is: Do the items represent different regions within the sets, and if so, how do they contrast with one another?

8.2 Theories of configuration

To answer the questions raised above, linguists belonging to different linguistic persuasions offer two solutions. One is the **Lexical Field** theory, in which the meaning of a linguistic item is described relative to the relationship it holds with its counterparts. Linguistic items acquire their meaning through their relationships to other items within the same field. This is a **dictionary theory**, which takes only linguistic phenomena into account. According to this theory, the core meaning of a linguistic item is the information contained in the item's definition. The other is the **Cognitive Domain** theory, whereby the meaning of a linguistic item is analysed in terms of the domain in which it is embedded. A **domain** is a coherent structure of concepts, in which each item represents conceptual knowledge based on human experience. This is an **encyclopaedic theory**, which takes linguistic and non-linguistic phenomena into account. According to this theory, the meaning of a linguistic item includes everything that is known about its referent. In what follows, I expand on the two theories of relationship.

8.2.1 Lexical Field

A Lexical Field, also called Semantic Field, is a theory of meaning which goes back to Trier in the 1930s. Basic to the theory is the view that the vocabulary of a language forms clusters of interrelated meanings rather than inventories of independent items. The vocabulary of a language is not simply a listing of independent items, like the lexemes in a dictionary. Rather, it is organized into fields within which lexical items interrelate and define each other in various ways. The precise meaning of any lexical item can be understood only by placing it in relation to others. That is, the semantic value of any lexical item is circumscribed by those of the other lexical items in the field. Examples of semantic fields include *vehicles, colour, fruit, clothing, plants, temperature, vision*, and so on. For example, the field of *vision* includes words like *gape, gawk, gaze, peer, stare*, to name just a few. These words constitute the lexical field, within which the words define themselves in contrast to each other. The lexical field of an item reflects its meaning.

8.2.1.1 Premises

The Lexical Field theory is based on focal premises, which can be summarized as follows:

1. Language is not a haphazard collection of concepts. Instead, it is a mosaic of concepts placed together, where each concept occupies a semantic space within the language. The meaning of any concept is affected by the other concepts to which it is related. A concept makes no sense outside its field. For example, on the basis of their meanings the concepts *carve, chop, crack, divide* and *split* cluster together to form the lexical field of *breaking* or *cutting*. Each concept takes up a position within the field. Each concept affects a different entity. However, the theory stops short of disclosing further details. People carve wood or stone, chop onions or carrots, crack paint or glass, divide money and split cost or prize.

2. The concepts in a field are related to each other directly. The meaning of an individual concept is dependent upon the meaning of the rest of the concepts in the same field. The meaning of a concept is internally determined by the set of relations which hold between the concept in question and the other concepts with which it contrasts. Namely, the meaning of a concept derives from the totality of relationships the concept has with other concepts in the language. Speakers understand a concept by understanding the other concepts that are in the same field. For example, the concepts *boo, cheer, groan, scream* and *sob* form the lexical field of *noise*. However, the theory is deficient in revealing any precise details. People cheer in approval, scream in fear, groan in pain, boo in disapproval, and sob from sadness.

3. The lexical field is exhaustively partitioned among its members, that is to say, there are no gaps. The field is complete in terms of the relevant meaning relations. Each member occupies a certain space within the field. If a single concept undergoes a change in meaning, then the whole structure of the lexical field changes. If there is an extension in the sense of one concept, it narrows the meaning of the neighbouring concepts. For example, the verbs *murmur, mutter* and *whisper* form the lexical field of *speaking*. However, the theory does not divulge any details how the change takes place. People murmur when they speak quietly so as not to disturb others. People mutter when they grumble in a low voice to themselves. People whisper when they speak so that only one person can hear.

8.2.1.2 Repercussions

The adoption of the Lexical Field theory to the description of linguistic items has the following repercussions.

1. The theory does not recognize the role of context in assigning a lexical item to a field. Contrary to this premise, the use of context is crucial as it is the best evidence available in accounting for the interpretation of an item. A lexical item has not just a semantic meaning, but also a pragmatic meaning. In view of the Lexical Field theory, the grammatical expressions *quite, rather* and *fairly* form the lexical field of *comparison*. However, the description is low on contextual details. *Quite* means completely or wholly, as in *The food at the restaurant was quite good; you should go there. Rather* means slightly or somewhat, as in *The food was rather good though the restaurant looked ordinary from the outside. Fairly* means nearly or practically, as in *The food was fairly good though we ate better at the other restaurant last night.*

2. The theory ignores the role of speaker in conceptualizing the world. It is true that one aspect of knowing an item is to know how that item is used in relation to other words. However, if this is the sole criterion, then the semantic structure of a language becomes a vast calculus of internal relations, with no contact at all with the way speakers conceptualize the world. The use of an item reflects the intention of the speaker and is a response to the communicative needs of the discourse. In light of the Lexical Field theory, the grammatical expressions *can, may* and *might* denote possibility. However, the description is lacking in conceptual details. *Can* form the lexical field of *possibility* that is always present, as in *Everyone can make mistakes. May* denotes possibility in a particular case, as in *The cause of the accident may never be discovered. Might* denotes possibility that is less likely, as in *I might visit you next year if I can save enough money.*

3. The theory does not draw a sharp distinction between the lexical items within the lexical fields. It does not tell the exact differences between lexical items belonging to a field. It does not take into account the contribution made to meaning by each lexical item. In virtue of the Lexical Field theory, the grammatical expressions *must, have to, should/ought* form the lexical field of *obligation* or *necessity.* However, the description is short of specific details. *Must* suggests obligation that comes from the speaker, as in *I must take my medicine.*

Otherwise I'd be very ill. Have to suggests obligation that comes from the outside, as in *I have to take the medicine. The doctor told me to. Should* and *ought to* suggest obligation that comes in the form of advice and that may not be carried out, as in *I should/ought to take my medicine, but I often forget.* Of the two, *ought to* is less frequent than *should.*

The Lexical Field theory equates roughly with the **dictionary view** of meaning, whereby a lexical concept represents a neatly packaged bundle of meaning. The core meaning of a word is the information contained in the word's definition, and this is the proper domain of **Lexical Semantics**. This view is consistent with the modularity hypothesis adopted within Formal Linguistics. The dictionary view is based on a number of premises. First, there is a distinction between the linguistic (literal) meaning and the non-linguistic (non-literal) meaning of a word. The linguistic meaning of a word includes the context-independent information. The non-linguistic meaning of a word includes the context-dependent information. From this premise, it follows that meaning is divorced from language use. Second, all aspects of meaning accessible in a given word are equal. The aspects are structured in terms of positive or negative values. Third, the core meaning of a word is a function of semantics. It is separated from the use of a word which is a function of pragmatics. Fourth, knowledge of word meaning is distinct from cultural, social, and physical knowledge. Fifth, the knowledge that a word provides access to is stable. It is this knowledge which is stored in the mental lexicon.

Given the inadequacies of the Lexical Field theory, cognitive semanticists have put forth a new theory, named Cognitive Domain, about the nature of lexical relationships.

8.2.2 Cognitive Domain

This theory of meaning was formulated by Langacker in the 1980s. The basic insight of the theory is that concepts cannot be understood independently of the domains in which they are embedded. A **domain** is a knowledge background with respect to which concepts can be properly described. The structure of a domain usually has a number of facets. A **facet** is a portion of a domain which is associated with a particular experience. In the area of language, the meaning of a lexical item cannot be understood independently of the domain with which it is associated. A domain is a conceptual structure with respect to which the meaning of a lexical item can be described.

A domain contains a set of facets, each of which describes a certain human experience, and each of which is realized by a lexical item. To understand the meaning of an item, it is necessary to associate it with the appropriate facet within a domain. The lexical items which occupy different facets are not in complementary distribution. A close investigation of their behaviour makes it clear they have distinct meanings.

Let us take an example to illustrate this. The meanings of the expressions *foresee, foretell* and *forecast* can best be understood against the domain of *prediction*, which the speaker activates as the conceptual knowledge for the description. *Prediction* means saying that something will happen in the future. Within the domain of *prediction*, each expression profiles a certain facet. Without understanding the details of the domain, we would not be able to use these expressions properly. *Foresee* implies prediction that comes as a result of ordinary reasoning and experience, as in *Economists should have foreseen the recession*. *Foretell* implies prediction that is made by using religious or magical powers, especially in literature and stories, as in *The prophet had the gift of foretelling the future*. *Forecast* implies prediction that is based on technical or scientific knowledge, as in *They forecast a large drop in unemployment over the next two years*.

A similar but not identical theory of meaning is **Frame Semantics**. This is a theory of meaning which was initiated by Fillmore in the 1980s. Fundamental to the theory is the assumption that word meanings can only be properly understood and described against the background of a particular body of knowledge known as a **frame**. The meaning associated with a particular lexical item cannot be understood independently of the frame with which it is associated. A frame represents a knowledge structure which relates the lexical items linked with a particular scene. Frames are based on recurring human experience. They allow us to understand, for example, a group of related lexical items, playing a role in explicating their usage in language. An example that is often cited is that of the commercial transaction frame. One would not be able to understand the lexical item *sell* without knowing anything about the situation of commercial transfer, which involves, among other things, a seller, a buyer, goods, money and so on. For example, the lexical item *sell* views the situation from the perspective of the seller, while the lexical item *buy* views it from the perspective of the buyer.

8.2.2.1 Premises

The Cognitive Domain theory is based on focal premises with reference to the nature of concepts, which can be summarized as follows:

1. Concepts do not exist in isolation in the mind of the speaker, but gather together with other concepts in conceptual fields, called cognitive domains. Domains represent human knowledge of a language, which correspond to background beliefs and perceptual experiences. A **domain** refers to a body of knowledge which provides background information for understanding and interpreting a given concept. A domain has specific facets of meaning. A **facet** is a portion of a domain which represents a particular aspect of experience. For example, the words *hobby, pastime* and *recreation* belong to the domain of *pursuit*, but each emphasizes a different activity. *Hobby* emphasizes activities that last over a long period of time such as collecting things, making models, and so on. *Pastime* emphasizes activities that make time pass agreeably such as doing jigsaw puzzles, playing dominos, and so on. *Recreation* emphasizes physical activities such as jogging, playing golf, and so on.

2. Concepts are not related to each other directly. They are linked to cognitive domains, and the particular facets within such domains which their meanings highlight. The meaning of any concept is established first by understanding the domain which it evokes and second by identifying the facet within the domain which it represents. Namely, concepts in a domain are not independent but are conceptually related. Concepts are understood by the way they stand in a relation of contrast or affinity to each other in a domain. For example, the words *instrument, implement* and *equipment* belong to the domain of *tool*, but each has a different use. *Instrument* refers to a tool used in the area of medicine or science. *Implement* refers to a tool used in the area of agriculture or building trades. *Equipment* refers to a tool used in the area of sports or electricity.

3. Concepts evoke domains which are encyclopaedic in nature. Domains are very broad; they include everything that is known about the referents of concepts. They cover a large range of knowledge of concepts, often in great detail. The encyclopaedic meaning of a concept may vary from one speaker to another, but there exists a common core that most speakers from a particular community might tend to share. Due to this, a domain helps to reveal all the semantic differences between concepts which are small but important. For example, the words *assignment, chore* and *task* belong to the domain of *jobs*, but each implies a different type of work to be done. *Assignment* implies a definite limited work assigned by one in authority like a teacher. *Chore*

implies a minor routine work necessary for maintaining a household or farm. *Task* implies work imposed by a person in authority or an employer.

8.2.2.2 Repercussions

The adoption of the Cognitive Domain theory has vital repercussions with reference to linguistic items as shown below.

1. Lexical items are dependent on domains. A **domain** is a coherent area of conceptualization relative to which the meanings of lexical items are characterized. A domain is a context of background knowledge with respect to which lexical items are understood. For example, the meanings of the adjectives *accidental, fortuitous* and *casual* can be derived from the domain of *chance* to which they belong, but each adjective stresses a different facet. *Accidental* stresses chance, as in *The site was located after the accidental discovery of bones in a field.* *Fortuitous* stresses a lucky chance connoting the entire absence of cause, as in *His success depended on a fortuitous combination of circumstances. Casual* stresses lack of real intent, as in *It was just a casual comment, I meant no harm.*

2. The scope of a lexical item is subdivided into two aspects, both of which are indispensable for understanding its meaning. These are the profile and its base, or alternatively figure and ground. The **profile** is the conceptual referent within the array of conceptual content invoked by the item, and the **base** is the domain relative to which the profile or figure is understood. One consequence of the profile-base relation is that the same base can provide different profiles. For example, the domain of *value* acts as a base for the adjectives *precious, (in)valuable* and *priceless*, within which each profiles a different facet. *Precious* profiles an object that is rare and worth a lot of money, as in *precious jewels. (In)valuable* profiles an action that is extremely useful, as in *(in)valuable discovery. Priceless* profiles an object that is extremely important, as in *priceless family photos.*

3. Lexical items can activate different domains for their interpretation. A lexical item can be conceptualized in relation to more than one domain. The set of domains which provide the context for the full understanding of a semantic unit is referred to as **matrix**. The domains evoked by the lexical item do not exist as separate patterns of knowledge. Rather, they interact with and react to each other in

numerous ways. For example, the morpheme *-y* participates in multiple domains. The morpheme together with the host provides access to a large inventory of domains. The first is the domain of *action* as in *scary*. The second is the domain of *causation*, as in *chilly*. The third is the domain of *possession*, as in *bushy*. The fourth is the domain of *evaluation*, as in *doggy*. The fifth is the domain of *resemblance*, as in *woody*.

The Cognitive Domain theory equates roughly with the **encyclopaedic** view of meaning, which focuses on both linguistic and non-linguistic knowledge in defining lexical items. The encyclopaedic view is based on a number of claims. First, it draws no distinction between semantic and pragmatic knowledge. The meaning of a lexical item subsumes knowledge both of what it means and how it is used. From this premise, it follows that pragmatic meaning is the real meaning of a lexical item. Second, encyclopaedic knowledge is organized as a network. Aspects of meaning associated with a given lexical item are not equal. Some aspects are more central than others. Third, meaning is a a consequence of context. The context in which a lexical item is used contributes to the encyclopaedic information that it evokes. Fourth, lexical items do not represent neatly pre-packaged bundles of meaning. Instead, they provide access to vast repositories of knowledge relating to a particular concept. Fifth, the encyclopaedic knowledge that a lexical item provides access to is dynamic. New experiences always increase one's knowledge about a given lexical item.

8.2.2.3 Advantages

The adoption of the domain model of configuration to the description of linguistic items has the following practical advantages.

One advantage pertains to definition. A domain is an area of knowledge which contains information about linguistic expressions, and so is a mechanism for defining their meanings. Extended to morphological expressions, a domain can serve to define the meanings of affixes. To define an affix, it is necessary to understand the entire domain to which it belongs and see which of its facets it picks out. For example, to define the meanings of the suffixes *-ous* and *-some*, we need to think of the domain of *possession* which they evoke. The suffixes exhibit comparison by sharing the main features of the domain and contrast by marking different facets of it. Thus, the domain provides accurate descriptions of their features. The suffix *-ous* may or may not imply indiscretion, as in *The adventurous manoeuvre of the staff secured* *the firm profits.* By contrast, the suffix *-some* implies only indiscretion, as in *They don't like drivers to be so adventuresome as to wreck cars.* Accordingly, affixes should not be defined on individual bases, as dictionaries usually do. Instead, affixes should be defined in terms of their respective domains.

Another advantage concerns comparison. A domain is a sphere of knowledge within which a number of linguistic expressions can be located, and so is a tool for comparing one expression with another. Applied to morphological expressions, a domain can serve to explicate similarities and differences among its members, and so is a convenient way of coding information about the distributions of the affixes and the patterns in which they occur. It shows the language user that understanding the meaning of an affix facilitates understanding the meaning of a counterpart affix in the domain. For example, to compare the suffixes *-ish* and *-like*, we need to think of the domain of *evaluation* which they evoke. The domain highlights their contrastive inherent meanings. The suffix *-ish* is used when one evaluates somebody or something in a negative way, as in *None of his friends tolerates his childish outbreaks of temper.* The suffix *-like* is used when one evaluates somebody or something in a positive way, as in *At 85, she retains a childlike curiosity about her environment.* Accordingly, affixes should not be tackled in isolation, as dictionaries usually do. Instead, they should be put in juxtaposition and tackled in terms of appropriate domains.

A further advantage belongs to construal. A domain is a realm of knowledge which provides the speaker with the linguistic expressions required to construe a situation in different ways, and so is a means of symbolizing conceptualization. Related to morphological expressions, a domain can serve to show that the use of a particular affix represents a particular construal of content. The construal coded is subjective in nature because it is based on experience that a human encounters, undergoes, or lives through. In construing a situation, two steps are thus involved. The first concerns the construal chosen which reflects the way the speaker conceptualizes the situation. The second concerns the linguistic form which the speaker chooses to represent the construal. For example, the suffixes *-able* and *-ful* represent different domains. The suffix *-able* elicits the domain of *voice*. It means 'capable of undergoing the action referred to in the verbal root', as in *forgettable.* By contrast, the suffix *-ful* elicits the domain of *possession*. It means 'likely to do the action denoted by the verbal root', as in *forgetful.* Accordingly, lexical choice provides a different way of describing a situation, giving rise to a different construal.

8.2.2.4 Applications

The Cognitive Domain theory can be applied to different areas of language with equal effect. To construct a domain for a group of linguistic items, the following steps should be taken:

1. Selecting the linguistic expressions which evoke domains by relying on their definitions. Domains explain and unify meaning at both conceptual and linguistic levels. The former is about conceptual content, which is in the mind of the speaker. The latter is about lexical content, which is represented by linguistic symbols. Because of polysemy, it is quite natural to find that some linguistic expressions appear in more than one domain, each time serving a different purpose.

2. Explaining the semantic structures of the domains, and identifying their facets. Domains constitute knowledge structures which serve to organize the lexicon. They do so by embracing various facets and the linguistic expressions which represent them. They uncover the properties of the structured inventory of knowledge associated with linguistic expressions. As reflections of subjective experience, the facets are necessary in describing the semantic contribution of linguistic expression.

3. Stating which linguistic expression represents which facet by comparing it with the other linguistic expressions. Domains are interpretative devices by which we understand a linguistic expression's deployment in a given context. To define an expression, it is best to compare it with the other expressions that belong to the same domain. In language, however, it is not surprising to find cases of overlap between the meanings of linguistic expressions. The focus, however, is on the general patterns in which the linguistic expressions occur.

A number of objectives lie behind drawing the semantic structure of linguistic items, the most important of which are:

1. Showing that domains mirror the reality of the mental lexicon and provide a natural means of organizing it. Domains construe reality in myriad ways and account for variability in conceptual representations. Domains are realms of knowledge which provide speakers with the flexibility to construe a situation in different ways. A domain serves to show that the use of a particular expression represents a particular construal of content. Domains allow speakers to symbolize their conceptualizations.

2.   Demonstrating that domains group together conceptually-related linguistic expressions and account for their meanings. Domains are spheres of knowledge within which a number of linguistic expressions can be located, and so are tools for comparing one expression with another. A domain serves to explicate similarities and differences among its linguistic expressions, and so is a convenient way of coding information about the distributions of the expressions and the patterns in which they occur.

3.   Indicating that domains serve as a means of encoding information pertinent to our understanding of linguistic expressions. Domains represent specific information about linguistic expressions and give an account of their exact behaviour. Domains serve to provide information about the linguistic expressions, and so function as mechanisms for defining their meanings. To define an expression, it is necessary to understand the entire domain and see which of its facets the expression stands for.

Morphology

The meaning of a bound morpheme, prefix or suffix, is best captured in terms of the domain in which it is positioned. A morphological domain is a conceptual configuration which encodes knowledge about morphological items with special provision for the roles they play in language. A domain is a context in which a number of bound morphemes are positioned, each having a distinctive function. As a pillar of meaning, domain is important at two levels. At a general level, it groups together bound morphemes that are associated with one concept. At a specific level, it reveals the characteristic behaviour of each of the bound morphemes. As a collection, bound morphemes are so related that in order to understand the meaning of one it is necessary both to understand the domain in which it occurs as well as the meanings of the other morphological participants. That is, the meaning of a bound morpheme can be interpreted by setting it in contrast with the other morphological participants of the domain.

Let us take an example to clarify this. The suffixes *-ette, -kin, -let* and *-ling* evoke the domain of *diminution*, an area of knowledge in which somebody or something is made small in size, young in age, or less in value. The suffix *-ling* is used mostly to form animate derivatives. It is used chiefly to describe persons, animals or plants. For example, *princeling* is a prince who rules a small or unimportant country, *duckling* is a young duck, and *seedling* is a young plant that has grown from a seed. By contrast, the suffixes *-ette, -kin* and *-let* are used mostly to form inanimate derivatives. The suffixes, however, differ in that each has a particular nuance. The suffix *-ette* is used chiefly to describe places or works of literature. For example, *kitchenette* is a small kitchen, and *novelette* is a short novel. The suffix *-kin* is used chiefly to describe fabric. For example, *napkin* is a small piece of cloth or paper used at a meal for wiping fingers or lips and protecting garments. The suffix *-let* is used chiefly to describe things. For example, *droplet* is a small drop of liquid, and *booklet* is a small, thin book with paper covers. The domain of diminution is diagrammed in Figure 8.1.

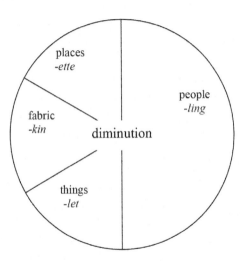

Figure 8.1: The domain of diminution

Exercise 8.1

The prefixes listed below evoke the domain of *distinction*. Yet, each represents a particular facet. What is it?

1. non-
2. a-
3. dis-
4. un-
5. in-

Syntax

The meaning of a grammatical item cannot be known without taking into account the domain to which it belongs. A grammatical domain is a knowledge structure which comprises a set of grammatical items. A domain is a conceptual structure which singles out the individual behaviour of a grammatical item. A domain has a twofold import. First, it houses the grammatical items under one umbrella. Second, it diagnoses the specificity of the grammatical items that make up the domain. Grammatical items form a domain in the sense that to understand the meaning of one grammatical item it is necessary to understand the meaning of the other grammatical items in the domain. The meaning of any grammatical item consists of the way it contrasts with the other grammatical items in the domain. Meaning is constituted out of concept contrasts. The meaning of a grammatical item is the concept which it stands for or the context in which it occurs. The participants in the domain then help to uncover the meanings of one another.

Let us take an example to make this clear. The expressions *all, any, each* and *every* evoke the domain of *quantification*: an area of knowledge which refers to the act of specifying the quantity of an instance of a thing. The quantity of an instance is specified in two different ways: in terms of a set (relative) or in terms of a scale (absolute). *Set quantification* refers to the magnitude of something measured against a full set. *Scalar quantification* refers to the magnitude of something measured against a scale. A set is divided into a full set (whole) and a subset (part). The above-mentioned expressions refer to full-set quantification: a collection of elements that forms a whole. The set quantifiers of English allow us to conceptualize the set's composition in different ways. The quantifier *all* is used to describe collectivity. In *All teachers need training*, *all* denotes all the individual elements of a set as a collection. The quantifier *any* is used to describe selectivity. In *Any teacher needs training*, *any* denotes a randomly selected element as representative for the full set. The quantifiers *each* and *every* are used to describe distributiveness, denoting each single element in relation to the full set. *Each* refers to two or more entities as individuals. In *Each teacher needs training*, *each* means each of the teachers considered separately. *Every* refers to three or more entities as a group. In *Every teacher needs training*, *every* means all the teachers considered as a group. The domain of set quantification is diagrammed in Figure 8.2.

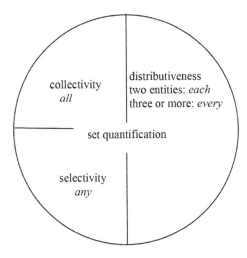

Figure 8.2: The domain of set quantification

Exercise 8.2

The prepositions listed below evoke the domain of *time*. Yet, each represents a particular facet. What is it?

1. on
2. in
3. at
4. by
5. for

Lexicology

The meaning of a lexical item can be defined in terms of the domain which it activates. The basic idea is that one cannot understand the meaning of a lexical item independently of the semantic knowledge it evokes, which usually involves other items. A domain shows that the use of a particular lexical item represents a particular construal of content. A domain is a coherent structure which relates lexical items together, captures their semantic specifications and shows how they correspond to different facets. Lexical items are organized as knowledge configurations in which each has a specific role to play and a specific task to fulfil. The notion of domain shows that what may appear to be hard-to-predict variations among lexical items can be treated as instances of conceptual representations. A domain is a device whereby the choice of a lexical item is guided by its meaning, which is the outcome of the concept it represents, rather than by its formal property.

Let us take an example to clarify this. The verbs *brush, scrub, sweep, wipe* and *scour* evoke the domain of *cleaning*, but each is used in a different context. *Brush* means cleaning something or making something smooth with a brush. It is used with hair, teeth and clothes, as in *Have you brushed your teeth yet?* and *You should brush your jacket, it is covered in dust*. *Scrub* means cleaning something by rubbing it hard with a brush and some water or soap. It is used with stains, as in *He is trying to scrub the stain from the carpet*. *Sweep* means cleaning the floor or the ground using a brush with a long handle. It is used with floors, as in *When everyone had left, she swept the floor*. *Wipe* means cleaning the surface of something by sliding something, especially a piece of cloth, over it. It is used with porcelain crockery for serving food and drink, as in *She has washed up, and wiped the cups, saucers and plates*. *Scour* means cleaning a cooking pan or hard surface by rubbing with a piece of rough material. It is used with metal containers for cooking food, as in *I scoured the bowls, pots and pans*. The domain of cleaning is diagrammed in Figure 8.3.

Figure 8.3: The domain of cleaning

Exercise 8.3

The verbs listed below evoke the domain of *employment*. Yet, each represents a particular facet. What is it?

1. hire
2 employ
3. engage
4. recruit
5. appoint

8.3 Summary

In this chapter, I have investigated **configuration**, the mental act of grouping together a number of linguistic expressions into a cognitive domain, in which each occupies a specific facet. A **domain** is a knowledge background with respect to which a concept is described. A domain contains a number of facets, each of which is linked to a particular experience. The knowledge is based on experience derived from beliefs, customs and practices. It is a coherent area of conceptualization which provides the basis for the characterization of a linguistic expression. A **facet** is a portion of a domain which is associated with a particular concept. Each facet is expressed by an appropriate form of language. To understand the meaning of any expression, it is necessary first to identify the cognitive domain that it evokes and second to relate it to the specific facet within the domain.

Table 8.1 presents a comparison between the Lexical Field theory and the Cognitive Domain theory.

Table 8.1 Lexical Field theory versus Cognitive Domain theory

Lexical Field theory	Cognitive Domain theory
1. Concepts are related to each other directly. The meaning of a concept is dependent upon its relation to the rest of the concepts in the same field.	1. Concepts are not related to each other directly. The meaning of a concept is dependent on the cognitive domain to which it belongs, and the particular facet within the domain which it highlights.
2. The theory does not recognize the role of context in assigning a linguistic expression to a field.	2. The theory recognizes the role of context in assigning a linguistic expression to a field. The use of context helps to indicate what speakers do in their natural use of language.
3. The theory ignores role of speaker in conceptualizing the world.	3. The theory emphasizes role of speaker in conceptualizing the world.
4. The theory is dictionary based. It solicits linguistic knowledge in defining the meaning of a linguistic expression.	4. The theory is encyclopaedia based. It solicits non-linguistic knowledge in defining the meaning of a linguistic expression.
5. The procedure relates to the discipline of Lexical Semantics. The definitions are stored in the mental lexicon.	5. The procedure relates to the discipline of Pragmatics. The definitions are governed by principles of language use.

Conceptualization

Chapter 9 evaluates the effect of **conceptualization** on the explanation of pairs of linguistic expressions acting as rivals. The aim is to discover the meaning differences between apparently similar linguistic expressions. The chapter is organized as follows. Section 9.1 explores the phenomenon of construal and underlines its significance. **Construal** refers to the mental ability of a speaker to describe a situation in alternate ways and express them in language by using different linguistic expressions. Section 9.2 weighs two theories of explanation: reference and construal. In the reference theory, meaning equals reference. This theory treats meaning as existing outside the mind. In the construal theory, meaning equals conceptualization. This theory treats meaning as existing in the mind. In both sections, I pursue three steps. First, I establish the essence of the theory. Second, I disclose its axioms and ramifications. Third, I provide examples to demonstrate its application to different areas within language. Section 9.3 gives a summary of the main points of the chapter.

9.1 Introduction

An intriguing aspect of the lexicon is **synonymy**, the tendency of linguistic expressions to have similar meaning, and so interchange freely in the context in which they occur. The word **synonymy** comes from Greek *syn* (with) and *onoma* (name). A **synonym** is an expression that has the same or nearly the same meaning as another in the same language. Expressions that are supposedly equivalent in meaning are **synonymous**. The verbs *disdain, hate, loathe, despise* and *detest*, for instance, are considered by some linguists to be synonymous. They are alternative forms or variants of the concept of *dislike*. Most theories agree on the fact that two or more expressions may have the same meaning, but they differ as to exactly how they should be used. The difference revolves around two questions. The first question is: Do seemingly similar expressions have different readings, and if so, in what respect are they different? The second question is: Is the difference between such expressions supported by evidence, and if so, where does it come from?

9.2 Theories of explanation

To solve the riddle of semantic equivalence and explain the meanings of seemingly similar pairs of expressions, linguists belonging to different linguistic persuasions offer two theories of explanation. One is the **reference** theory, which regards meaning as objective in nature. Lexical meaning is a matter of relationships holding between words and mind-independent worlds. To count two words as non-synonymous, the choice between them relies on a difference in the objects in the external world which they represent. The other is the **construal** theory, which considers meaning as subjective in nature. Meanings tend to refer less to objective situations and more to subjective ones; less to the described situation and more to the discourse situation. The construal theory is concerned with how human beings use language to represent, or even construct, reality. The meaning of an expression represents the way the speaker describes a situation.

In what follows, I briefly survey the two theories of explanation which are prevalent in modern linguistics.

9.2.1 Reference

The reference theory of meaning is an approach to language in which the meaning of an expression equals its reference. The meaning of an expression resides in the relationship between the expression and aspects of an objective world. This theory focuses exclusively on the referential properties of language. Language is seen as corresponding to the external world in an almost literal sense. The meaning of an expression involves applying it appropriately to an object in the world. This theory has given rise to a more sophisticated version, referred to as **truth-conditional** theory. Truth-conditional theory, which is adopted in Generative Linguistics, is an approach to language that sees the meaning of an expression as being the same as, or reducible to, its truth conditions. The meaning of an expression is identified with the conditions in the world under which it is true or false. Speakers of language are concerned with the conditions which allow them to determine the objective truth, or otherwise, of expressions. For example, the statement *Snow is white* is true if and only if snow is white.

9.2.1.1 Axioms

The reference theory is based on principal axioms, which can be summarized as follows:

1. Meaning is defined in terms of the conditions in the real world under which an expression is used to make a true statement. This is in contrast to approaches which define meaning in terms of the use of expressions in communication, or the speaker's role in describing a scene. In terms of the reference theory, the two expressions *wound* and *injury* refer to physical damage to the body, and so are freely interchangeable. However, there is a difference in usage which the theory ignores. *Wound* is the result of an intentional action. It is caused by a weapon, as in *The victim suffered a severe stab wound. Injury* is the result of an accident. It is caused by a crash, as in *The train passenger sustained a serious injury in the crash.*

2. Meaning is described by means of mechanical devices. Such mechanical devices are stated in terms of complex formalisms inspired by work in mathematics, computer science or logic. On the basis of such devices, speakers can judge the statement to be either true or false. On the basis of the reference theory, the two expressions *assembler* and *collector* share the components [human] + [adult] + [+/− male]. However, there is a difference in usage which the theory neglects. *Assembler* means a person who assembles a machine or its parts. *Collector* means a person who collects things either as a hobby like stamps, or as a job like taxes.

3. Meaning equates roughly with denotation, referring to objects in the external world. Meaning resides in the relationship between a linguistic expression and the explicit entity which it denotes. In virtue of the reference theory, the two expressions *referee* and *umpire* denote a person who makes sure that the rules are followed in a sports game. However, there is a difference in usage which the theory disregards. A *referee* controls contact sports games such as football, basketball and handball. An *umpire*, by contrast, controls non-contact sports games such as cricket, tennis and baseball.

9.2.1.2 Ramifications

The adoption of the reference theory to the description of linguistic items has the following ramifications.

1. Propositional meaning is the centre of attention. The propositional meaning of a linguistic expression is that part of its meaning which determines its truth conditions. It thus excludes non-propositional meaning including descriptive, expressive and social content. In virtue

of the reference theory, the expressions *false* and *untrue* share the same proposition: lack of veracity. In usage, however, they are different. The former as in *She was charged with giving false evidence in court* is more disapproving than the latter as in *Their story was completely untrue*. The non-propositional content of *false* includes the notion of deliberateness.

2. When two expressions occur in the same position, they are in **free alternation**, which refers to the substitutability of one expression for another in a given environment. In this way, synonymous expressions are considered free alternatives. In view of the reference theory, the two expressions *defender* and *defendant* are derived from *defend*, and so can be used interchangeably. In usage, however, they are distinguishable. *Defender* means a person who defends someone or somewhere against attack, as in *She has finally found a defender of her viewpoints*. *Defendant* means a person who defends a legal charge in a court of law, as in *The defendant has been convicted of a petty crime*.

3. Concrete entities which have truth conditions are the main focus of analysis. In this way, abstract entities which have no truth conditions lie outside the scope of investigation. In light of the reference theory, the two expressions *benefactor* and *beneficiary* denote concrete entities and so are equal in meaning. That is, they have the same truth conditions. In usage, however, they are clearly different. *Benefactor* means a person who gives benefits, as in *The benefactor is generous, donating $2 million*. *Beneficiary* means a person who receives benefits, as in *The beneficiary is grateful, receiving all the money in her father's will*.

Owing to such limitations, the reference theory is no longer a solution to semantic problems. Such a state of affairs paves the way for a new theory of meaning, named construal.

9.2.2 Construal

The construal theory of meaning is an approach to language that links the meaning of an expression with the idea in the mind of the person who produces it. The meaning of a lexical item is the function of both conceptual content and construal. **Conceptual content** is the property inherent in a situation. It is the meaning that is conventionally associated with an expression. **Construal** is the way the content is conceived relative to the communicative needs. It is the ability of the speaker to conceptualize a situation differently and use different linguistic expressions to represent them in discourse. When two linguistic expressions share the same conceptual content, they differ semantically in terms of the alternate ways the speaker construes their common content. Each alternative encodes a distinct meaning. Each alternative serves to highlight a different aspect of the content. Each alternative is realized in language differently. The expressions *non-person* and *unperson* are truth-conditionally equivalent, i.e., they describe the same objective situation, but they have nevertheless different meanings. The first refers to one who is ignored. The second refers to one who is non-existent. Construal is then a matter of how a situation is conceptualized and how it is linguistically encoded.

9.2.2.1 Axioms

The construal theory is based on principal axioms, which can be summarized as follows:

1. A difference in form always indicates a difference in meaning. Lexical or grammatical items are not in **free variation**. Variants usually display subtle differences in meaning or unequal functions in discourse, which can be observed in certain contexts. Variation in language is not random. Pairs of expressions are neither identical in meaning nor equal in use. According to the **Principle of Contrast**, every two forms contrast in meaning. The two expressions *authentic* and *genuine* denote something real, but they are not synonymous. They construe the thing differently. *Authentic* construes something as traditional, as in *It is a friendly restaurant offering authentic Greek food. Genuine* construes something as natural, as in *Is the painting a genuine Picasso?*

2. A semantic structure includes both conceptual content and a particular way of construing that content. Two expressions may invoke the same conceptual content, yet differ semantically by virtue of the construals they represent. The ability of the speaker to construe an objective situation in different ways is fundamental to lexical and grammatical organization. The choice of an expression correlates with the particular construal imposed on a situation. The two expressions *empathy* and *sympathy* have to do with understanding and caring about someone else's problems, but they are not synonymous. They construe the situation differently. *Empathy* focuses on sharing someone else's feelings, while *sympathy* focuses on being sorry for someone.

3. Meaning equates roughly with connotation, referring to ideas in the internal world. Meaning resides in the association between a linguistic expression and the indirect or implicit message which it suggests. The two expressions *jealous* and *envious* mean feeling angry or unhappy because one wishes one had the advantage that somebody else has. Yet, they are not synonymous. They construe the situation differently. *Jealous* means feeling hostile towards someone who enjoys an advantage, as in *You are just jealous of me because I got better marks.* *Envious* means wishing to have the advantage which someone else has, as in *She has always been envious of her sister's good looks.*

9.2.2.2 Ramifications

The adoption of the construal theory to the description of linguistic items has the following crucial ramifications.

1. Both propositional and non-propositional meanings count. Speakers of a language do not accept two linguistic forms of the same proposition as synonyms. When language provides two apparently equal expressions, speakers should find a way to discriminate between them. Each linguistic expression corresponds to a distinct meaning. The difference in meaning is argued to be the outcome of a given dimension of construal. The two expressions *allude* and *refer* share the same proposition, but they differ in construal. *Allude* is used to state things indirectly, as in *The reporter alluded to the president's secret fortune.* *Refer* is used to state things directly, as in *The reporter referred to the $250 million in the president's bank account.*

2. When two expressions occur in the same position, they are not in free alternation. Alternatives reflect different conceptualizations, and as a result are realized linguistically differently. Differences in linguistic form are not arbitrary, but signal differences in meaning. The two expressions *pick* and *select* have the same proposition: choose something from a number of possibilities. Yet, they differ in construal. *Pick* means to choose something without thinking very carefully about it, as in *Pick a card from the pack.* *Select* means to choose something by thinking very carefully about it, as in *How do you select people for promotion?*

3. Seemingly similar expressions, abstract or concrete, are subject to analysis. They are not derived from the same underlying structure. Nor is one derived from the other. Rather than being regarded as linguistic

variants, they are attributed distinct semantic values. Semantics is associated directly with surface form. The form of a linguistic expression reflects its meaning. Although the two expressions *freedom* and *liberty* mean more or less the same, they are distinguishable in use. *Freedom* means the right to live the way one wants without restraint, as in *He enjoys freedom of speech*. *Liberty* means release from former restraint, as in *The released prisoner enjoys his new liberty*.

9.2.2.3   Advantages

The construal theory employed in Cognitive Semantics is capable of resolving many of the difficulties encountered by previous proposals, and offers a number of advantages over their analyses. It provides a revealing account of lexical and grammatical structure.

First, the construal theory allows the speaker to conceptualize and express a situation in alternate ways, which result in different linguistic manifestations. When there is a one-to-one mapping between a construal and its linguistic representation, the construal theory plays a crucial part in differentiating between one expression and another. In complementation, for example, there is a case in which a complement clause represents a particular construal and follows a different verb. In *He desires to achieve fame*, and *He enjoys achieving fame*, for example, prominence is accorded to the main clause subject, and his essential interaction with the complement event. The main clause subject explicitly relates himself to the content of the situation depicted in the complement clause. There is, however, a difference in construal, which is realized by the use of a different complement type. The *to*-infinitive makes reference to a future action, describing the achievement of fame as a longed-for goal. The *-ing* gerund refers to an action taking place at the moment of speaking, describing the achievement of fame as a pleasurable activity.

Second, the construal theory solicits semantic as well pragmatic factors in determining the selection of a linguistic expression, particularly when there is a one-to-many mapping between a construal and its linguistic representations. In complementation, for example, there is a case in which the same verb is followed by two types of complement clause. Despite following the same verb, each complement type represents a different construal. For example, among differences in construal between *to*-infinitive and *-ing* gerund complement clauses, one relates to potentiality vs. actuality. In *It is hard to come to terms with being unemployed*, the *to*-infinitive complement clause refers to a situation which has not yet occurred or is about to occur. Pragmatically, the success of the action is not guaranteed. By contrast, in *It* *is hard coming to terms with being unemployed*, the *-ing* gerund complement clause refers to a situation that has actually occurred, or is occurring at the moment of speaking. Pragmatically, the success of the action is guaranteed.

Third, the construal theory focuses both on the form and the distribution of linguistic expressions. The form of an expression is characterized in terms of the particular construal imposed on its conceptual content. The distribution of an expression is the result of the semantic compatibility that exists between its internal parts. In the cognitive framework, the issues of form and distribution are considered inseparable. By accounting for the distributional difference between one linguistic expression and another, and by explaining why one linguistic expression is chosen over another, the cognitive analysis represents a departure from the current trend in linguistic research which tends to focus only on the structural specificity of expressions. For example, in *Working in the garden cheered him up*, the *-ing* gerund is coherent. This is so because it refers to an actual event, which is supported by the use of the past marker *-ed*. In this context, the *to*-infinitive is incoherent. This is so because the *to*-infinitive refers to a non-actual event.

9.2.2.4 Applications

The construal theory can be applied to different areas of language with equal effect. To help interpret the meaning of an expression, the following steps should be taken:

1. Collecting pairs of expressions that share the same conceptual content. The use of a pair has double import. Theoretically, it achieves emphasis by placing focus on a particular segment within an expression, and provides evidence that the segments compared have different meanings. Empirically, it helps, by relying on a corpus, to determine the contextual preferences of the pair members, and to stress the role of the distinguishing segments in signalling the meaning differences between them.

2. Distinguishing the pairs of expressions by examining their structures. To achieve this, first their mode of formation are identified and second their component parts are defined. Their uses are demonstrated through examples of sentences. Through these examples, it becomes easy to see how a difference in structure brings about a difference in meaning. Precisely, it becomes easy to see how the segments serve as a locus of difference in meaning, how related expressions are used in different ways, and how appropriate they are in different contexts.

3. Identifying the construals that are responsible for disambiguating the meanings of pairs of expressions. One great advantage of construal is that it captures differences between apparently similar expressions. Construal serves to show how a conceptual content is viewed in numerous ways and how these views are realized in language. The meaning of an expression is not just the conceptual content it evokes. Equally important is how that content is construed. As part of its semantic value, every expression construes its content in a certain fashion.

A number of objectives lie behind drawing the use of the construal theory, the most important of which are:

1. Confirming the absence of synonymy in language, a phenomenon whereby word pairs are assumed to have similar meanings. It is very rare that words are randomly interchangeable. Although word pairs may share some features, they are still distinguishable in actual use. Word pairs may be truth-conditionally similar, but they are subtly different. Such is the nature of language that there is essentially some difference. For example, the difference between *tasty* and *tasteful* is often encoded morphologically through the use of a different suffix. Each suffix affects the character of the word by adding a special meaning to it. *Tasty* is used to construe food as in *tasty soup*, whereas *tasteful* is used to construe objects as in *tasteful décor*. Each suffix represents a different conceptualization of experience.

2. Verifying the multiplicity of word meanings in language, a phenomenon whereby a word base has a wide range of meanings. Meanings are not fixed entities, but rather constitute different subsets of semantic components. Meaning represents a highly motivated process, whereby word pairs can be derived from the same bases. For example, the same state of affairs like *closure* can be linguistically encoded in different ways by means of different prepositions. *The shop closed up* means 'stop operating temporarily', whereas *The shop closed down* means 'stop operating permanently'. Although the word pairs are based on the same content, each has a different meaning, and so hosts a different preposition. The word pairs acquire special meanings, which differ with respect to how they construe a given situation.

3. Substantiating the role of construal in language, a phenomenon whereby a speaker conceives of and expresses a situation. The speaker is endowed with the ability to construe a situation in alternate

ways, and choose the language resources available to express them. For example, the difference between the word pair *personable* and *personal* can be explained by the different construals imposed on their common content, which is *person*. *Personable* means showing personality, whereas *personal* means relating to a person. The specific form of each word reflects the particular way in which the speaker chooses to describe its scene. Thus, seemingly similar words are not free variants. The distinction between them is not a function of formal rules; it is exclusively a property of construal. Each represents a different construal.

9.2.2.5 Dimensions

One of the central ideas in **Cognitive Semantics** relates to the way a speaker chooses to encode a conceptual representation in language. This is achieved by imposing a particular construal upon a scene. **Construal** refers to the cognitive ability to conceive a situation in alternate ways and use the appropriate linguistic expressions to stand for them. The meaning of an expression is therefore characterized in terms of both its content and the particular construal the speaker imposes on the content. Expressions differ in meaning depending on not only the entities they designate but also the images employed to structure their contents. Alternate expressions reflect contrasting images on a conceived situation. For example, one can construe the conceptual content of dreaming in two ways and use different linguistic structures to represent them. When one imagines and thinks while one is asleep about something that one would like to happen, one uses *dream of*, as in *She dreams of running her own business*. When one imagines and thinks while one is asleep about something in the past, one uses *dream about*, as in *She dreamed about him last night*.

Construal is a multifaceted phenomenon whose various dimensions reflect some of our basic cognitive abilities. The dimensions of construal enable us to make focal adjustments, thereby transforming one conceptualization into another that is roughly equivalent in terms of content but different in terms of construal. Speakers can conceive of a situation according to different dimensions, which result in different expressions to describe the same conceived situation. An essential aspect of the semantic value of linguistic expressions resides in the dimensions of construal imposed on their content. In choosing a particular expression, the speaker selects a particular dimension from a range of alternatives to structure its conceptual content for expressive purposes. The selection relates to the way in which attention is differentially focused on a particular aspect of a given scene and the way different linguistic expressions are used to describe that scene.

Before embarking on a classification of the construal operations, two notes are in order. First, it is very difficult to organize a comprehensive system of classification for the construal operations. The assignment of a particular construal operation under one rubric rather than another cannot always be entirely justified. In the literature, a number of classification systems have been proposed for the construal operations. The one presented here, however, provides a unifying framework in terms of which many semantic phenomena can be captured. It attempts to organize the construal operations into basic types. Second, several dimensions of construal can be involved in the meaning of a single linguistic expression. Each dimension views the conceptual content of the expression in a different way. The dimensions of construal apply to different areas of language. They can be grouped under three main headings: prominence, perspective and focusing.

9.2.2.5.1 Prominence

Prominence refers to the quality of eminence given, often in different degrees, to the substructures of a conception relative to their importance. Linguistically, the substructures are placed in different positions within the construction. Three types of prominence are distinguished: profiling, trajector/landmark alignment and salience.

1. Profiling

Within its base, every expression singles out a substructure which functions as the focal point of attention. This substructure, the **profile**, is the one that the expression designates. The base constitutes the larger structure of which the profile constitutes a substructure. The base is essential for understanding the meaning of the profile. The process whereby an aspect of some base is designated is referred to as **profiling**. In order to illustrate this, consider the following examples, where the action chain is realized linguistically differently, where the speaker chooses to profile different segments of it. In a three-element action chain like *Floyd broke the glass with a hammer*, the entirety of the action chain is in profile; the agent *Floyd* is coded as subject, the patient *the glass* as object, and *a hammer* as instrument. The success of the action is attributed to *Floyd*. In a two-element action chain like *The hammer broke the glass*, the agent is left unprofiled, while the rest of the chain is in profile; the instrument is coded as subject and the patient as object. The success of the action is inherent in the nature of the *hammer*. In a single-element action chain like *The glass broke*, the agent and the instrument are left unprofiled, while the patient alone is in profile, and hence coded as subject. The success of the action is inherent in the nature of the *glass*.

Morphology

In morphology, the significance of the dimension of profiling can be appraised by probing the function of prefixes or suffixes. For example, the bound morphemes *-able* and *-ful* can attach to the root *respect* to form *respectable* and *respectful*. Yet, they profile different relationships characterizing the relationship of the trajector to the verbal process, and so denote different meanings. In *She is a respectable woman from a good family*, the adjective *respectable* is derived from the verb *respect*, which means 'can be respected by others for having good qualities'. The suffix *-able* means 'capable of undergoing the action referred to in the verbal root'. A respectable woman deserves respect by reason of good character, appearance or behaviour. In *He taught his son to be respectful of other people*, the adjective *respectful* is derived from the noun *respect*, which means 'showing respect to others for having good qualities'. The suffix *-ful* means 'full of the thing denoted by the nominal root'. A respectful son has deference for other people and their beliefs.

Exercise 9.1

Show what segment in the conceptual content of the following expressions the rival affixes profile.

1.	earthen	earthly
2.	childish	childlike
3.	compulsive	compulsory
4.	documental	documentary
5.	adventurous	adventuresome

Syntax

In syntax, the dimension of profiling can be evaluated by reviewing non-extraposed vs. extraposed, raised vs. non-raised, and active vs. passive expressions. These variants are meaningful expressions which are used in different contexts despite the fact that they evoke the same conceptual content. In an active construction like *Nigel helped Kathy to make a presentation*, the most important participant *Nigel*, which is the agent of the main event, is in profile and consequently chosen as subject. In a passive construction like *Kathy was helped to make a presentation*, the most important participant *Nigel* is bypassed in favour of a less important participant *Kathy*, which is in profile and consequently chosen as subject. This shows that in Cognitive Semantics the selection of an entity as subject or object arises as a result of different conceptualizations. In other words, the function of subject or object assigned to an entity ensues from profiling, and not from semantic role.

Exercise 9.2

The non-equivalence of the following pairs of expressions is the result of placing different parts in profile. Discuss.

1. a. I expect that Susan will leave.
    b. I expect Susan to leave.
2. a. That Anna will resign is likely.
    b. Anna is likely to resign.
3. a. To entertain Catherine is difficult.
    b. Catherine is difficult to entertain.
4. a. To argue about a trivial issue is unwise.
    b. It is unwise to argue about a trivial issue.
5. a. They released the shoplifter on bail.
    b. The shoplifter was released on bail.

Lexicology

In lexicology, the dimension of profiling can be estimated by perusing instances in which profiling designates different aspects of a scene. Linguistically, the lexical item used evokes a distinct domain. For instance, in the following examples the different uses of the lexical item *close* invoke different domains as the basis for meaning. This is due to the semantic flexibility which the lexical item *close* displays. In *Our new house is close to the school*, it profiles the domain of space. In *The children are close to each other in age*, it profiles the domain of time. In *The new library is close to completion*, it profiles the domain of state. In *The child is very close to her mother*, it profiles the domain of relationship. In *His feeling for her was close to hatred*, it profiles the domain of similarity. In *She's always been very close with her money*, it profiles the domain of meanness. In *He was so close about his past*, it profiles the domain of secrecy. In *Can I open the window? It's very close in here*, it profiles air conditions, in which it is uncomfortably warm.

Exercise 9.3

Identify the cognitive domain which the adjective *far* activates in each of the following expressions.

1. She does not live far from here.
2. They worked far into the night.
3. You are getting far too cheeky!
4. I read as far as the third chapter.
5. The story sounds very far-fetched.
6. He is the most far-sighted politician.
7. The law has far-reaching benefits for workers.
8. She was so far-gone that she could hardly walk.
9. The advantages far outweigh the disadvantages.
10. He's a very talented writer. I'm sure she'll go far.

2. Trajector/landmark alignment

Within every expression, the profiled participants stand in a relationship, where one is more salient than the other. One participant, termed the **trajector**, is analysed as the primary figure within the relationship. It is the focal, or most prominent, participant in a profiled relationship. The other participant, termed the **landmark**, is analysed as the secondary figure. This distinction between trajector and landmark in linguistic expressions reflects the more general perceptual phenomenon of figure-ground organization. The assignment of the function of trajector (subject) or landmark (object) to an entity arises as a result of different conceptualizations. For instance, take the spatial relation expressed in *The mirror is above the washbasin*. In this relationship, both *the mirror* and *the washbasin* are profiled. However, *the mirror* is the trajector, whereas *the washbasin* the landmark. *The mirror* is the focus of attention, whereas *the washbasin* functions only as a spatial reference point, and is relatively backgrounded. In *The washbasin is below the mirror*, the situation is reversed. The trajector status is given to *the washbasin*, whereas the landmark status is conferred on *the mirror*.

Morphology

In morphology, the dimension of trajector/landmark alignment can be verified by investigating the functions of prefixes or suffixes. For example, the suffixes *-er* and *-ee* can attach to the verbal root *employ* to form new words, but they align the trajector/landmark status differently. The suffix *-er* derives a noun which profiles the trajector of the verb it combines with. The suffix means 'a person who performs the action named by the verbal root'. For example, an *employer* is a person or organization that employs people, as in *We need a reference from your former employer*. By contrast, the suffix *-ee* is added to verbal roots to form patientive nouns, and so assigns the landmark status to the new formation. The suffix means 'a person who is affected by the action named by the verbal root'. For example, an *employee* is someone who is paid to work for someone else, as in *She is a former employee of the local council*. In this example, the human person is the direct object of the verb, and so the target of the influence.

Exercise 9.4

Which status, trajector or landmark, do the rival suffixes confer on each of the following pairs?

1. trainer   trainee
2. rescuer   rescuee
3. adopter   adoptee
4. examiner   examinee
5. interviewer   interviewee

Syntax

In syntax, the dimension of trajector/landmark alignment can be assessed by examining the functions of prepositions. For example, the spatial prepositions *above* and *below* designate what is referentially the same relationship. The semantic contrast between them resides in their choice of trajector and landmark, not in content or profiling. They confer different trajector/landmark statuses on the members of the profiled relationship. In *She's rented a flat above a shop*, the *flat* is the focus of attention, while the *shop* is relatively backgrounded, and so functions only as a spatial reference point. In this relationship, the *flat* is the trajector, whereas the *shop* is the landmark. In *She's rented a shop below a flat*, the situation is reversed. In this sentence, the *shop* is brought into focus, and so functions as the trajector, whereas the *flat* functions as the landmark. As can be seen, the two prepositions bring about a change in focus, and so assign different statuses to the entities involved in the profiled relationship.

Exercise 9.5

The semantic non-equivalence of the following pairs of expressions resides in their choice of trajector and landmark. Discuss.

1. a. The lamp is above the table.
   b. The table is below the lamp.
2. a. The sculpture resembles a seashell.
   b. The seashell resembles a sculpture.
3. a. She ordered the driver to fetch the car.
   b. She ordered the car to be fetched.
4. a. The phone box is in front of the house.
   b. The house is behind the phone box.
5. a. Some of the guests had left before we arrived.
   b. We arrived after some of the guests had left.

---

3. Salience

Within every perceptual field, something becomes more salient than its surroundings. This is so because it requires less cognitive effort to bring it to the centre of attention. In linguistics, a substructure of a conception becomes more significant and eminent than the rest. Within its base, an expression places some participants on stage. These participants are accorded a special quality termed **salience**, referring to the quality of a participant of an expression of being noticeable, obvious and conspicuous. When there are two landmarks in a profiled relationship, they differ in the degree of salience they receive. The primary landmark receives what is called **initial salience**, referring to the most significant participant within a scene. Linguistically, the participant, standing out from the ground, is placed in a certain position in the expression relative to its importance. The secondary landmark has least salience.

To illustrate this, let us have a look at an example on the dative shift, as in *He sent a letter to Susan*, and *He sent Susan a letter*. According to theories of autonomous syntax, the two sentences have the same source, with the second being derived from the first. Because they have the same source, the two sentences are equivalent in meaning. In Cognitive Semantics, each sentence symbolizes a different construal of the same conceptual content, with the grammatical morphemes contributing to its meaning. In terms of salience, in *He sent a letter to Susan* it is the direct object *a letter* which is initially salient, whereas in *He sent Susan a letter* it is the indirect object *Susan* which is initially salient. Therefore, the two sentences embody different meanings. Only the second implies that *Susan* has received the letter. The meaning of each sentence is reflected by its structure, i.e., symbolized by the presence of *to* and by the juxtaposition of the nominals.

Syntax

In language, the attachment of varying degrees of salience to the profiled entities within the same content results in various syntactic structures. In a sentence with two entities in profile, the dimension of **salience** determines which entity is construed as initially salient by the speaker. In construing a causative situation, grammar provides the speaker with two sentential options. If the speaker construes the situation in such a way that s/he selects the complement clause for salience, s/he chooses the bare infinitive as in *They made her accept low-paid jobs*. By contrast, if the speaker selects the subject of the complement clause for salience, s/he chooses the to-infinitive as in *They forced her to accept low-paid jobs*. Semantically, the bare infinitive denotes an action that is direct, whereas the *to*-infinitive denotes an action that is indirect. Temporally, in the bare infinitive sentence the main and complement verbs refer to the same stretch of time, while in the to-infinitive sentence the complement verb refers to a time posterior to that of the main verb.

Exercise 9.6

Apply the dimension of salience to the following expressions and write what difference in meaning it causes.

1. a. She ordered them to join the club.
   b. She persuaded them to join the club.
2. a. She let the kids play in the garden.
   b. She allowed the kids to play in the garden.
3. a. I had the gardener plant some trees.
   b. I had the gardener to plant some trees.
4. a. He saved the boy drowning in the canal.
   b. He saved the boy from drowning in the canal.
5. a. They gave a chance to the applicant.
   b. They gave the applicant a chance.

9.2.2.5.2 Perspective

In the sphere of perception, a perceiver can see a visual scene from different angles. In the sphere of language, by analogy, a speaker can view a situation differently and adapt his/her viewpoint accordingly. The particular way of viewing a situation, which can shift according to one's intention, is referred to as **perspective**. Describing a situation often involves shifting attention or emphasis from one part to another depending on the needs of the discourse. Perspective relates to the way in which a scene is viewed, including the relative prominence of its participants. The relationship between the perceiver and the perceived entity in the perceptual realm corresponds in the linguistic realm to the conceptual relationship between the speaker and his or her object of conceptualization. The distinction between *Have you seen a giraffe?* and *Have you seen the giraffe?* relates conceptually to a shift in definiteness and linguistically to the use of different articles. The first sentence construes the *giraffe* as unknown to the speech participants, whereas the second sentence construes the *giraffe* as part of their common knowledge.

Exercise 9.7

The way each member of the following pairs is described depends on the viewpoint taken by the speaker. Discuss.

1. a. The table was covered with glass.
   b. The table was covered with glasses.
2. a. A few people can afford to buy a house.
   b. Few people can afford to buy a house.
3. a. Our next-door neighbour is a nuisance.
   b. Our next-door neighbour is being a nuisance.
4. a. The dog was chewing the bone happily.
   b. The dog was chewing on the bone happily.
5. a. By the time I leave work, the sun will be setting.
   b. By the time I leave work, the sun will have set.

The perspective imposed on a conceptualized scene subsumes two factors: vantage point and viewing arrangement.

The **vantage point** refers to the position from which the same objective situation is observed and described, resulting in different construals and different structures. The vantage point is the actual location of the participants in the speech situation: either of the speaker or the hearer. The importance of vantage point is twofold. Conceptually, it serves as a window through which the speech-act participants can observe the described scene, and so helps to specify which participant is involved in the described scene. Syntactically, it yields a distinction between expressions where the scene is construed from an external vantage point, i.e., from outside its scope of predication, and expressions where the scene is construed from an internal vantage point, i.e., from inside its scope of predication. The different wordings in *Sara came in* and *Sara went in* reflect a shift in perspective. The first involves the vantage point of the person who is inside the place, whereas the second involves the vantage point of the person who is outside the place.

Exercise 9.8

The following expressions describe the same situation but differ in terms of vantage point. Account for the meaning of each.

1. a. Come up into the tower.
   b. Go up into the tower.
2. a. Shall I come to your place?
   b. Will you come to my place?
3. a. Andy is sitting to the left of Jane.
   b. Andy is sitting to the right of Jane.
4. Context: On Monday Sally says 'I'm pregnant'.
   a. On Tuesday: Sally said she was pregnant.
   b. On Tuesday: Sally said she is pregnant.
5. a. The door slowly opened and two thieves sneaked in.
   b. Two thieves slowly opened the door and sneaked in.

The **viewing arrangement** refers to the relationship between the speaker and the situation being described. The importance of the viewing arrangement is twofold. Conceptually, it shows how the speaker relates himself or herself to the scene s/he describes, and so yields two basic types of viewing arrangements, respectively called the **Optimal Viewing Arrangement** (OVA), and **Egocentric Viewing Arrangement** (EVA). In the OVA, the speaker excludes himself or herself from the scene s/he describes. In the EVA, the speaker includes himself or herself as part of the scene s/he describes. Syntactically, it yields a distinction between expressions which are objectively construed and expressions which are subjectively construed. In admonishing her child, an annoyed mother may say either *Don't lie to me!*, or *Don't lie to your mother*! In the first sentence, the mother includes herself as part of the scene she describes. Linguistically, she uses the deictic pronoun me. This gives a subjective perspective of the scene conceptualized. In the second sentence, the mother displaces herself from the person speaking. Linguistically, she uses the descriptive noun phrase mother in referring to herself. This gives an objective perspective of the scene conceptualized.

Closely related to the viewing arrangement and vantage point are the two dimensions of subjectivity and objectivity, which result from imposing two different descriptions on a situation.

1. Subjectivity

With reference to the dimension of **subjectivity**, the speaker expresses involvement in the situation being described. There is a close relationship between the speaker and the content of the situation. Subjectivity represents the EVA, where the speaker includes himself or herself as part of the scene s/he describes. The scene is construed from an internal vantage point, where the attention is fully focused on the self. Subjectivity concerns a specific situation or a particular person and the private areas of his/her life. In the area of language, a subjectively-construed expression is one in which the speaker relates the situation described exclusively to the self. The above-mentioned example *Don't lie to me*! is subjectively-construed because conceptually the mother is included in the scene and linguistically the deictic pronoun *me* is used.

2. Objectivity

In connection with the dimension of **objectivity**, the speaker expresses distance from the situation being described. There is distant relationship between the speaker and the content of the situation. Objectivity represents the OVA, where the speaker excludes himself or herself from the scene s/he describes. The scene is construed from an external vantage point, where the attention is fully focused on some external entity. Objectivity concerns a general situation shared by or affecting most people, and not only the speaker who is describing it. In the area of language, an objectively-construed expression is one in which the speaker relates the situation described exclusively to the public. The above-mentioned example *Don't lie to your mother*! is objectively-construed because conceptually the mother is displaced from the scene and linguistically the noun phrase *mother* is used.

Syntax

In syntax, the dimensions of subjectivity-objectivity can be validated by comparing personal and impersonal complement expressions. The two expressions can be analysed as different choices in the construal imposed on the complement scene, where difference in choice results from a difference in the vantage point taken and from a difference in the viewing arrangement between the conceptualizer and the conceptualized scene. A personal complement expression codes a subjective construal of the complement scene judged from the vantage point of the main clause subject, who includes himself/herself in the scene s/he describes. An impersonal complement expression, by comparison, signals an objective construal of the complement scene judged from the vantage point of a general conceptualizer, who excludes himself/herself from the scene s/he describes as if it were none of his/her concern.

To illustrate the distinction, let us look at a pair of expressions. The sentence *Robert desires to have some familiarity with computers* is a personal complement expression because its subject position is occupied by the lexical noun phrase *Robert*. Therefore, the construction represents the perspective of *Robert*. This sentence stands for EVA and gives a subjective perspective of the event, which is conceptualized from the vantage point of the main clause subject, namely from inside the complement's scope of predication. The sentence *It is desirable to have some familiarity with computers* is an impersonal complement expression because its subject position is taken up by the pronoun *it*. *It* does not refer to a specific individual or person. Therefore, the expression represents the perspective of anyone. This sentence represents OVA and gives an objective perspective of the event, which is conceptualized from the vantage point of the speaker, namely from outside the complement's scope of predication.

Exercise 9.9

Compare the following pairs of expressions in terms of the alternative construals imposed on their conceptual content.

1. a. He enjoys going on holiday.
   b. It is enjoyable going on holiday.
2. a. Lesley abhors killing animals for food.
   b. It is abhorrent killing animals for food.
3. a. He strains to reach the pinnacle of his career.
   b. It is a strain to reach the pinnacle of a career.
4. a. She dreams of living on a tropical island.
   b. It is a dream living on a tropical island.
5. a. Alice prefers to travel/travelling around by train.
   b. It is preferable to travel/travelling around by train.

3. Dynamicity

This dimension pertains to how a conceptualization unfolds through processing time. It illustrates how the specific course of development is a significant aspect of our mental experience. Dynamicity can be observed in three cases: mode of scanning, order of presentation and course of direction.

In the **mode** of scanning, the difference relates to whether the scene described is in motion or not. Speakers demonstrate flexibility by construing a complex scene either temporally or atemporally. In the temporal construal, the component states are conceived individually and experienced successively with the passage of time. The speaker employs the cognitive mode of **sequential scanning**, which is defined as the cognitive process of construing a situation serially as it evolves through time. At the linguistic level, this is manifested on the verb by tense and agreement. In the atemporal construal, the component states are conceived collectively and experienced simultaneously as a single gestalt. The speaker employs the cognitive mode of **summary scanning**, which is defined as the cognitive process of construing the entire situation simultaneously in a cumulative fashion. At the linguistic level, this is manifested by morphemes such as *-ed* past participle and *-ing* present participle, and complementizers such as *to*-infinitive and *-ing* gerund.

To clarify the point, let us take an example. In the sentence *The tourists viewed the exhibition*, the verb *view* profiles a process which comprises a series of component states distributed through a continuous span of conceived time. The component states are processed in series rather than in parallel and construed as different. The conceptualizer moves his mental eyes successively from one point in the series to another. This is similar to the ability we display when examining a motion picture. In *The tourists like to view/viewing the exhibition*, the verb *view* requires the support of the *to*-infinitive or the *-ing* gerund complementizers, which serve to atemporalize the expression by imposing summary scanning, where the component states are processed in parallel and construed as identical. The conceptualizer moves his mental eyes along the path in one go, and simultaneously accumulates his impressions into one image. This is similar to the ability we display when examining a still picture. The complementizers differ only in the semantic effect they have on the base. The *to*-infinitive refers to time subsequent to the time of the main verb, whereas the *-ing* gerund refers to time simultaneous with the time of the main verb.

Exercise 9.10

Sequential scanning is characteristic of verbs, whereas summary scanning subsumes everything but verbs. Apply this to the following:

1. a. The bridge collapsed suddenly.
   b. The collapse of the bridge was sudden.
2. a. She called me this morning at the office.
   b. She gave me a call this morning at the office.
3. a. He had seen the children playing in the yard from the window.
   b. He kept seeing the children playing in the yard from the window.

In **order** of presentation, the difference relates to the different order of words. The order in which events occur fits with the order in which they are conceptualized. Alternate word orders embody different construal strategies for presenting a scene. A case in point is the semantic effect of preposing a locative expression, as illustrated by *A dead rat lay on the counter* and *On the counter lay a dead rat*. The two expressions are not semantically equivalent, despite using the same words to characterize the same objective situation. The semantic non-equivalence resides in how the situation is mentally accessed. Precisely, it resides in the general discourse tendency: given vs. new information. In the first expression, the mental access starts with the subject *a dead rat* which marks the new information in the discourse. In the second expression, the mental access starts with the locative phrase *on the counter* which marks the given information in the discourse.

Exercise 9.11

A difference in word order, spatial as in (1) or temporal as in (2), always implies a semantic contrast. Apply this principle to the following examples.

1. a. The document is in the study, on the desk, in the briefcase.
   b. The document is in the briefcase, on the desk, in the study.
2. a. I finished my studies, found a job and got married.
   b. I got married, found a job, and finished my studies.

In the course of **direction**, the difference relates to the route in which an event is viewed. Speakers exercise flexibility by construing a complex scene, adopting contrasting directions. This can be seen from a pair of examples like *The hill gently rises from the bank of the river* and *The hill gently falls to the bank of the river*. The two expressions have the same content, they are nevertheless semantically nonequivalent. They describe the same spatial configuration but have contrasting meanings, nonetheless. The contrast lies in the direction of mental scanning, where the distinct directions are realized lexically differently. The conceptualizer constructs an image of *the hill* by tracing a mental path along it in either an upward or a downward direction. The direction of the scanning is determined by the meanings of the words used: *rises from* induces upward mental scanning, and *falls to* downward scanning.

Exercise 9.12

The following pairs of examples differ in contrasting directions, relative to the different viewpoints of the speaker. How?

1. a. The washing line extends from the backyard to the gate.
   b. The washing line extends from the gate to the backyard.
2. a. The country from east to west is rural.
   b. The country from west to east is rural.
3. a. Lilly gave the doorman a tip before she left the hotel.
   b. Before she left the hotel, Lilly gave the doorman a tip.

9.2.2.5.3 Focusing

This dimension entails giving attention to one particular part of an expression rather than another. Focusing includes foreground vs. background and scope. One reason for grouping these dimensions under the rubric of focusing is that they are a matter of selection.

1. Foreground vs. background

The act of perception usually involves the foregrounding of some portion of the perceptual field called the **figure** and the backgrounding of the rest called the **ground**. Attention is focused on the figure, which is thereby more fully present to consciousness than the ground. In language, **foregrounding**, sometimes called **highlighting**, refers to giving the most importance to a particular part in an expression. **Foregrounding** is used for specific communicative purposes. It can be achieved grammatically by means of different structures, as in *It was Mark who posted the letter yesterday, It was yesterday that Mark posted the letter, What Mark posted yesterday was the letter*, and *It was the letter that Mark posted yesterday*. These structures are called **focusing devices**, and the foregrounded part of the utterance is called the **focus**. The cognitive notions of **profile** and **base**, and **trajector** and **landmark** are developments of the notions of foregrounding and backgrounding.

Syntax

In syntax, the organization of linguistically encoded spatial scenes reflects figure-ground organization. The **figure**, also known as **trajector**, is the focal or most prominent participant in a profiled relationship. The **ground**, also known as **landmark**, is the secondary participant in a profiled relationship. The subject position corresponds to the figure, whereas the object position corresponds to the ground. The sentences *The football fans swarmed onto the pitch* and *The pitch swarmed with football fans* describe the same situation. Yet, they are different. The difference resides in the organization of the information as figure and ground. In the first sentence, the speaker accords the status of figure to the football fans and ground to the pitch. In the second, the speaker accords the status of figure to the pitch and ground to the football fans. Imposing different views on a situation is rampant in all areas of language, and it is these areas that Cognitive Semantics attempts to analyse.

Exercise 9.13

The members in each of the following pairs of expression denote the same objective situation but place different parts in focus. What are they?

1. a. John lives in Hamburg city.
   b. John is living in Hamburg city.
2. a. She sent a postcard to her mother.
   b. She sent her mother a postcard.
3. a. The city council built a new mall.
   b. A new mall was built by the city council.
4. a. After the police left, violence erupted.
   b. The police left before violence erupted.
5. a. The children had smeared mud on the wall.
   b. The children had smeared the wall with mud.

2. Scope

The scope of an expression comprises the array of conceptual content that it specifically evokes and relies upon for its characterization. Scope contains the profile and represents the general focus of attention. An expression has a **maximal scope**, i.e., the full extent of its coverage, and an **immediate scope**, the portion directly relevant for a particular purpose. The immediate scope is thus foregrounded *vis-à-vis* the maximal scope. The maximal scope is vague and non-delimited in reference. It comprises everything a speaker is aware of at a given moment to assess the meaning of an expression. The speaker's scope of awareness is referred to as **field**, i.e., everything evoked in describing a situation. The immediate scope is the one with the highest degree of prominence and relevance. It is the general locus of viewing attention with respect to which an expression is interpreted. The term *elbow*, for instance, evokes as the maximal scope the conception of human body, and as the immediate scope the conception of *arm* for its characterization. It is specifically the *arm* which is prominent and immediately relevant to the concept *elbow*. The immediate scope is therefore describable as the context necessary for the characterization of the profile.

Syntax

In syntax, the dimension of scope can be corroborated by scrutinizing extraposed and non-extraposed expressions. The distinction is not based on the operation of generative rules; it is exclusively a property of construal which gives the speaker the flexibility to construe his or her conceptualization in alternate ways. The choice as to which alternative to use is motivated by the construal of scope. One way in which the speaker exercises choice in construing a situation is by taking either a narrow or a broad view of it, which can change relative to the change of the aim one has in mind. In the **narrow view**, the speaker considers a minimal range of content in describing the situation. In the **broad view**, the speaker considers a maximal range of content in describing the situation. The type of scope chosen by the speaker is then deemed crucial for the characterization of a given situation.

A non-extraposed complement expression like *To build a house nowadays is easy* takes a narrow view of a situation. The reason is ascribed to the absence of a field represented by *it*. In this type of construal, the complement clause is considered the sole factor in inducing the experience in the speaker. That is, the reason for the experience expressed by the main predicate is unilateral, which is attributed solely to the complement content and does not involve anything else. By contrast, an extraposed complement expression introduced by the pronoun *it* like *It is easy to build a house nowadays* takes a broad view of the situation. In this type of construal, the speaker relies on different kinds of knowledge in making the evaluation, in which the complement content is the most important. *It* is the locus of factors inducing the experience in the speaker, and so the reason for the experience expressed by the main predicate is multilateral. The source of the evaluation in the extraposed expression is therefore somewhat larger in scope than in the non-extraposed one, and goes beyond mere observation.

Exercise 9.14

The non-extraposed alternatives in (a) differ from the extraposed alternatives in (b) in scope. Explain.

1. a. To win the game is possible.
   b. It is possible to win the game.
2. a. To follow the guidelines is mandatory.
   b. It is mandatory to follow the guidelines.
3. a. To remember old acquaintances is nice.
   b. It is nice to remember old acquaintances.
4. a. To argue about a trivial issue is unwise.
   b. It is unwise to argue about a trivial issue.
5. a. To make a momentous decision is tough.
   b. It is tough to make a momentous decision.

9.3 Summary

In this chapter, I have investigated **conceptualization**, the mental act of construing and expressing a situation in alternate ways. **Construal** refers to the mental ability of a speaker to conceive a situation in alternate ways and express them in language by using different linguistic structures. Two linguistic expressions may have the same conceptual content, but still contrast semantically. The semantic contrast between them is attributable to the imposition of alternate construals on their content. Each linguistic expression designates a different construal. An expression's meaning is not just the conceptual content it evokes. Equally important is how that content is construed. Speakers can conceive of a situation according to different dimensions, which result in different expressions to describe the same conceived situation. Construal is thus a multifaceted phenomenon, consisting of various dimensions which reflect basic human cognitive abilities.

Table 9.1 presents a comparison between the Reference theory and the Construal theory.

Table 9.1 Reference theory and Construal theory

Reference theory	Construal theory
1. Meaning is defined in terms of the conditions in the real world under which an expression is used to make a true statement.	1. Meaning is defined in terms of the use of an expression in communication.
2. Meaning is described by means of complex formalisms inspired by work in mathematics, computer science or logic.	2. Meaning is described by means of construal dimensions imposed conceptual content of a situation.
3. Meaning equals denotation, referring to objects in the external world.	3. Meaning equals connotation, referring to ideas in the internal world.

Glossary

A

accommodation The phenomenon in which a component substructure adjusts itself when integrated with another to form a composite structure.

affective The speaker's feelings *vis-à-vis* an expression, which differs from one person to another.

agent The entity performing the action expressed by the verb.

ambiguity A phenomenon whereby an expression has more than one meaning, and may therefore cause confusion.

analogy The formation of a new word on the basis of a unique expression or pattern.

analysability The process of matching up the substructures of a composite structure phonologically and semantically. Linguistic expressions undergo two types of analysability: *full analysability* and *partial analysability*.

analytic sentence A sentence which is necessarily true because of the meanings of the words in it.

anaphor The word, typically a pronoun, which maintains reference to an entity that is mentioned.

anaphora The use of a word that refers to or replaces another word which comes earlier in the discourse.

anomaly The lexical relation in which a word does not match the context in which it is used.

antecedent The word which gives anaphor its meaning.

anti-antonyms Pairs of words which mean the same thing although they look the opposite of each other.

antonymy The lexical relation between two words in which one is the opposite of the other.

arbitrariness The phenomenon where the form of a sign bears no resemblance to its meaning.

assertives An assertive, or representative, is a speech act which commits the speaker to the truth of the expressed proposition.

atomistic The assumption that the meaning of a word can be determined in isolation by its semantic components.

auto-antonyms Pairs of words which are homographs and mean the opposite of each other.

autonomous The component subpart of an expression that exists on its own without need of a dependent structure to complete its meaning.

B

backgrounding   The act of paying less attention and so less importance to a part of a sentence.

base   Also called *ground*. The domain relative to which the profile or figure is understood.

base space   The real space that serves as the starting point for a particular stage in discourse.

blend   Also known as *blended space*. The created space that results from the interaction of input spaces. The blend has emergent meaning of its own that is not contained in either of the inputs.

blending   Also called *Conceptual Integration*. The device by which selected elements from two mental spaces are combined to create a new space, the blend.

benefactive   The entity which benefits from an action.

broad view   The view in which the speaker considers a maximal range of content in describing a situation.

C

cataphor   The word, typically a pronoun, which maintains reference to an entity that is mentioned later.

cataphora   The use of a word that refers to or replaces another word which comes later in the discourse.

categorization   The mental act of grouping together the multiple senses of a linguistic item into a category. In the cognitive approach to language, categorization is based on prototypes.

category   A network of distinct but related senses of a given linguistic item. The senses gather around a prototype, are defined by their resemblance to it, and are arranged in terms of distance from it.

causer   The thing which makes something happen.

classical   Also called *check-list*. The theory of linguistic meaning where humans categorize concepts by means of necessary and sufficient conditions.

clause   A major unit of grammar which may contain a subject, verb phrase, object, complement and adverbial.

cliché   A non-compositional expression that has a particular meaning that is different from the meanings of the individual words which it contains. It is used by people to give advice or express feelings.

cognitive   In Cognitive Linguistics, it means that language is seen as an integral facet of cognition. Knowledge of language is based on experience.

The mind is initially a blank slate and cognitive development is a matter of learning. In Generative Linguistics, it means that language is seen as an autonomous component of the mind. Knowledge of language is innate. The mind has a blueprint for language.

cognitive commitment   The characterization of linguistic structures should reflect principles from other cognitive sciences like philosophy, psychology and neuroscience.

Cognitive Linguistics   The general approach to language study which characterizes language as being non-modular, symbolic, usage based, meaningful and creative.

cognitive operations   Processes which reflect capabilities of the mind or functions of the brain in producing and interpreting linguistic expressions.

Cognitive Semantics   The specific approach to linguistic meaning which characterizes linguistic meaning as being embodied, motivated, dynamic, encyclopaedic and conceptualized.

cohesion   The act of connecting one piece of language to another.

co-hyponyms   The set of words which share the same superordinate term.

colligation   A grammatical pattern which shows the position of a word in a sentence and/or delimits the types of its complements.

collocation   The case when two or more words go together and form a common expression.

co-meronyms   Words which name the parts of the same whole.

commissives   A commissive is a speech act which commits the speaker to performing some action in the future.

communicative strategy   A plan adopted by the speaker to achieve a particular purpose.

compatibility   The tendency of words to co-occur in certain positions due to sharing specific syntactic and semantic features.

complement   The subpart that elaborates a schematic entity in the semantic structure of the dependent head. It adds intrinsic conceptual substance to the head.

complex sentence   A sentence which consists of a main clause and at least one subordinate clause linked by a subordinator.

complex word   Also called *composite/polymorphemic*. A word that is composed of two or more substructures, which is morphologically divisible.

Componential Analysis   A type of definitional analysis in which the meaning of an expression is decomposed into a finite set of semantic components.

composite structure   A structure formed by unifying corresponding sub-parts which overlap conceptually.

compositionality   An expression is compositional when its meaning is made up or composed of the meanings of its constituent parts. Linguistic expressions undergo two types of compositionality: *full compositionality* and *partial compositionality*.

compound   A blend formed by integrating two substructures, or a composite structure that is made up of two, or more, free morphemes.

compounding   The process of putting together two free morphemes, be they nouns, adjectives or verbs, to make a compound word, a brand-new word.

compound sentence   A sentence which consists of two or more main clauses linked by a coordinator.

compound word   A word that is composed of two words which is morphologically divisible.

concept   A mental representation which is realized in language by means of symbolic structures. It is the abstract meaning which a linguistic expression represents.

conceptual   In the light of the conceptual conception, the meaning of an expression that is a concept in the speaker's mind.

conceptual content   The property inherent in a situation. It is the meaning that is conventionally associated with an expression.

conceptualization   The mental act of construing and expressing a situation in alternate ways.

conceptualized   The claim that the meaning of a linguistic expression is a reflection of concepts, and not directly of things. It serves as a prompt for an array of mental processes.

conceptual structure   The concept in the conceptual system which stands for the thing experienced. It is knowledge representation assembled for purposes of meaning construction.

conceptual system   Our knowledge of the world. It is the repository of the concepts available to a human being.

configuration   The mental act of grouping together a number of linguistic items, be they lexical or grammatical, into a cognitive domain. The linguistic items share the same conceptual area but differ in the specifics.

connotation   The figural, cultural or emotional meaning associated with an expression.

connotative   The additional meaning that a word has which goes beyond its denotative meaning.

constancy under negation The property of a presupposition remaining true even when it is negated.

constituency The order in which the subparts are successively integrated to yield a composite structure.

construal The mental ability of a speaker to describe a situation in alternate ways and express them in language by using different linguistic items. The construal theory considers meaning as subjective in nature.

container An image schema which is derived from the experience of having something inside something else or including something as a part of something else.

containment The act of keeping an entity in an enclosed space and consequently restricting its movement.

context The physical environment in which a linguistic expression is used. It refers to the location where the discussion takes place.

contextual meaning The meaning which a linguistic expression has in a context.

contradiction A semantic relation between a pair of sentences in which the second is a complete opposite of the first, thus triggering a change in meaning.

contradictory sentence A sentence which is false because of the meanings of certain words in it.

co-operative principle Principles which speakers and hearers have to comply with in order to make the conversation work.

correspondence The factor which relates to how the component subparts of a composite structure fit together and form a coherent assembly when they have certain elements in common at both semantic and phonological levels.

co-text The linguistic environment in which a linguistic expression is used. It refers to that which precedes or follows the linguistic expression, and so determines its actual meaning.

conventional The quality of linguistic units being established in the lexicon through repeated usage.

conventional implicature An implicature that is made irrespective of context, where the additional meaning is arrived at by the use of discourse markers.

conversational implicature An implicature that is made with respect to context, where the additional meaning is deduced from particular knowledge, general knoweldge or scalar knowledge.

conventionalized metaphors   Metaphors whose meanings have been so deeply entrenched in the speech community through repeated usage that they become automatic.

converse antonyms   The relation between two words in which the existence of one implies the existence of the other.

creative   The ability of speakers to coin a novel expression from a conventional expression, or construe the same situation in alternate ways using different linguistic expressions.

D

declaratives   A declarative is a speech act which causes a change of some sort in the world.

decomposition   The analysis of an expression in terms of semantic components.

deictic expressions   Also called indexicals. The linguistic forms which are interpreted with reference to the speaker's position in place and time.

deixis   The mechanism which encodes the personal, spatial and temporal dimensions of language by means of linguistic forms relative to the speaker's standpoint.

denotation   The literal, constant and basic meaning of an expression. It is the relationship between an expression and the kind of thing it refers to in the world. It is the core meaning which an expression has, as described in a dictionary.

denotative   The literal meaning of a word.

dependent   The component subpart of an expression that is dependent on the autonomous structure to complete its meaning.

descriptive   The meaning of a word which bears on reference and truth. It includes the act of both referring to something and stating its truth.

determinacy   The factor relating to which of the component subparts determines the profile of the composite structure as a whole. A composite structure consists of two or more subparts. Of the two or more subparts, one lends its profile to the entire composite structure.

dictionary theory   The theory according to which the core meaning of a linguistic item is the information contained in the item's definition. It focuses on linguistic knowledge in defining lexical items.

diminution   An area of knowledge in which somebody or something is made small in size, young in age, or less in value.

direction   A case of dynamicity which describes the route in which an event is viewed.

directives   A directive is a speech act in which the speaker attempts to get the hearer to do something.

direct speech acts   Speech acts in which an explicit relationship exists between the linguistic form and the communicative function of an utterance.

disambiguation   The process of establishing a single interpretation for an ambiguous word or sentence.

distal form   The deictic form that means away from the speaker like *that*, *there* or *then*.

domain   A knowledge background with respect to which concepts can be properly described. It is a coherent area of conceptualization relative to which the meanings of lexical items can be characterized.

dynamic   The meaning of a linguistic expression is flexible in the sense of extending its scope to express new experiences.

dynamicity   The dimension which shows how a conceptualization unfolds through processing time. It illustrates how the specific course of development is a significant aspect of our mental experience.

E

Egocentric Viewing Arrangement   The view in which the speaker includes himself or herself as part of the scene s/he describes.

elaboration   The factor which relates to how one component subpart contains a schematic hole which the other component subpart serves to elaborate.

elaboration site/e-site   The hole within the semantic structure of a dependent substructure, which is filled by an autonomous substructure.

embodied   The structure of reality, as reflected in language, is a product of the human mind and human embodiment. The meaning of a linguistic expression is determined in large measure by the nature of our bodies.

emotive   The strong feelings, especially of anger, which a subject, statement or use of language has on the people.

encyclopaedic knowledge   The structured body of non-linguistic knowledge to which a linguistic expression such as a word potentially provides access.

encyclopaedic theory   The theory according to which the meaning of a linguistic item includes everything that is known about its referent. It focuses on both linguistic and non-linguistic knowledge in defining lexical items.

endocentricity   The case where the meaning of a compound is a specialization of the meaning of its head.

entailment   A semantic relation between a pair of sentences in which the second is the implicit consequence of the first.

essential condition   A felicity condition which compels the speaker to perform an act.

euphemism   The phenomenon in which a word or phrase is used instead of another to avoid being unpleasant, indecent or offensive.

experiencer   The entity which is psychologically affected by an action.

expression   The meaningful unit of language such as an affix, word, phrase or sentence.

expressive   The semantic quality of an expression which is used independently of context.

expressives   An expressive is a speech act in which the speaker expresses feelings or attitudes about something.

extension   The set of things which an expression applies to.

F

facet   A portion of a domain which is associated with a particular concept. Any facet is expressed by an appropriate form of language.

felicity conditions   Certain criteria which must be met if the speech act is to achieve its purpose.

field   The speaker's scope of awareness, i.e. everything evoked in describing a situation.

figure   The entity which is distinguished from a background, i.e., the *ground*.

focus   The central point of a sentence in which speakers are most interested and to which they pay a special attention.

focusing   The mental act of giving attention to one particular part of an expression rather than another.

focusing devices   The grammatical structures used to express foregrounding.

foregrounding   Also called *highlighting*. The act of highlighting a part of a sentence by making it the main point of attention and consequently emphasizing its importance.

form   The orthographic representation associated with a linguistic expression. The form serves to express meaning.

formalist   The paradigm that focuses on the formal aspects of language. It includes the decompositional conceptions of meaning: componential, conceptual and primitive. It considers language a system which should be studied in isolation, both from its users and its cognitive processes.

Frame Semantics   A theory of meaning according to which word meanings can only be properly understood and described against the background of a particular body of knowledge known as a *frame*.

free alternation   The substitutability of one expression for another in a given environment. In this way, synonymous expressions are considered free alternatives.

free variation   The phenomenon in which two or more linguistic items can occur in the same environment without signalling any change in meaning.

full analysability   The case when the phonological substructures of a composite structure match up, one to one, with their semantic substructures.

full compositionality   The case when the meaning of a composite structure is fully determined by the meanings of its substructures and the manner in which they are combined.

function ambiguity   The case when a phrase in a sentence fulfils two or more grammatical functions.

G

generalization commitment   The characterization of linguistic structures should reflect principles from other aspects of human language like morphology, phonology, pragmatics, syntax and semantics.

goal   The entity towards which something moves.

gradable antonyms   The lexical relation between two words in which the degree of opposition is not absolute. Gradable antonyms normally have a *contrary* relation.

ground   The background against which the figure stands out.

grouping ambiguity   The case when a phrase in a sentence can be arranged in two ways, and so can have two readings.

H

head   The central element within an expression which determines its syntactic and semantic character.

holistic   The assumption that the meaning of a word is determined its relations with the other words in the language.

holonym   The word which names the whole and includes parts.

homography   The relation between two or more words which arc spelt alike but have different meanings and different pronunciations.

homonymy   The relation between two words which sound alike but differ in meaning, or the relation between two words which have the same spelling but different meaning.

homophony The relation between two or more words which are pronounced alike but have different spellings and meanings.

honorific markers Expressions used to show respect for the person you are speaking to.

hyperonym The superordinate word which has a general meaning.

hyponym The subordinate word which has a specific meaning.

hyponymy The lexical relation between two words in which the meaning of one is included in the meaning of the other.

I

iconicity The phenomenon where the form of a sign bears some resemblance to its meaning, or where the structure of language bears similarity to conceived reality.

idiom A non-compositional expression that has a particular meaning that is different from the meanings of the individual words in it.

idiomaticity The lexical relation that deals with a group of words whose meaning is different from the meanings of the individual words.

illocutionary act The act of producing an utterance which serves to communicate information such as advising, promising, stating, thanking, warning, and so on.

image schema A conceptual representation which emerges from human bodily interaction with the world. It is a dynamic pattern which is grounded in human bodily movements through space.

immediate scope The portion in an expression which is directly relevant for a particular purpose.

implication The act of suggesting something without saying it directly.

implicature A semantic relation between a pair of sentences in which the first is said but the second is meant.

indeterminacy The difficulty of identifying the referent in an expression.

indirect speech acts Speech acts in which an implicit relationship exists between the linguistic form and the communicative function of an utterance.

inference A conclusion which a hearer draws about something unsaid based on existing evidence or general knowledge.

initial salience The quality of a participant of being the most significant participant within an expression.

instances Specific units which represent situations or events. They are regarded as the basis on which schemas are built.

instrument The means by which something is done.

integration   The combination of the component subparts of a composite structure into a linear sequence. The integration process is conditioned by parameters such as correspondence, dependence, determinacy and constituency.

intension   The set of properties an expression has.

interpretation   The way the meaning of the resulting composite structure is explained. It resides in the two principles of compositionality and analysability.

inventory   A detailed list of all the linguistic resources which speakers exploit in constructing units for serving particular purposes.

J

juxtaposition   The ability of words to combine horizontally.

L

landmark   The secondary participant in a relationship.

language   A structured inventory of linguistic units defined as form-meaning pairings used for communicating ideas and feelings.

language user   A member of a particular linguistic community who uses language for the sake of communication.

lattice   The set of mental spaces which arise when talk unfolds and thought proceeds.

lexical ambiguity   The case when a word has more than one meaning.

lexical concepts   The meanings associated with words. The conventional form which conceptual structure assumes when encoded in language.

lexical field   (I) A network which subsumes words that are related in meaning, each of which represents a special feature. (II) The theory according to which the meaning of a linguistic item is described relative to the relationship it holds with its counterparts.

lexical/sense relation   A pattern of association that exists between words in a language. Two types of lexical relation exist: paradigmatic and syntagmatic.

lexical semantics   The branch of semantics which deals with the meanings of words.

lexical triggers   Certain words in the first sentence which presuppose the truth of the information stated in the second sentence.

linguistic unit   Also called *symbolic structure*. Any unit which consists of a semantic structure, a phonological structure and a symbolic relationship between them.

linguistics   The scientific study of language. It studies the cognitive processes involved in producing and understanding language.

location   The place where an action happens.

locutionary act   The act of simply producing an utterance which follows the grammatical rules of language.

M

matrix   The set of domains which provide the context for the full understanding of a semantic unit.

maximalist   An approach to meaning in which differences between semantics and pragmatics are not recognized.

maximal scope   The full extent of the coverage of an expression.

maxim of manner   The principle that requires speakers and hearers to be brief, clear and orderly.

maxim of quality   The principle that requires speakers and hearers to be truthful.

maxim of quantity   The principle that requires speakers and hearers to be economical and informative.

maxim of relevance   The principle that requires speakers and hearers to be relevant.

maxims   Basic rules which participants should adhere to in any ordinary conversation.

meaning   The semantic content associated with a linguistic expression. The meaning is expressed by form.

meaningful   The claim that all language elements have semantic values. Language is a means of conveying meaning; therefore all its resources serve to carry out this function.

mental space   A form of conceptual structure in which a particular mental construct is set up on the basis of a general scenario to understand a message. It is a temporary package of knowledge structure, which is built up through ongoing discourse for interpretive purposes.

meronym   The word which names the part of another word.

meronymy   Also called *partonymy*. The lexical relation between two words in which the meaning of one names a part of the meaning of the other.

metaphor   The form of conceptual structure that involves mapping between two things from distinct areas of knowledge, where one is compared with the other.

metonymy The form of conceptual structure that involves mapping between two things within the same area of knowledge, where the name of one is substituted for the name of the other with which it is connected in some respect.

mode A case of dynamicity which describes the scene as being in motion or not.

modifier The subpart that has a schematic entity in its semantic structure which is elaborated by the head. It adds non-intrinsic or additional information to the head.

mood The form of a verb in a sentence which expresses the speaker's attitude towards the content of an utterance.

motivated The relationship between the form and meaning of a linguistic expression is often motivated or inseparable. The meaning of a linguistic expression arises as the outcome of stimulation to achieve a desired goal.

N

narrow view The view in which the speaker considers a minimal range of content in describing a situation.

non-gradable antonyms Also called *complementaries* or *binary antonyms*. The lexical relation between two words in which the degree of opposition is absolute. Non-gradable antonyms normally have a *contradictory* relation.

non-modular An approach to language which claims that there is no autonomous portion of the brain which is specialized for language. Linguistic abilities are inseparable from other cognitive abilities.

O

objectivism The theory which stipulates that symbols used in language get their meaning via correspondence with things in the external world.

objectivity The dimension in which the speaker expresses distance from the situation being described. There is distant relationship between the speaker and the content of the situation. Objectivity represents the OVA, where the speaker excludes himself or herself from the scene s/he describes.

Optimal Viewing Arrangement The view in which the speaker excludes himself or herself from the scene s/he describes.

order A case of dynamicity which describes the order in which events occur.

P

pairing   The act of mating the phonological and semantic poles of a linguistic expression for communicative purposes.

paradigmatic relation   A pattern of relationship between the morphemes of a composite structure in a vertical order. It is based on the criterion of substitution.

paraphrase   The semantic relation between a pair of sentences in which the second is an alternative version of the first without changing its propositional meaning.

partial analysability   The case when the phonological substructures of a composite structure fail to correspond with their semantic substructures.

partial compositionality   The case when the meaning of a composite structure is determined by both the semantic contribution of its substructures and the pragmatic knowledge behind what is actually symbolized.

patient   The entity which undergoes the action expressed by the verb.

periphery   The remaining members in a category that contain some, not all, of the attributes.

perlocutionary act   The act of producing an utterance which serves to make something happen such as convincing, deterring, misleading, persuading, surprising, and so on.

person deixis   The deictic form which is used to point to people.

perspective   The particular way of viewing a situation, which can shift according to one's intention.

pleonasm   The use of a word to emphasize what is clear without it.

polyseme   A word or phrase that has multiple meanings.

polysemy   The tendency of a linguistic item, lexical or grammatical, to have a range of different meanings that are related in some way. A word which has more than one distinct but related meaning is said to be polysemous or polysemic.

preparatory condition   A felicity condition which obliges the speaker not to exceed his/her authority in the performance of an act.

presupposition   The semantic relation between a pair of sentences in which the second is the implicit presumption of the first.

primitive   Regarding the primitive conception, known as *Natural Semantic Metalanguage*, the meaning of an expression can be defined in terms of a small set of semantic primes or primitives.

primitives   Indivisible atoms of meaning which combine to form a more complex meaning.

Principle of Contrast   The principle according to which every two forms contrast in meaning. Pairs of expressions are neither identical in meaning nor equal in use.

profile   Also called *figure*. The conceptual referent within the array of conceptual content invoked by the item. It is the substructure that an expression designates.

profile determinant   Also called *head*. The substructure which lends its profile to the entire composite structure. It determines its categorical status, establishes its core meaning, and selects its dependents.

profiling   The mental act of singling out a substructure which functions as the focal point of attention in an expression.

prominence   The quality of eminence given, often in different degrees, to the substructures of a conception relative to their importance.

proposition   The semantic content of an expression which describes a state of affairs in the world.

prototype   The ideal or central member of a category. It assembles the key attributes of the category.

proverb   A non-compositional expression whose meaning is different from the meanings of the individual words in it. It is meant as advice or warning.

proximal form   The deictic form that means near the speaker like *this*, *here* or *now*.

Q

quantification   An area of knowledge which refers to the act of specifying the quantity of an instance of a thing.

R

reference   (I) The theory of meaning according to which the meaning of a word is tied to an actual object in the world. (II) The act of using a word or phrase, either earlier or later in the discourse, to enable the hearer to identify an entity.

referring expression   The word or phrase that is used to refer to an entity.

referent   The specific entity which an expression stands for on any occasion of use.

referential   In view of the referential conception, the meaning of an expression derives from its reference to an actual object in the external world.

relational   In virtue of the relational conception, the meaning of an expression is determined by its position in a network in which it is related to other expressions.

relational antonyms   The lexical relation between two words which, unlike the gradable ones, are not susceptible to degrees of opposition, and, unlike the non-gradable ones, they are not an either-or matter in character.

representational   In connection with the representational conception, known as *Cognitive* Semantics, the meaning of an expression is linked to a particular mental representation, termed a *concept*.

reversive antonyms   The relation between two words which involves opposition in direction.

rivalry   The case when two or more affixes or lexical expressions occur in the same environment but convey different messages.

S

salience   The quality of a participant of an expression of being noticeable, obvious and conspicuous.

scalar quantification   The magnitude of something measured against a scale.

schema   A pattern which is specified in general terms and elaborated by its instances in detailed ways. It is a mental representation with a general meaning, whose specifics are elaborated by its instances in contrasting ways.

scope   The array of conceptual content that an expression specifically evokes and relies upon for its characterization.

selection restrictions   Syntactic-semantic restrictions which govern the co-occurrence of words. It is the tendency of a word to select another word with which it can co-occur.

semantic components   The features of meaning which combine to form a complex meaning.

semantic primes   Indivisible atoms of meaning which combine to form a more complex meaning.

semantic prosody   The pattern in which a word co-occurs with other words that belong to a particular semantic set.

semantic roles   Also called *functional/thematic/participant*. The semantic relations that link a verb to its arguments.

semantic structure   The meaning which stands for the conceptual structure. It is the meaning that is conventionally associated with linguistic expressions.

sense   The concept represented by the meaning of an expression. It is the meaning of an expression that is basic to its individual identity.

sentence   A well-formed string of words put together by the grammatical rules of a language.

sentence meaning   The literal meaning of a sentence taken out of context, which is built up from the meanings of the words it contains.

sentential ambiguity   Also called *structural* or *grammatical.* The case when the structure of a sentence has two or more meanings.

sentential relation   The pattern of association that exists between sentences in a language.

sentential semantics   The branch of semantics which deals with the meanings of phrases and sentences.

sequential scanning   The cognitive process of construing a situation serially as it evolves through time.

set quantification   The magnitude of something measured against a full set.

simple sentence   A sentence which consists of only one clause.

simple word   Also called *monomorphemic.* A word that is composed of only one lexical structure, which is morphologically indivisible.

sincerity condition   The felicity condition which requires the speaker to be sincere in the performance of an act.

social   The meaning of a word that is governed by the social rules of interaction. It refers to the use of a particular expression in language which indicates the social relationship between the speaker and the addressee.

social deixis   The social relationship between speaker and hearer which is encoded by certain linguistic forms.

source   (I) The entity from which something moves. (II) In metaphor, aspects of a more familiar area of knowledge are placed in comparison with aspects of a less familiar area of knowledge, called the *target.*

space builders   The linguistic elements that serve as triggers for opening new mental spaces or shifting focus to existing ones.

space deixis   The deictic forms which are used to point to location.

speech act   The act which a speaker performs by using an utterance to communicate.

structured   The property of units being related to one another in organized ways.

subjectivism   Also called *experientialism.* The theory which stipulates that symbols used in language get their meaning via correspondence with conceptualizations of the world.

subjectivist   The theory of meaning which emphasizes the importance of world experience to the representation of linguistic expressions and recognises the speaker's capacity to construe a situation in alternative ways.

subjectivity   The dimension in which the speaker expresses involvement in the situation being described. There is a close relationship between the speaker and the content of the situation. Subjectivity represents the EVA, where the speaker includes himself or herself as part of the scene s/he describes.

subordinate   The meaning of a word which display a high degree of specificity.

substance   The form and meaning which an expression has. The form is the phonological representation. The meaning is the idea conventionally associated with it.

substitution   The ability of morphemes to replace each other vertically within a particular context.

summary scanning   The cognitive process of construing an entire situation simultaneously in a cumulative fashion.

superordinate   The meaning of a word which displays a high degree of generality.

symbolic   The claim that language is a set of symbols or conventional means that are available to language users for representing ideas or communicating thought.

synecdoche   The process of using a part of something to represent the whole or vice versa.

synonymy   The lexical relation between two words in which the meaning of one is similar, but not identical, to the meaning of the other. A word is said to be a synonym of another word when one of its senses is the same or nearly the same as the other.

synonym   An expression that has the same or nearly the same meaning as another in the same language.

syntagmatic relation   The pattern of relation between the words of a linguistic structure in a linear order. It is based on the criterion of *juxtaposition*.

synthetic sentence   A sentence which may be true or false depending on the way the world is.

T

target   In metaphor, aspects of a less familiar area of knowledge are placed in comparison with aspects of a more familiar area of knowledge, called the *source*.

tautology   A kind of expression in which you repeat the same word twice, conveying an additional meaning which goes beyond what the words mean.

taxonomy Also called *lexical hierarchy*. The systematic way of classifying words by arranging them into categories.

time The time when an action happens.

time deixis The deictic forms which are used to point to time.

trajector The focal, or most prominent, participant in a relationship.

truth conditions The conditions of objective external reality against which an expression can be judged true or false.

truth-conditional The theory which sees the meaning of an expression as being the same as, or reducible to, its truth conditions. The meaning of an expression is identified with the conditions in the world under which it is true or false.

U

unit Any simple or composite expression which is frequently used and thoroughly mastered, thus acquiring the status of a habit. It carries a lexical or grammatical pattern and serves a particular purpose.

usage based The quality of linguistic units being authentic. Knowledge of language is knowledge of how language is used. Language patterns emerge as a result of generalizations made from actual instances of language use.

usage event An actual utterance used to serve a particular purpose in communication.

use The way the language user construes content.

utterance A particular piece of language, be it a word, phrase or sentence, spoken by a specific speaker on a specific occasion.

utterance meaning Also *speaker meaning*. The non-literal meaning of an expression, word or sentence, which is derived from the context in which it is used.

V

vagueness Lack of referential clarity, which results from giving little information about something.

valence The mechanism whereby two grammatical expressions combine to form a composite expression.

vantage point The position from which the same objective situation is observed and described, resulting in different construals and different structures.

viewing arrangement The relationship between the speaker and the situation being described.

vocatives   The deictic forms which point to the social status of the addressee.

W

word   A symbolic unit which has an identifiable meaning and a phonological shape. It is a combination of meaning and form.

word meaning   The literal meaning of a word taken out of context, which is derived from the morphemes it consists of.

Z

zeugma   The use of a word which has to be interpreted in two different ways at the same time in order to make sense.

Further Reading

1 General Topics

Cognitive Linguistics

Croft, W., & Cruse, D.A. (2004). *Cognitive Linguistics*. Cambridge: Cambridge University Press. http://dx.doi.org/10.1017/CBO9780511803864

Dirven, René. & Marjolijn Verspoor. (eds) (1998). *Cognitive Explorations of Language and Linguistics*. Amsterdam: John Benjamins.

Evans, V., & Green, M. (2006). *Cognitive Linguistics: An Introduction*. Edinburgh: Edinburgh University Press.

Lee, D. (2001). *Cognitive Linguistics:Aan introduction*. Oxford: Oxford University Press.

Ungerer, F., & Schmid, H.-J. (2006). *An Introduction to Cognitive Linguistics*. Harlow: Pearson Longman.

Cognitive Grammar

Langacker, R. (1987). *Foundations of Cognitive Grammar*. (Vol. 1). *Theoretical Prerequisites*. Stanford: Stanford University Press.

Langacker, R. (1991). *Foundations of Cognitive Grammar*. (Vol. 2). *Descriptive Application*. Stanford: Stanford University Press.

Langacker, R. (2008). *Cognitive Grammar: A Basic Introduction*. New York: Oxford University Press. http://dx.doi.org/10.1093/acprof:oso/9780195331967.001.0001

Radden, G., & Dirven, R. (2007). *Cognitive English Grammar*. Amsterdam: John Benjamins. http://dx.doi.org/10.1075/clip.2

Taylor, J. (2002). *Cognitive Grammar*. Oxford: Oxford University Press.

Cognitive Morphology

Bybee, J. (1985). *Morphology: An Inquiry into the Relation Between Meaning and Form*. Amsterdam: John Benjamins. http://dx.doi.org/10.1075/tsl.9

Hamawand, Z. (2007). *Suffixal Rivalry in Adjective Formation. A Cognitive-Corpus Analysis*. London: Equinox.

Hamawand, Z. (2008). *Morpho-Lexical Alternation in Noun Formation*. London: Palgrave Macmillan. http://dx.doi.org/10.1057/9780230584013

Hamawand, Z. (2011). *Morphology in English. Word Formation in Cognitive Grammar*. London. Continuum.

Tuggy, D. (2005). Cognitive approach to word formation'. In Pavol Stekauer & Rochelle Lieber. (eds) *Handbook of Word-Formation*, 233–265. Netherlands: Springer http://dx.doi.org/10.1007/1-4020-3596-9_10

Semantics

General Semantics

Cruse, D. Alan. (1986). *Lexical Semantics*. Cambridge: Cambridge University Press.

Cruse, D. Alan. (2004). *Meaning in Language: An Introduction to Semantics and Pragmatics*. Oxford: Oxford University Press.

Hofmann, T. (1993). *Realms of Meaning: An Introduction to Semantics*. London: Longman.

Hurford, J., & Heasley, B. (1983). *Semantics: A Coursebook*. Cambridge: Cambridge University Press.

Löbner, S. (2002). *Understanding Semantics*. London: Arnold.

Lyons, J. (1977). *Semantics* (2 Vols). Cambridge: Cambridge University Press.

Lyons, J. (1995). *Linguistic Semantics: An Introduction*. Cambridge: Cambridge University Press. http://dx.doi.org/10.1017/CBO9780511810213

Saeed, J. (1997). *Semantics*. Oxford: Blackwell.

Cognitive Semantics

Hamawand, Z. (2009). *The Semantics of English Negative Prefixes*. London: Equinox.

Lakoff, G. (1988). Cognitive semantics. In Umberto Eco, Marco Santambrogio & Patrizia Violi (eds). *Meaning and Mental Representations*, 119–154. Bloomington, IN: Indiana University Press.

Langacker, R. (1988). A view of linguistic semantics. In Brygida Rudzka-Ostyn. (ed.) *Topics in Cognitive Linguistics*, 49–90. Amsterdam: John Benjamins. http://dx.doi.org/10.1075/cilt.50.04lan

Langacker, R. (1997). The contextual basis of cognitive semantics. In Jan Nuyts & Eric Pederson. *Language and Conceptualisation*, 229–232. Cambridge: Cambridge University Press.

Talmy, L. (2000). *Toward a Cognitive Semantics,* (2 Vols). Cambridge, MA: MIT Press.

Formal Semantics

Allan, K. (2001). *Natural Language Semantics*. Oxford: Oxford University Press.

Cann, R. (1993). *Formal Semantics: An Introduction*. Cambridge: Cambridge University Press. http://dx.doi.org/10.1017/CBO9781139166317

Heim, I., & Kratzer, A. (1998). *Semantics in Generative Grammar*. Oxford: Blackwell.

Jackendoff, R. (1990). *Semantic Structures*. Cambridge, MA: MIT Press.

Portner, P., & Partee, B. (Eds) (2002). *Formal Semantics: The Essential Readings*. Oxford: Blackwell. http://dx.doi.org/10.1002/9780470758335

Pragmatics

Austin, J.L. (1962). *How to Do Things with Words*. Oxford: Clarendon Press.

Davis, S. (Ed.). (1991). *Pragmatics: A Reader*. Oxford: Oxford University Press.

Grice, H.P. (1975). Logic and conversation. In P. Cole & J.L. Morgan (Eds), *Syntax and Semantics* (Vol. 3). *Speech Acts,* 41–58. New York: Academic Press.

Grundy, P. (2000). *Doing Pragmatics*. London: Arnold.

Levinson, S.C. (1983). *Pragmatics*. Cambridge: Cambridge University Press.

Mey, J. (2001). *Pragmatics: An Introduction*. Oxford: Blackwell.

Searle, J. (1969). *Speech Acts: An Essay in the Philosophy of Language*. Cambridge: Cambridge University Press. http://dx.doi.org/10.1017/CBO9781139173438

Verscheuren, J. (1999). *Understanding Pragmatics*. London: Arnold.

2 Specialized Topics

Category

Rosch, E. (1977). Human categorisation. In Neil Warren (Ed.) *Studies in Cross-Cultural Psychology 1*, 3–49. London: Academic Press.

Rosch, E. 1978. Principles of categorisation. In Eleanor Rosch & Barbara B. Lloyd (Eds) *Cognition and Categorisation*, 27–48. Hillsdale, NJ: Lawrence Erlbaum.

Rosch, E., & Mervis, C. (1975). Family resemblances: Studies in the internal structure of categories. *Cognitive Psychology*, *7* (4), 573–605. http://dx.doi.org/10.1016/0010-0285(75)90024-9

Taylor, J. (1989). *Linguistic Categorisation. Prototypes in Linguistic Theory*. Oxford: Clarendon Press.

Tsohadzidis, S.L. (Ed.). (1990). *Meanings and Prototypes: Studies in Linguistic Categorisation*. London: Routledge.

Domain

Barsalou, L. (1992). Frames, concepts and conceptual Fields. In Adrienne Lehrer and Eva Feder Kittay (Eds.), *Frames, Fields and Contrasts: New Essays in Semantic and Lexical Organisation*, 21–74. London: Routledge.

Clausner, T., & Croft, W. (1999). Domains and image schemas. *Cognitive Linguistics*, 10 (1), 1–31. http://dx.doi.org/10.1515/cogl.1999.001

Croft, W. (1993). The role of domains in the interpretation of metaphors and metonymies. *Cognitive Linguistics*, 4 (4), 335–370. http://dx.doi.org/10.1515/cogl.1993.4.4.335

Fillmore, C. (1977). Scenes-and-frames. In Antonio Zampolli (Ed.) *Linguistic Structures Processing*: 55–81. Dordrecht: Springer.

Fillmore, C. (1982). Frame semantics. In Linguistic Society of Korea (Ed.) *Linguistics in the Morning Calm*: 111–138. Seoul: Hanshin.

Construal

Casad, E. (1995). Seeing it in more than one way. In John Taylor & Robert Maclaury (Eds) *Trends in Linguistics, Language and the Cognitive Construal of the World*, 23–45. Berlin: Mouton de Gruyter. http://dx.doi.org/10.1515/9783110809305.23

Croft, W., & Wood, E.J. (2000). Construal operations in linguistics and artificial intelligence. In Liliana Albertazzi (Ed.), *Meaning and Cognition: A Multidisciplinary Approach*, 51–78. Amsterdam: John Benjamins. http://dx.doi.org/10.1075/celcr.2.04cro

Hamawand, Z. (2002). *Atemporal Complement Clauses in English: A Cognitive Grammar Analysis*. München: Lincom.

Langacker, R. (1988). A view of linguistic semantics. In Brygida Rudzka-Ostyn. (Ed.) *Topics in Cognitive Linguistics*, 49–90. Amsterdam: John Benjamins. http://dx.doi.org/10.1075/cilt.50.04lan

Verhagen, A. (2007). Construal and perspectivisation. In Dirk Geeraerts & Hubert Cuyckens (Eds) *The Oxford Handbook of Cognitive Linguistics*, 48–81. Oxford: Oxford University Press.

Mental Spaces

Dancygier, B., & Sweetser, E. (2005). *Mental Spaces in Grammar: Conditional Constructions*. Cambridge: Cambridge University Press. http://dx.doi.org/10.1017/CBO9780511486760

Fauconnier, G. (1994). *Mental Spaces*. Cambridge: Cambridge University Press. http://dx.doi.org/10.1017/CBO9780511624582

Fauconnier, G. (1997). *Mappings in Thought and Language*. Cambridge: Cambridge University Press. http://dx.doi.org/10.1017/CBO9781139174220

Fauconnier, G., & Sweetser, E. (1996). *Spaces, Worlds and Grammar*. Chicago: University of Chicago Press.

Fauconnier, G., & Turner, M. (2002). *The way We Think: Conceptual Blending and the Mind's Hidden Complexities*. New York: Basic Books.

Image Schemas

Clausner, T.C., & Croft, W. (1999). Domains and image schemas. *Cognitive Linguistics*, 10 (1), 1–31. http://dx.doi.org/10.1515/cogl.1999.001

Gibbs, R., Jr., & Colston, H. (1995). The cognitive psychological reality of image schemas and their transformations. *Cognitive Linguistics*, 6 (4), 347–378. http://dx.doi.org/10.1515/cogl.1995.6.4.347

Hampe, B. (Ed.). (2005). *From Perception to Meaning: Image Schemas in Cognitive Linguistics*. Berlin: Mouton de Gruyter. http://dx.doi.org/10.1515/9783110197532

Johnson, M. (1987). *The Body in the Mind: The Bodily Basis of Meaning, Imagination and Reason*. Chicago: Chicago University Press.

Mandler, J. (2004). *The Foundations of Mind: Origins of Conceptual Thought.* Oxford: Oxford University Press.

Blending

Coulson, S. (2000). *Semantic Leaps: Frame-Shifting and Conceptual Blending in Meaning.* Cambridge: Cambridge University Press.

Coulson, S., & Oakley, T. (Eds.) (2000). Special issue on conceptual blending. *Cognitive Linguistics*, 11 (3/4), 175–360.

Fauconnier, G., & Turner, M. (2002). *The Way We Think: Conceptual Blending and the Mind's Hidden Complexities.* New York: Basic Books.

Gibbs, R. (2000). Making good psychology out of blending theory. *Cognitive Linguistics*, 11 (3/4), 347–358.

Sweetser, E. (2000). Blended spaces and performativity. *Cognitive Linguistics*, 11 (3/4), 305–334.

Conceptual Metaphor

Gibbs, R. (1994). *The Poetics of Mind.* Cambridge: Cambridge Universit Press.

Lakoff, G. (1987). *Women, Fire and Dangerous Things: What Categories Reveal about the Mind.* Chicago: University of Chicago Press. http://dx.doi.org/10.7208/chicago/9780226471013.001.0001

Lakoff, G., & Johnson, M. (1980). *Metaphors We Live By.* Chicago: University of Chicago Press.

Lakoff, G., & Turner, M. (1989). *More than Cool Reason: A Field Guide to Poetic Metaphor.* Chicago: University of Chicago Press. http://dx.doi.org/10.7208/chicago/9780226470986.001.0001

Paprotté, W. & Dirven, R. (Eds.), *The Ubiquity of Metaphor: Metaphor in Language and Thought.* Amsterdam: Benjamins. http://dx.doi.org/10.1075/cilt.29

Conceptual Metonymy

Barcelona, A. (2003). 'Introduction. The cognitive theory of metaphor and Metonymy'. In A. Barcelona (ed.), *Metaphor and Metonymy at the Crossroads: A Cognitive Perspective*: 1–30. http://dx.doi.org/10.1515/9783110894677.1

Dirven, R., & Pörings, R. (2002). *Metaphor and Metonymy in Comparison and Contrast.* Berlin: Mouton de Gruyter.

Kövecses, Z., & Radden, G. (1998). Metonymy: developing a cognitive linguistic view'. *Cognitive Linguistics*, 9(1), 37–78. http://dx.doi.org/10.1515/cogl.1998.9.1.37

Panther, K.-U., & Radden, G. (Eds) (1999). *Metonymy in Language and Thought.* Amsterdam: Benjamins. http://dx.doi.org/10.1075/hcp.4

Panther, K.-U., & Thornburg, L. (Eds) (2003). *Metonymy and Pragmatic Inferencing.* Amsterdam: John Benjamins. http://dx.doi.org/10.1075/pbns.113

3 Dictionaries

Language Dictionaries

Cambridge Advanced Learner's Dictionary Online Available at: http://dictionary.cambridge.org/

C.O.B.U.I.L.D. (1998). *English Dictionary,* Glasgow: Harper Collins Publishers.

Longman Dictionary of Contemporary English. (1995). (3rd ed.). London: Longman.

Online, M.-W.D. Available at: http://www.m-w.com.

Oxford Advanced Learner's Dictionary. (1995). (5th ed.). Oxford: Oxford University Press.

Linguistics Dictionaries

Bauer, L. (2004). *A Glossary of Morphology.* Edinburgh: Edinburgh University Press.

Bussman, H. (1996). *Routledge Dictionary of Language and Linguistics.* London: Routledge.

Crystal, D. (2002). *A Dictionary of Linguistics and Phonetics.* Oxford: Blackwell.

Matthews, P. (1997). *The Concise Oxford Dictionary of Linguistics.* Oxford: Oxford University Press.

Trask, R. (1993). *A Dictionary of Grammatical Terms in Linguistics.* London: Routledge.

4 Usage manuals

Fowler, H. (1996). *Modern English Usage.* Oxford: Oxford University Press.

MacKaskill, S. (1981). *A Dictionary of Good English: A Guide to Current Usage.* London: The Macmillan Press Ltd.

Partridge, E. (1961). *Usage and Abusage. A Guide in Good English.* London: Hamish Hamilton.

Peters, P. (2004). *The Cambridge Guide to English Usage.* Cambridge: Cambridge University Press. http://dx.doi.org/10.1017/CBO9780511487040

Treble, H.A., & Vallins, G.H. (1961). *An ABC of English Usage.* Oxford: Clarendon Press.

Answer Key

Chapter 1

Exercise 1.1

1. Said as the tool one is using comes apart in one's hands.
2. His actions or words caused a disaster.
3. She really thought it would not be useful at all.
4. You are not a tidy cook.
5. You have done nothing.

Exercise 1.2

1. dirty   2. tricky   3. stubborn   4. Submissive   5. evil

Exercise 1.3

1. relax (v): to rest after work or effort: event
2. ring (n): a piece of jewellery that you wear on your finger: object
3. blue (adj): a colour we associate with a clear sky or sea: quality
4. linguist (n): a scientist who studies language: entity
5. I am sick (s): physically or mentally ill: situation

Exercise 1.4

1. The interjection *ah* expresses surprise.
2. The interjection *alas* expresses distress.
3. The interjection *hey* expresses indifference.
4. The interjection *ugh* expresses disgust.
5. The interjection *wow* expresses admiration.

Exercise 1.5

1. greeting   informal/formal
2. asking about health   informal/formal
3. acknowledging   informal/formal
4. asking for repetition   informal/formal
5. request   informal/formal

Exercise 1.6

1. indisposed   2. slim   3. economical   4. disabled   5. curious

Exercise 1.7

1. viewer: a person who watches television.
2. sightseer: a person who watches tourist places.
3. observer: a person who watches a meeting without taking an active part in it.
4. onlooker: a person who watches an incident in a street.
5. spectator: a person who watches a sports event.

Exercise 1.8

1. *Frail* implies delicacy and slightness of structure, as in *The teenager is too frail to enjoy sports.*
2. *Weak* applies to deficiency or inferiority in strength or power of any sort, as in *She felt weak after the surgery.*
3. *Feeble* suggests extreme weakness inviting pity or contempt, as in *She made a feeble attempt to walk.*
4. *Fragile* suggests frailty, brittleness and inability to resist rough usage, as in *The reclusive poet is too fragile for the rigours of this world.*
5. *Decrepit* implies being worn-out or broken-down from long use or old age, as in *A decrepit elderly man sat on a park bench.*

Exercise 1.9

1. juror: a member of a jury who decides the verdict in a trial.
2. referee: an official who controls the game in certain sports.
3. reviewer: a person who writes reviews of books, films or plays.
4. surveyor: a person who measures and records the details of a piece of land.
5. arbitrator: a person who is chosen to settle a disagreement.

Exercise 1.10

1. shun: implies avoiding something as a matter of habitual practice or policy and may imply repugnance or abhorrence, as in *She has shunned publicity since she retired from the theatre.*
2. avoid: stresses forethought and caution in keeping clear of danger or difficulty, as in *They built a wall to avoid soil being washed away.*

3. evade: implies adroitness, ingenuity or lack of scruple in avoiding something, as in He *evaded the question by changing the subject.*
4. escape: stresses the fact of getting away or being passed by not necessarily through effort or by conscious intent, as in *She was lucky to escape serious injury.*
5. eschew: implies deliberately avoiding or keeping away from something as unwise or distasteful, as in *We won't have discussions with this group unless they eschew violence.*

Exercise 1.11

1. bag: a container made of cloth, plastic or leather, used for carrying shopping or travelling items.
2. box: a container made of wood, cardboard or metal, used for holding books, tools or matches.
3. sack: a container with made of strong paper or plastic, used for storing flour or coal.
4. packet: a small container made of paper or cardboard used for packing biscuits, cigarettes or crisps.
5. wallet: a small container made of leather or plastic used for keeping paper money or credit cards in.

Exercise 1.12

1. forcible: involving the use of physical power, as in a forcible measure.
   forceful: involving the use of mental power, as in a forceful argument.
2. displace: to move away people from their home to another place.
   misplace: to put something somewhere and then be unable to find it again.
3. triumphal: action done in order to celebrate a great success or victory.
   triumphant: a person who is successful in a way that causes great satisfaction.
4. observance: the practice of obeying a law, celebrating a festival or behaving according to a particular custom.
   observation: the act of watching somebody or something carefully for a period of time, especially to learn something.
5. international: involving two or more countries.
   intranational: involving one country.

Chapter 2

Exercise 2.1

1. expelled 2. discharged 3. evicted 4. banished 5. dismissed

Exercise 2.2

1. non-gradable 2. gradable 3. relational 4. non-gradable
5. relational

Exercise 2.3

1. plain: 1. simple in style as in *The rooms are quite plain.* 2. honest as in *I will be plain with you.* 3. clear as in *The instructions were very plain.*
2. over: 1. above or more as in *Children of 14 and over are invited to the programme.* 2. across a street, an open space, etc. as in *I stopped and crossed over.* 3. remaining, not used or needed as in *If there's any food left over, put it in the fridge.*
3. foot: 1. the lowest part of the leg as in *What size foot have you got?* 2. the bottom of something as in *There is a note at the foot of the page.* 3. a measure of length as in *She is five feet two inches tall.*
4. run: 1. to move using your legs, going faster than when you walk as in *I had to run to catch the bus.* 2. to go in a particular direction as in *The road runs along the side of a lake.* 3. to organize or be in charge of something as in *They run a restaurant in Leeds.*
5. mouth: 1. the opening in the face used for speaking, eating, etc. as in *Don't talk with your mouth full.* 2. a person considered only as somebody who needs to be provided with food as in *The world will not be able to support all these extra hungry mouths.* 3. the entrance or opening of something as in *They took a picture near the mouth of the cave.*

Exercise 2.4

1. *Thankful* is used especially for feelings of relief at having avoided a danger or at having come through an unpleasant experience, as in *I am thankful that we got home before the storm started.* *Grateful* is used especially for people's reactions to kindness, favours, etc. as in *I am very grateful for all your help.*
2. *Accurate* implies property of precision acquired by training as in *He gave an accurate description of the event.* *Exact* implies property of

precision that is inherent or native as in *They need an exact measurement of blood volume.*

3. *Repair* is formal as in *They are repairing the surface of the road. Fix* is informal as in *He is trying to fix my old computer.*

4. *Quick* stresses immediacy of response which is native rather than acquired as in *She was quick to point out that it wasn't her fault. Prompt* stresses immediacy of response which is acquired by training as in *They are prompt in providing medical assistance.*

5. *Steal* means to take something illegally from a person, shop, etc. It is followed by the thing stolen, as in *She admitted stealing the money from her employers. Rob* means to take money or property illegally from a place, organization or person, often using violence. It is followed by person or place, as in *They robbed the bank of £2 million* and *My wallet's gone! I've been robbed*!

Exercise 2.5

1. knife, fork, spoon   2. cups, plates, bowls   3. train, car, plane
4. cod, salmon, trout   5. sparrow, hawk, fowl

Exercise 2.6

1. flash, lens, tripod   2. monitor, keyboard, mouse
3. wheel, engine, tyre   4. ceiling, door, window
5. cellar, kitchen, study

Exercise 2.7

1. *burning* occurs with *desire*, *blazing* occurs with *row*
2. *broad* occurs with *shoulders*, *wide* occurs with *eyes*
3. *make* occurs with *trouble*, *do* occurs with *exercise*
4. *profound* occurs with *book*, *deep* occurs with *well*
5. *powerful* occurs with *drug*, *strong* occurs with *smell*

Exercise 2.8

1. Mutton is meat from sheep.   2. I heard a lion roaring.
3. The man passed away.   4. A stallion is a male horse.
5. The engine needs petrol.

Exercise 2.9

1. achieve a goal, defeat an opponent
2. highly unlikely, utterly ridiculous
3. bitterly complain, strongly object
4. go bald, become extinct   5. fail miserably, smile proudly

Exercise 2.10

1.	recall -ing gerund	I can't recall meeting her before.
2.	intend -ing gerund/to-infinitive	I intend staying/to stay long.
3.	make bare infinitive	She always makes me laugh.
4.	pledge to-infinitive	They pledged to continue campaigning.
5.	like -ing gerund/to-infinitive	I like swimming/to swim.

Exercise 2.11

1. watch or look after something or someone
2. accept something unpleasant without complaining
3. sound familiar or you have heard before
4. avoid getting into trouble
5. hear something from other people

Exercise 2.12

1. hire a car   2. let a room   3. lease a video   4. rent a cottage
5. charter a boat

Chapter 3

Exercise 3.1

1. She was not only clever but also honest.
   Apart from being clever, she was honest.
2. Staying indoors all the time is unhealthy.
   It is unhealthy to stay indoors all the time.
3. It is believed that they knew the answer.
   They are believed to have known the answer.
4. I will not leave under any circumstances.
   Under no circumstance will I leave.

5. It is a pity they live so far away.
    I wish they didn't live so far away.

Exercise 3.2

1. contradictory   2. analytic   3. contradictory   4. analytic
5. synthetic

Exercise 3.3

1. The fox is dead.   2. The man is sleeping.   3. She was tired.
4. She bought a bird.   5. They were selling flowers.

Exercise 3.4

1. The furniture needed cleaning.
2. The children were complaining before.
3. I was ill.   4. There is an investigation.   5. She drove the car.

Exercise 3.5

1. She does not love him.   2. They went there as visitors.
3. The talk show was not that good.
4. Others don't like playing dominos.
5. He can't answer the call now.

Exercise 3.6

1. Quantity. The speaker has not provided enough information.
2. Relevance. The speaker's answer is not related to the question.
3. Manner. The speaker's answer is not orderly. B.A. should be 1980 and
    M.A. 1982.
4. Quality. The speaker has failed to tell the truth.

Exercise 3.7

1. bank: margin of a river/a financial institution
2. backward: a place that is behind/less developed
3. take: give me a lift/take a legal action against me
4. glasses: drinking vessels/a pair of lenses in a frame
5. record: a disc on which music is recorded/the best result especially in
    sport

Exercise 3.8

1. Either we talked about the party which was held last night, or we talked last night about the party.
2. Either small boys only and other girls, or small boys and small girls.
3. Either the chicken is ready to eat something, or the chicken is ready for us to eat.
4. Either the idea is crazy, or the lawyer is crazy.
5. Either I like the café, or I like the district.

Exercise 3.9

1. Either the relatives who visit us are boring, or our visiting them is boring.
2. Either the hunters are shooting something which is appalling, or someone is shooting the hunters which is appalling.
3. Either planes which fly are dangerous, or flying the planes is dangerous.
4. Either I like them separately or together.
5. Either she likes pets more than he likes them, or she likes pets more than she likes him.

Exercise 3.10

1. He is not here. He is there in the garden.   person, space
2. She agreed to visit them next summer.   person, time
3. Would you like to see the menu, sir?   person, vocative
4. There's a car park in front of the hotel.   space
5. Is Jim coming to tomorrow's meeting?   person, time

Exercise 3.11

1. expressive   2. directive   3. assertive   4. declarative
5. commissive

Exercise 3.12

1. agent   2. patient   3. instrument   4. beneficiary   5. location
6. time

Chapter 4

Exercise 4.1

1. loveable child: a child who has attractive qualities. Presumably, all children can be loved, but not every child is loveable.
2. watchable film: a film that is enjoyable. Presumably, all films can be watched, but not every film is watchable.
3. agreeable deal: a deal that is suitable. Presumably, all deals can be agreed upon, but not every deal is agreeable.
4. readable book: a book that is enjoyable. Presumably, all books can be read, but not every one is readable.
5. drinkable water: water that is safe to drink. Presumably, pond water can be drunk, but it is not drinkable.

Exercise 4.2

1. iso-:/iː.zəʊ/, [ISO], equal
2. eco-:/iː.kəʊ/, [ECO], environment
3. -itis: /aitis/, [ITIS], illness
4. hydro-: /haidrəʊ/, [HYDRO], water
5. -ology: /-ɒl.ə. dʒi/ [OLOGY], study of

Exercise 4.3

1. big occasion, large salary   2. quick meal, fast food
3. right decision, correct answer   4. strong evidence, powerful drug
5. dangerous mission, perilous road

Exercise 4.4

1. fresh   2. pleasant   3. polite   4. spotless   5. accurate
6. lawful   7. fair   8. empty   9. smooth   10. complete

Exercise 4.5

1. a. The present simple tense expresses habitual or everyday activity.
   b. The present continuous tense expresses an activity that is in progress at the moment of speaking.
2. a. The present perfect expresses an action that happened at an unspecified time in the past.

  b. The present perfect continuous expresses an action that began in the past and continues to the present.

3. a. The present perfect expresses a situation that began in the past and continues to the present.

  b. The present perfect expresses a situation that began in the past and finished recently.

4. a. *Will* is used to express a willingness to do an action in the future, no prior plan has been made.

  b. *Going to* is used to express a prior plan which the speaker intends to do in the future.

5. a. The present simple tense expresses a timeless truth or condition.

  b. The present continuous tense expresses a temporary condition.

Exercise 4.6

1. COMPULSION 2. BLOCKAGE 3. DIVERSION
4. ENABLEMENT 5. ATTRACTION

Exercise 4.7

1. a. The sentence implies that the family received the letter.

  b. The sentence implies that it is not sure if the family received the letter.

2. a. The helper participates directly in the action for which he is giving assistance.

  b. The assistance is felt as mediate or indirect.

3. a. The sentence implies direct means of achieving a result are employed.

  b. The sentence implies indirect means of achieving a result are employed.

4. a. The subject is closely concerned with the action of attending the baby.

  b. The subject is less concerned with the action of attending the baby.

5. a. The sentence describes an event in which the speaker has the power or the legal right to make the confession happen.

  b. The sentence describes an event in which the speaker merely claims that a certain obligation existed.

Exercise 4.8

1. Preference   2. Advice   3. Invitation   4. Opinion   5. Request

Exercise 4.9

1. rim   cup, glasses, wheel
2. edge   knife, cliff, table
3. fringe   city, hair, woodland
4. frame   bicycle, picture, glasses, window
5. border   country, garden, pillowcase

Exercises 4.10

1. a. means he jumped on the surface of the table, i.e. touching it.
   b. means he jumped from one side of the table to the other without touching it.
2. a. means she moved within the garden.
   b. means she moved from a position outside the garden into the garden.
3. a. means at exactly the correct time, neither early nor late.
   b. means with enough time to spare, before the last moment.
4. a. means the grass is short.
   b. means the grass is long.
5. a. means the street is at the back of the station.
   b. means the street is further away in distance from the station.

Chapter 5

Exercise 5.1

1. He holds a thought.   2. Time is passing quickly.
3. I am crazy about her.   4. He clings to his beliefs.
5. Your argument is vacuous.

Exercise 5.2

1. CONSCIOUS IS UP   2. UNCONSCIOUS IS DOWN
3. VIRTUE IS UP   4. BAD IS DOWN   5. HEALTH IS UP

Exercise 5.3

1. The state of being in love is construed as a container.
2. Violence is construed as an entity.
3. Law is construed as a person.
4. The depression is construed as a container.
5. Unemployment is construed as an entity.

Exercise 5.4

1. CONTAINER FOR CONTENT
2. PLACE FOR EVENT (the name of a place is used for the event that occurred in that place)
3. PRODUCER FOR PRODUCT (The name of film director is used for his films)
4. MATERIAL FOR OBJECT
5. PLACE FOR INSTITUTION (the British parliament and government)

Exercise 5.5

1. STATES ARE LOCATIONS   2. SIMILARITY IS NEARNESS
3. QUANTITY IS VERTICAL ELEVATION
4. DESIRE IS HUNGER   5. PURPOSES ARE DESTINATION

Exercise 5.6

1. This sentence can set up two spaces which we can identify as speaker's reality and the film. In the first interpretation, there is a kind of referential shifting between the two mental spaces: *Catherine* is the name of a person in reality, but the speaker uses her name to describe the film images of her acting the role of a psycho. This kind of interpretation can be described as: real-life Catherine plays the film part of a psycho. In the second interpretation, there is no referential shifting between the two mental spaces: Catherine is the name of a character in the film space and we predicate of this character that she is a psycho. This kind of interpretation can be described as: in the film the character Catherine is a psycho.
2. This sentence can set up two spaces which we can identify as a reality space and a wish space. In the wish space which is unlikely or impossible, Nancy wants to marry a film star. In the reality space, we have two interpretations. In the specific interpretation, there is a film star,

but Nancy has not yet married him. In the non-specific interpretation, there is no such film star.

3. If *I* were *you*, *I* would accept the offer. This sentence sets up two spaces: a reality space and a counterfactual space. It contains the conditional conjunction *if* and is in the past tense. In the reality space, the person is described as being hesitant. In the hypothetical space, the speaker is firm.

4. This sentence sets up two mental spaces, one representing the now of the speaker, the other representing the time 1985. The first identifies a wife in the 1985 time space, and is consistent with the speaker either having the same wife in the now space or not. The second is that the person who is speaker's wife now was not his wife in 1985, but is referred to as my wife by a shift linking the mental spaces.

5. This sentence is ambiguous. It could mean that every time we see your father's car, some aspect of the car has changed. For example, it might have had some new spare parts. Alternatively, it could mean that your father has a new car every time we see him.

Exercise 5.7

1. motor + hotel
2. The word *brunch* is morphologically composed of breakfast and lunch. Semantically, certain elements of the input spaces *breakfast* and *lunch* are projected into the blended space *brunch*, in which some additional meanings emerge. A brunch is typically a meal eaten late in the morning on Saturday and Sunday. It may include alcoholic drinks such as champagne.
3. motor + pedal
4. breath + analyser
5. information + entertainment

Exercise 5.8

1. Just as the soul is the heart of something so is brevity is the essence of intelligence.
2. A root is the primary source of everything just as money is the source of all evil.
3. Quicksand is a potential trap for the traveller just as vanity is a potential trap for beauty.
4. A mirror reflects an object just as speech reflects the mind.

5. A mother gives birth to children just as necessity gives birth to invention.

Chapter 6

Exercise 6.1

1. For example, a phrase like *red carpet* brings together two semantic poles: *pink* designates or profiles a subpart of the COLOUR SPECTRUM, and brings with it as part of its structure a schematic TR. This schematic TR is specified only as PHYSICAL OBJECT, which is a schematic instance of THING. In other words, part of the meaning of *red*, which is an instance of the lexical class adjective, is that it relates to some entity, a TR, which is red. While the TR is not specified, we know that pink is relational in this way (it has to be a property of something), which is part of what it means for *red* to be an adjective. *Carpet* designates a specific type of PHYSICAL OBJECT among its other far richer semantic specifications. The association of these two semantic poles within the phrase maps the semantically specific *carpet* onto the schematic semantic TR of *red*. At the phonological pole, the association of the two simplex symbolic units entails that they are pronounced sequentially, one after the other.
2. vandalism
3. under the bed
4. our friend James Joyce
5. This is an example of a nominal apposition, involving the juxtaposition of two expressions each of which profiles a thing. Both component structures her husband and the lawyer profile things, and their profiles correspond, so both correspond to the composite-structure profile.

Exercise 6.2

1. As a composite whole, *jar lid* profiles the same entity as *lid*: a *jar lid* is a kind of lid, not a kind of jar. *Lid* is thus the profile determinant in *jar lid* because the profiles of *lid* and *jar lid* correspond (whereas neither corresponds to the profile of *jar*).
2. As a composite whole, *boredom* designates a thing. The suffix *-dom* functions as the profile determinant.

3. As a composite whole, *inessential* profiles a relationship. The prefix *in-* functions as the profile determinant.

4. As a composite whole, *in the drawer* designates a relationship of spatial inclusion, not the closet. *In* functions as the profile determinant because the relationship it profiles corresponds to the relationship profiled by *in the drawer*.

5. As a composite whole, the phrase *send the letter* designates a relation. The verb *send* functions as the profile determinant.

Exercise 6.3

Autonomous: leak, leisure, qualify, sprinkle, budget
Dependent: -age, -ly, dis-, be-, -ary

Exercise 6.4

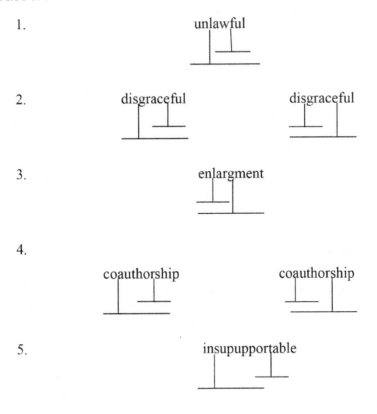

Exercise 6.5

1. Care that is given during the day.
2. Feeling that is situated in the heart.   3. Hunt for a criminal.
4. Plate made of silver.   5. Bowl used for holding sugar.

Exercise 6.6

1. A person who does not like spending money.
2. A book that is in stiff covers.   3. A type of personal stereo.
4. A person who lacks experience.   5. A shark.

Exercise 6.7

1. The area in a courtroom wherein the jury sits.
2. A box in which documents are kept.
3. A section, as in a stadium, kept for reporters to work in.
4. A small confined place in which there is a public phone.
5. A box that plays a musical tone when you open it.

Exercise 6.8

1. A very intelligent person.
2. Someone who is very successful at their job and soon becomes powerful or rich.
3. Someone who complains all the time and is never happy.
4. A story that someone has invented in order to deceive people.
5. A business or product that makes a lot of money for someone.

Exercise 6.9

1. By repairing a small tear now we avoid the necessity of repairing a large tear later. The moral of this proverb is that prompt action at an early stage may prevent serious trouble in the future.
2. Do not judge a thing by its attractive appearance. The lesson this proverb teaches is that never base your opinion of anything merely on what it looks like for appearances are deceptive.
3. The religious meaning is that you will be punished or rewarded according to whether you have led a virtuous or a sinful life. In much the same way, all of us are responsible for the consequences of our actions, so we must put up with them.

4. Do not wait until tomorrow, for rain may ruin the harvest. By extension, the proverb means that we should always take advantage of favourable circumstances. When an opportunity to do a thing arises, you should take full advantage of it for you may never get another one.

5. Birds of the same kind travel in company. In the same way, people with similar tastes or interests tend to come together in groups.

Exercise 6.10

1. To have a problem.   2. To be very easy.   3. Strong and healthy.
4. To make extremely angry.   5. Difficult to believe.

Exercise 6.11

1. An illness that affects the nose, eyes and throat and is caused by pollen from plants that is breathed in from the air.
2. A container that is used for coffee.
3. A place in which fruit is sold.
4. Bread that is made from wheat.
5. The people who work at a college.

Exercise 6.12

1. A person who is outside normal society, i.e. a criminal.
2. A person who spoils other people's enjoyment.
3. A book which is bound in flexible covers.
4. A very stupid person.
5. A poisonous snake.

Exercise 6.13

1. To be very eager to hear what someone is going to say.
2. Stop work for the day.
3. To be in charge of an organization or an activity.
4. To be more successful than anyone you are competing against.
5. To be unable to speak because you are so surprised.

Exercise 6.14

1. Events, especially misfortunes, always come together. One misfortune is followed closely by another.

2. It is what is behind the man, namely his character, which really matters.
3. A person who never stops long in a place or constantly changes his job will never make money. People whose love affairs are so casual and frequent gain no real or enduring affection.
4. Do not make a fuss about nothing. Do not turn a trifling matter into a major disaster.
5. It is better to accept something small than to reject it and hope to get more later on.

Exercise 6.15

1. To do something if necessary in a difficult situation.
2. The thing was silly or not valuable to do.
3. Being unpleasant or frightened.
4. It is their turn to take action or to reply.
5. Agree with each other.

Chapter 7

Exercise 7.1

un-

Prototypically, the prefix *un-* is tied to adjectival bases to express distinction, having the following semantic variants: **(a)** 'the antithesis of what is specified by the adjectival base'. This meaning proceeds when the prefix is tied to adjectives, simple or complex, describing humans. The formations are gradable and express contrariety. In some cases, it describes traits. For example, *uncooperative* is the antithesis of cooperative. In some cases, it describes nationality. For example, *unAmerican* means the antithesis of an American national in characteristics. **(b)** 'distinct from what is specified by adjectival base'. This meaning proceeds when the prefix is tied to adjectives, simple or complex, describing non-humans. The formations are gradable and express contrariety. For example, *unofficial* is distinct from being official. **(c)** 'not subjected to what is specified by adjectival base'. This meaning proceeds when the prefix is tied to complex adjectives denoting quality, participles ending in *-ed* or *-ing*. For example, *undressed* means not dressed.

Peripherally, the prefix *un-* is tied to other bases to express other meanings, having the following semantic variants: **(a)** 'inverting what is specified by the verbal bases'. The meaning of reversal proceeds when the prefix is

tied to verbal bases denoting action, meaning that the object has the physical ability to undergo change. For example, *unclose* means inverting the
action of closing. **(b)** 'taking away what is specified by the nominal base'.
The meaning of removal proceeds when the prefix is tied to concrete nouns,
with the resulting formation denoting separation or release. For example,
unchain means taking away a chain from somebody or something. **(c)** 'bereft
of what is specified by the nominal base'. The meaning of privation proceeds when the negative prefix is tied to abstract nouns. In some formations,
the nouns imply non-action. For example, *unease* means something which
is bereft of ease. In other formations, the nouns imply action. For example,
unbelief means lacking belief.

The figure below presents a graphical representation which captures the
multiple uses of the negative prefix *un-*. Note that the solid arrow represents
the prototypical sense, whereas the dashed arrows represent the semantic
extensions.

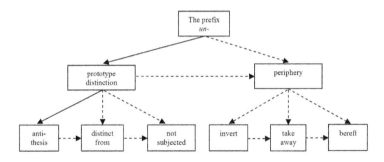

The semantic network of the negative prefix *un-*

-ure

Prototypically, the suffix *-ure* is tacked on to verbs to form nouns. Its meaning
is founded on the semantic property of transitivity. Relative to the nature of
the root, the suffix acquires the following senses: **(a)** 'the action of performing the thing described in the root'. This sense emerges when the verbal roots
are transitive. For example, *closure* is the act of closing something, *erasure*
is the act of removing something. **(b)** 'the result of the action described in the
root'. This sense appears when the verbal roots are transitive. For example,
enclosure is the result of being surrounded. **(c)** 'the body which performs
the thing described in the root'. This sense follows when the verbal roots are
intransitive. For example, *judicature* is a body of persons having the power
to make decisions.

Peripherally, the suffix *-ure* is attached to nouns to form nouns. Its meaning is founded on the semantic distinction concrete vs. abstract. Based on the nature of the root, the suffix acquires the following senses: **(a)** 'the position, rank or office of the thing described in the root'. This sense proceeds when the nominal roots are concrete and the nouns describe things connected with people. For example, *prefecture* is the office, position or territory of a prefect. **(b)** 'the state of being the thing described in the root'. This sense surfaces when the nominal roots are concrete and the nouns describe conditions in which people are. For example, *candidature* is the state of being a candidate.

The multiple senses of the suffix *-ure* are diagrammed in the figure below. Note that the solid arrow represents the prototypical sense, whereas the dashed arrows represent the semantic extensions.

For the semantic network of the remaining prefixes in A, see Hamawand's book *The Semantics of English Negative Prefixes*.

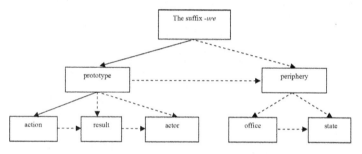

The semantic network of the suffix *-ure*

For the semantic network of the remaining prefixes in A and suffixes in B, see Hamawand's book *Morpho-lexical Alternation in Noun Formation*, and *Suffixal Rivalry in Adjective Formation: A Cognitive-Corpus Analysis*.

Exercise 7.2

Anticipatory it

Prototypically, the pronoun *it* is assigned the status of reference. In this role, *it* means 'referring back to an entity which has previously been mentioned in the discourse'. An entity is something that exists as a material object in the real world or a non-material concept in the imagined world. In this use, *it* is parallel with other third person pronouns. Relative to its nature, the entity is of the following types: **(a)** In some cases, the entity is concrete. In *Have you seen my book? Yes, it is on the table*, *it* refers back to a lifeless object represented by *book*. This sense can be semantically extended to anaphoric senses for other kinds of antecedents. In *Have you been to London? Yes, it was very crowded*, *it* refers back to a place represented by *London*. In *Many people watch the BBC. It started broadcasting in 1937*, *it* refers to an organization. In *The bear approached Patrick. It has thick fur*, *it* refers back to an animal, especially when its gender is not known. Some people use *it* to refer to babies in this way, as in *The mother feeds the baby. The father bathes it.* (b) In other cases the entity is abstract. In *Everyone is asking for love. Few seem able to provide it*, *it* refers back to an emotion. In *Truth is important. One must always speak it*, *it* refers back to a concept. In *Thousands live in poverty. We must combat it*, *it* refers back to a condition or state. In *I am trying to get a taxi. You won't find it easy*, *it* refers back to an entire situation, in which an event coded as a clause is reified as a kind of abstract thing. (c) In rare cases, *it* is cataphoric. In this role, *it* means 'referring forward to an entity which comes later in the discourse'. This is a case of right-dislocation, moving an element to the end of a sentence. It is found mainly in spoken language. It is used to add clarification to a noun phrase. The entity could be concrete, as in *I liked it, the food*. It could be abstract, as in *I enjoyed it, dancing the tango*.

Peripherally, the pronoun *it* is assigned the status of non-reference. In this role, *it* means 'profiling a setting within which an activity is introduced'. A setting represents the region within which an event unfolds or a situation obtains. It is an expanse within which an activity is introduced or a context within which it emerges. Depending on the nature of the complement, the setting is of two types: (a) In some instances, the setting is concrete. In *It is five o'clock* or *It is Tuesday*, *it* profiles a temporal setting, a location in time within which an action occurs. Recall that English allows sentences like *Monday witnessed a historic development*, in which Monday profiles a temporal setting within which the action of development is conceptualized to occur. Normally, one cannot conceptualize an event without connecting it with the time in which it occurs. In *It is freezing*, *it* profiles a spatial setting, a location in space represented by the environment, within which the action of freezing takes place. Recall that English allows sentences like *Chicago is freezing*. Naturally, one cannot conceptualize a meteorological event without connecting it with the environment causing it. (b) In further instances, the setting is abstract. In *It is tragic to hear the news of a plane crash*, *it* is used as an anticipatory subject, and so the construction is referred to as *a setting-subject construction*. *It* profiles an abstract setting within which a situation represented by a complement clause takes place. Moreover, *it* codes the general circumstances that surround the occurrence of the complement clause. In *I would hate it if they said so*, *it* is used as an anticipatory object, and so the construction is referred to as *a setting-object construction*. It profiles an abstract setting within which a situation represented by a complement clause takes place. Moreover, the presence of *it* serves to iconically distance the content of the complement clause from the main clause subject.

Complementizer -ing

To the *-ing* gerund, one can attribute precisely the same value that an *-ing* has in a progressive construction. In this function, the *-ing* refers specifically to an activity which is in progress at the moment of time serving as the reference point for the utterance. It imposes on a process a restricted immediate scope of predication comprising an arbitrary series of internal states. It confines the profile to these component states and portrays them as homogeneous. In *She is pruning the roses*, the *-ing* progressive refers to an ongoing activity which is happening at exactly the same speech time. The activity of pruning takes place over some period of time relative to the moment of speaking. Like the progressive, the *-ing* gerund takes an internal perspective on the action described by the verb stem, to the exclusion of the initial and final states. The only difference is that the former is grounded in time, whereas the latter is ungrounded.

I assume the meaning of the temporary ongoingness of an activity evoked by the *-ing* as central. This core meaning can be extended into two different values for the gerundial *-ing*.

The first extended value, which is closely related to the one above, is simultaneity, where two durative events happen at the same time. This value, which is the hallmark with complements marked by *-ing* gerund, is compatible with the notion of *happening now*, or *sameness of time*. It is found after two classes of verbs. In a sentence containing a verb expressing a mental activity like *She considers accepting the offer*, the complement event is mentally concurrent with the main event, but physically it is not necessarily so. In a sentence containing a verb expressing an emotional reaction like *Kate enjoys dancing the tango*, the value of something happening now is properly included in the description of the complement event. This implies that if one enjoys doing anything, one takes delight or pleasure in it at the very time one is doing it. To verify this value, the use of an adverb of time such as *yesterday* would render the sentence ungrammatical, but the use of *now* would not, as in *She considers now accepting the offer now/*yesterday*.

The second extended value is anteriority, where the complement event temporally precedes the time of the utterance expressed by the main verb.

This value is analogous with the notion of *factivity*, where the speaker of the sentence presupposes that the action expressed by the complement is true or has taken place. This sense is found after verbs expressing communication, as exemplified in *He admits tripping her up*. That is, the *-ing* clause describes a situation which is actual in relation to the process represented by the main verb *admit*. This implies that the event of making her fall, by putting his foot in front of her when she was moving, has actually occurred and happened before the event of admitting. To verify this value, it would be contradictory to use a follow-up expression rejecting the complement content, as in *He admits tripping her, *but he hasn't done it.*

For the semantic network of the remaining grammatical elements, see Hamawand's book *Atemporal Complement Clauses in English: A Cognitive Grammar Analysis*.

For convenience, I will summarize in the figure below the semantic structure of the *-ing* complementizer.

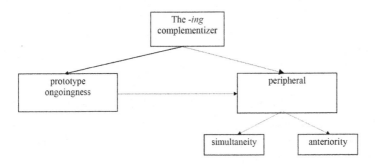

The semantic network of the complementizer -ing

Exercise 7.3

Drive

The verb *drive* is polysemous. Prototypically, it has the following senses. **(a)** 'to make a vehicle move along'. In this sense, the agent is human, while the thing driven is a concrete entity, as in *She drives a red sports car*. **(b)** 'to take someone somewhere in a car'. In this sense, the thing driven is a concrete human entity, as in *She drove Anna to London*. **(c)** 'to force something into a state'. In this sense, the thing driven is an abstract entity, as in *The government has driven the economy into deep recession*. **(d)** 'to force someone to go somewhere'. In this sense, both the agent and the thing driven are human, as in *They drove the occupying troops from the city*. **(e)** 'a short private road which leads from a public road to a house', as in *I parked in the drive*. **(f)** 'a journey in a car', as in *Shall we go for a drive this afternoon?*

Peripherally, the verb *drive* has the following senses. **(a)** 'to provide the power to keep something working. In this sense, both the agent and the thing driven are concrete non-human entities, as in *The engine drives the wheels*. **(b)** 'to force someone into a particular state, often an unpleasant one;. In this sense, the agent is an abstract entity, whereas the thing driven is a concrete human entity, as in *Love has driven men and women to strange extremes*. **(c)** 'to force someone into a particular state, often an unpleasant one. In this sense, both the agent and the thing driven are concrete human entities, as in *She's driving me crazy*. **(d)** 'energy and determination to achieve things', as in *We are looking for someone with drive and ambition*. **(e)** 'a planned effort to achieve something', as in *The latest promotional material is all part of a recruitment drive*. **(f)** 'to state something in a very forceful and effective way', as in *The speaker really drove his message home, repeating his main point several times*.

Chapter 8

Exercise 8.1

Non- and (to a lesser degree) *a-* favour a contradictory reading, which arises from non-gradable bases.

1. *Non-* conspicuously describes a choice between two different plans of action, as in *They were accused of non-observance of the terms of the contract*.

2. *A-* noticeably describes a choice between two opposing features of things, as in *They promote wound healing by adherence to aseptic technique*.

   By contrast, the negative prefixes *dis-*, *un-* and *in-* favour a contrary reading, which arises from gradable bases.

3. *Dis-* occupies the lowest level on the scale of contrariness. It is used mainly to evaluate attitudes of people. In this use, it is unfavourable in character, as in *Beware of dishonest traders in the tourist areas*.

4. *Un-* occupies a medium level on the scale of contrariness. It is used chiefly to evaluate properties of things. In this use, it is disapproving in character, as in *The small front garden is untidy; it is full of bushes*.

5. *In-* occupies the highest level on the scale of contrariness. It is used mostly to evaluate properties of situations. In this use, it is critical in character, as in *The contributions are statistically insignificant*.

Exercise 8.2

1. *On* means during a particular day, that is part of the week or date, as in *They'll be here on Tuesday, I was born on July 1st, We will see you on Christmas Eve*, etc.
2. *In* means during part or all of a period of time that belongs to month, season or year, as in *We are going to Italy in April. Some trees lose their leaves in autumn, I started working here in 1991*, etc.
3. *At* means an exact or a particular time that is part of the day, as in *There's a meeting at 6 o'clock, Are you free at lunchtime?, They will see each other at Easter*, etc.
4. *By* means not later than a special time, that is at or before it, as in *She promised to be back by five o'clock, We need a firm decision by the end of the week, The application must be in by the 31st to be accepted*, etc.
5. *For* is used to show an amount or period of time, as in *She's out of the office for a few days next week, I'm just going to bed for an hour or so, I haven't played tennis for years*, etc.

Exercise 8.3

1. *Hire* means to employ somebody for a short time to do a particular job, as in *They hired a firm of consultants to design the new system.*
2. *Employ* means to give somebody a job to do for payment, as in *The company employs 1200 people.*
3. *Engage* means to employ somebody to do a particular job, as in *He is currently engaged as a consultant.*
4. *Recruit* means to find new people to join a company, an organization, the armed forces, as in *They recruited several new members to the club.*
5. *Appoint* means to choose somebody for a job or position of responsibility, as in *They have appointed him (as) captain of the team.*

Chapter 9

Exercise 9.1

1. The adjective *earthen* means 'resembling earth in make', as in *The hut had an earthen floor and a thatched roof.* An earthen floor is floor that is made of soil or composed of baked clay. The adjective *earthy* means 'resembling earth in quality', as in *The old cellar was damp*

and had an earthy smell. An earthy cellar is a cellar that resembles earth in smell.

2.   The adjective *childish* means 'having the character of a child', as in *None of his friends tolerates his childish outbreaks of temper.* A person who is childish is immature, irrational and impatient. The adjective *childlike* means 'having the character of a child', as in *At 85, she retains a childlike curiosity about her environment.* A person who is childlike is innocent, fresh and honest.

3.   The adjective *compulsive* means 'tending to compel', as in *He suffers from the addictive disease of compulsive gambling.* Compulsive gambling is behaviour that is difficult to stop or control; the compulsion is due to internal urges. The adjective *compulsory* means 'tending to compel', as in *There are external exams at the end of compulsory schooling.* Compulsory schooling is something people are obliged to do because it is a law; the compulsion is due to external urges.

4.   The adjective *documental* means 'relating closely to document', as in *They have not produced documental proof of their identity.* Documental proof is proof that provides a crucial piece of information about the truth of something. The adjective *documentary* means 'relating closely to document', as in *We watched a documentary film on gold miners in Africa.* A documentary film is a film that provides simple or general information about something.

5.   The adjective *adventurous* means 'causing or inspiring adventure', as in *The adventurous manoeuvre of the staff secured the firm profits.* An adventurous manoeuvre is one that is difficult but exciting, so cleverly planned as to obtain an advantage. The adjective *adventuresome* means 'causing or inspiring adventure', as in *They don't like drivers to be so adventuresome as to wreck cars.* An adventuresome driver is a driver who tends to take excessive risks, so daring as s/he lacks discretion.

Exercise 9.2

1.   This is a case of subject-to-object raising. In (a), the non-raised variant, the overall complement clause *that Susan will leave*, which functions as the main clause landmark, is accorded the focal status. In (b), in the raised counterpart, the focal prominence is conferred on the trajector of the complement clause *Susan*, which also functions as the main clause landmark.

2. This is a case of subject-to-subject raising. In (a), in the non-raised variant, there is absence of a candidate for focal prominence. Instead, the whole complement clause, which functions as its trajector, is accorded the focal status. In (b), the focal status in the raised counterpart is conferred on the most salient participant in the complement clause *Anna*. This second meaning emerges only out of the use of a *to*-infinitival complement.

3. This is a case of object-to-subject raising. In (a), in the non-raised variant, the entire complement clause, which is located in the subject region, serves as the trajector of the adjective, whereas in (b), in the raised counterpart the landmark of the complement clause serves as its trajector.

4. This is a case of converting a non-extraposed into extraposed construction. In the non-extraposed version in (a), the complement clause is in profile and hence chosen as subject. The complement clause serves as the trajector of the adjective, and so is coded as subject. In this type of construction, the speaker takes a *narrow* view of the complement event. Semantically, the content of the complement clause is considered the only stimulus that induces the evaluation. So, the reason for the evaluation is deemed unilateral, in the sense that the complement content is held solely responsible for the evaluation made by the speaker. The act of arguing about a trivial issue functions as a sole stimulus, and consequently induces a certain judgement by the speaker.

    In the extraposed version in (b), the pronoun *it* is in profile and hence chosen as subject. The speaker's scope of awareness, i.e. *field*, profiled by *it* serves as trajector, and so is coded as subject. In this type of construction, the speaker takes a *broad* view of the complement event. Semantically, *it* represents a global stimulus subsuming the general circumstances which are responsible for the inducement of the evaluation. The global stimulus embraces two components: the complement content which is central and the general circumstances surrounding its occurrence, including its consequences such as severing ties with people or distorting one's image in the eyes of people. So, the reason for the evaluation is deemed multilateral.

5. This is a case of an active and passive pair of sentences. The distinction relates to a shift in perspective which entails changing the relative prominence attached to the participants in the profiled relationship. In

(a), in the active variant, the agent is the focal participant. In (b), in the passive variant, the patient is the focal participant.

Exercise 9.3

1. Distance   2. Time   3. Degree   4. Progress   5. Difficulty
6. Wise   7. Effect   8. Very drunk or ill   9. Importance
10. Success.

Exercise 9.4

1. A trainer is a person who trains people or animals for sport or work. A trainee is a person who is being trained for a job.
2. A rescuer is a person who saves someone or something from a situation of danger or harm. A rescuee is someone who is in a dangerous situation.
3. An adopter is a person who legally takes someone else's child into their own family and treats them as one of their own children. An adoptee is a child who has been legally been made as part of a family that s/he was not born into.
4. An examiner is someone who tests someone knowledge or skill in a particular subject. An examinee is someone whose knowledge or skill is being tested.
5. An interviewer is the person who asks questions in an interview. An interviewee is a person answers questions in an interview.

Exercise 9.5

1. In (a), the lamp is interpreted as the thing being located. The lamp has trajector status only by virtue of how the situation is linguistically expressed. It reflects the speaker's decision to say where the lamp is, and thus to use *above*, which puts primary focus on the vertically higher participant. In (b), the same lamp is only a landmark. The table is the entity being located.
2. In (a), the sculpture is the focal participant and the seashell is the secondary participant in the profiled relationship. Accordingly, the sculpture constitutes the trajector, whereas the seashell constitutes the landmark. In (b), the situation is reversed. The seashell is the focal participant and the sculpture is the secondary participant in the profiled relationship. Accordingly, the seashell constitutes the trajector, while the sculpture constitutes the landmark.

3. In (a), focus is placed on the trajector of the complement *the driver*, while in (b) focus is placed on the landmark *the car*. The difference is against which participant the order is being exerted; in the first it is *the driver*, whereas in the second it is *the car*.

4. Here, *in front of* and *behind* rely on vantage point to specify the trajector's location *vis-à-vis* the landmark. We use (a) when the phone box intervenes in the line of sight. In this case, the phone box is the trajector while the house is the landmark. We use (b) when the house intervenes in the line of sight. In this case, the house is the trajector while the phone box is the landmark.

5. This is a temporal relation. Both *before* and *after* designate what is referentially the same relationship. The semantic contrast between them resides in their choice of trajector and landmark, not in content or profiling. In (a), the status of trajector is conferred on the guests. In (b), it is conferred on the pronoun *we*.

Exercise 9.6

1. In (a), the main verb *order* represents potential reality in the sense that it evokes the subsequent potentiality of the complement event. The occurrence of the complement clause is futurized as compared to the time denoted by *order*. Potential reality: refers to a future event that possibly happens. In (b), the main verb *persuade* represents projected reality in the sense that it evokes the subsequent actualization of the complement event. Projected reality refers to a future event that certainly happens.

2. In (a), in the bare infinitive structure, the complement event of playing in the garden has initial salience, while the participant involved in that event *the kids* becomes salient only secondarily. In this type of construction, the whole complement clause elaborates the landmark of the main verb *let*. There is temporal coincidence between the event of the main verb and the event of the complement verb. In (b), in the *to*-infinitive structure, the complement subject *the kids* receives initial salience, and is therefore recognized as the primary landmark of the main verb *allow*, while the complement clause *to play in the garden* as its secondary landmark. There is temporal subsequence between the event of the main verb and the event of the complement verb.

3. In (a), the complement verb is not preceded by *to*. The bare infinitive construction evokes a realized event. It is characterized as a form

of non-subsequence involving coincidence in time between the two events: that of the main verb and that of the complement verb. In (b), the complement verb is preceded by *to*. The *to*-infinitive construction expresses a non-realized event. It is characterized as a form of subsequence. That is, the event expressed by the complement verb follows the event expressed by the main verb.

4. In (a), without *from*, direct means of achieving a result are employed. This sentence would be the appropriate thing to say if the main clause subject employed some direct means, e.g. jumping into the water and dragging the boy to the bank. In (b), with *from*, indirect means of achieving a result are employed. This sentence would be the appropriate thing to say if the main clause subject used indirect means, e.g. calling the attention of those swimming nearby, or throwing the boy a lifejacket.

5. In (a), where the two nouns in object position is separated by the preposition *to*, the implication drawn is that it is not sure if the applicant received the chance. In (b), where the two nouns in object position are juxtaposed, the implication drawn is that it is sure the applicant received the chance.

Exercise 9.7

1. In each sentence, the word *glass* is used differently. In (a), it is used as a mass noun. It refers to substance. A mass noun is non-count noun. In (b), it is used a count noun, It refers to distinct objects. This shows that many nouns, however, can be either count or non-count, depending on their meaning and context.

2. The two sentences are used to describe the same state of affairs but in a different fashion. Intuitively, the difference between *a few* and *few* is that the former is positive whereas the latter is somehow negative. As evidence, *any*, which requires a negative context, is compatible with few, but not with a few, as in *Few people can afford to buy any house. A few* means a small number of people or thing. *Few* means hardly any of people or thing.

3. The verb phrase in sentence in (a) is in present simple. It describes a general statement, implying that this is a habit or behavioural trait. The verb phrase in sentence in (b) is in present continuous. It describes a specific statement, implying that this is an activity that is going on at the present time.

4. In (a), the bone is being affected by the dog's action. In (b), it is only the meat and gristle on the bone that is being affected.
5. The verb phrase in (a) is in future continuous. It expresses an activity that will be in progress at a time in the future. The verb phrase in (b) is in future perfect. It expresses an activity that will be completed before another time or event in the future.

Exercise 9.8

1. These presuppose different speaker locations: In (a), the speaker is in the tower. In (b), the speaker is down below.
2. In (a), the coming is seen from the hearer's vantage point. In (b), it is seen from the speaker's vantage point.
3. In (a), Andy's position is reckoned from the speaker's vantage point. In (b), Andy's position is reckoned from the Jane's vantage point.
4. In these examples, the vantage point is extended to time. In (a), I describe the situation from Jill's vantage point. In (b), I describe the same ongoing situation from my own vantage point.
5. In (a), the vantage point is located inside the room. The subject of the sentence is *the door*, which is the theme: a passive entity whose location or state is described. In this example, *open* is an intransitive verb: it requires no object. The vantage point is located inside the room. In (b), the vantage point is located outside the room. The subject of the sentence is *two* thieves, which is the agent: the entity that intentionally performs the action of opening the door. In this example, *open* is transitive (it requires an object: *the door*). The vantage point is located outside to the room. What comes first in the sentence (the subject) corresponds to what is viewed first by the human experiencer, and this provides us with clues for reconstructing the vantage point.

Exercise 9.9

The personal complement clause construction in (a) codes a subjective construal of the complement clause seen from the vantage point of the main clause subject. Personal complement clause constructions convey the main clause subject's involvement in the event profiled in the complement clause. As the speaker of the scene, the main clause subject relates the scene he describes exclusively to himself, and consequently appears more committed to its realization. Such a sentence represents EVA (Egocentric Viewing Arrangement) and gives a subjective perspective of the scene conceptualized.

The experience of going on holiday in (1a), killing animals in (2a), reaching the pinnacle of career in (3a), living on a tropical island in (4a) and travelling around by train in (5a) is assigned to a specific entity (the main clause subject), the sentence is construed subjectively.

The impersonal complement clause construction in (b), which begins with *it*, codes an objective construal of the complement clause seen from the vantage point of the speaker. Impersonal complement clause constructions convey the speaker's distance from the event denoted in the complement clause. As the speaker of the scene, the speaker adopts an external vantage point of the scene and displaces himself from the person engaged in the activity. Consequently, the speaker appears less committed to its realization. Such a sentence represents OVA (Optimal Viewing Arrangement) and gives an objective perspective of the scene conceptualized. Because the experience of going on holiday in (1b), killing animals in (2b), reaching the pinnacle of career in (3b), living on a tropical island in (4b) and travelling around by train in (5b) is assigned to a non-specific entity (general), the sentence is construed subjectively.

Exercise 9.10

1. The event in (a) is scanned sequentially over time. This is due to the use of a verb. The event in (b) is scanned summarily as a whole without being scanned through time. This is due to the use of a noun.

2. The verb *call* in (a) profiles a process. It comprises a series of component states scanned successively from one point in the series to another. The series are construed as different. The noun *call* in (b) comprises a series of component states which are scanned summarily in one go. The series are construed as identical.

3. The example in (a) invokes a stationary perspective. This has to do with distance, where distal correlates with stationary. If the perspective point is stationary, it is in synoptic mode. The example in (b) invokes a motion perspective, as a result of which the children are seen one or some at a time. This has to do with distance, where proximal correlates with motion. If the perspective point is moving, it is in sequential mode.

Exercise 9.11

1. The two sentences evoke the same overall spatial configuration, but they build it up in different ways, thereby providing very different

conceptual experiences. The difference is that the (a) variant zooms in from the largest area to successively smaller ones, whereas the (b) variant starts from the smallest area and zooms out to a larger area.

2. The two sentences evoke the same overall temporal configuration, but they contrast semantically because each conceptualization has its own time course, unfolding in a particular way through processing time. The contrast is that in the (a) variant the sequence in which the component expressions occur correlates with an ordering of the conceptualizations they symbolize, while in the (b) variant the sequence diverges from their order of occurrence or even runs directly counter to it. The contrast is in the order from most important things to less important ones.

Exercise 9.12

1. The sentences are not semantically equivalent, despite using the same words to characterize the same objective situation. The order of words induces us to access the conceptions they symbolize in the corresponding order. In (a), it starts with the backyard and ends in the gate. In (b), it starts with the gate and ends with the backyard.

2. The sentences symbolize two scanning paths which run counter to each other. The difference in word order correlates with the difference in attention. In (a), the scanning path starts at the east and ends at the west. In (b), the scanning path starts at the west and ends at the east.

3. The difference relates to the direction from which the two events are viewed. The direction in (a) is prospective. The event-sequence is viewed from the perspective of the first event, i.e. giving the tip. That is, the perspective point is located at the temporally earlier event (giving the tip), from which the speaker looks forward to the later event (leaving the hotel). The direction in (b) is retrospective. The event-sequence is viewed from the perspective of the second event, i.e. leaving the hotel. That is, the perspective point is located at the temporally later event (leaving the hotel) and the viewing direction is backwards, towards the earlier event (giving the tip).

Exercise 9.13

1. The form of the verb imposes a particular profile on the interpretation of the each expression. In (a), the present simple foregrounds the endpoints of the designated process. This sentence is used when

someone views the whole process. In (b), the -ing progressive back-grounds the endpoints (beginning and end) of the designated process. This sentence is used when someone views only the internal part of the process.

2. The meaning of each construction is reflected by its structure, i.e. symbolized by the presence of *to* and by the juxtaposition of the nominals. In terms of initial salience, in the (a) version it is the direct object *a postcard*, whereas in the (b) version it is the indirect object *her mother*. Therefore, the two constructions embody different meanings. Only the second implies that *her mother* has received the letter.

3. In the active sentence in (a), the most important participant, i.e. the city council, is in profile and consequently chosen as subject. In the passive sentence in (b), the less important participant, i.e. the new mall, is in profile and consequently chosen as subject.

4. In (a), the leaving of the police is presumed to cause the violence to erupt. In (b), the police left before the violence broke out.

5. The two sentences have different syntactic structures, and so have different semantic values. The two sentences share the same semantic content, but that content is construed differently by the speaker. In (a), the implication drawn is that only part of the wall is smeared. This is reflected by the fact that the wall is separated from the verb by a preposition. In (b), the implication drawn is that the whole wall is smeared. This is reflected by the fact that the wall, being a direct object, is close to the verb.

Exercise 9.14

In the non-extraposed version in (a), the complement clause is in profile and hence chosen as subject. The complement clause serves as the trajector of the adjective, and so is coded as subject. In this type of construction, the speaker takes a narrow view of the complement event. Semantically, the content of the complement clause is considered the only stimulus that induces the evaluation. So, the reason for the evaluation is deemed unilateral, in the sense that the complement content is held solely responsible for the evaluation made by the speaker. The complement content functions as a sole stimulus, and consequently induces a certain judgement by the speaker. A construction of this type simply highlights the role of the situation as a target of evaluation. The reason is that in this type of construction the speaker's scope of awareness is limited.

In the extraposed version in (b), the pronoun *it* is in profile and hence chosen as subject. The speaker's scope of awareness, i.e. field, profiled by *it* serves as trajector, and so is coded as subject. In this type of construction, the speaker takes a broad view of the complement event. Semantically, *it* represents a global stimulus subsuming the general circumstances which are responsible for the inducement of the evaluation. The global stimulus embraces two components: the complement content which is central and the general circumstances surrounding its occurrence. So, the reason for the evaluation is deemed multilateral. A construction of this type, which is introduced by *it*, subsumes the range of considerations that can be brought to bear for the evaluation. The reason is that in this type of construction the speaker's scope of awareness is non-delimited.

Index

CPSIA information can be obtained at www.ICGtesting.com
Printed in the USA
BVOW06s2152181215

430593BV00001B/1/P